D0769053

A Catalogue of the Compositions of
S. Rachmaninoff

В. И. Россинскій.

S. V. Rachmaninoff in March 1917
(Drawing by V. I. Rossinsky)

A Catalogue of the Compositions of

S. Rachmaninoff

by

Robert Threlfall and

Geoffrey Norris

London

Scolar Press

First published 1982 by
SCOLAR PRESS
James Price Publishing Ltd
90/91 Great Russell Street London WC1B 3PY

British Library Cataloguing in Publication Data
Threlfall, Robert
A Catalogue of the Compositions of S. Rachmaninoff.
1. Rachmaninoff, Sergei – Bibliography
I. Title II. Norris, Geoffrey, b.1947
016.78 '092' 4 ML134.R12

ISBN 0 85967 617 X

Printed in England by
Whitstable Litho Ltd
Whitstable Kent

Contents

Illustrations

Introduction
(on a personal note)

The joint authors of the present volume first became acquainted with each other in 1973. In that year, which marked the centenary of the birth of Rachmaninoff, each – quite unknown to the other – had prepared articles for subsequent publication on very similar aspects of his work (see p. 133 below) and each was working on a more general book on the composer. A slim volume by RT appeared from Boosey & Hawkes that same year, in their projected second series of biographies of composers (since discontinued); GN's book, wherein SR ultimately achieved recognition as a Master Musician (doubtless to the considerable posthumous discomfiture of some earlier editors of that series), followed in 1976. We had already been introduced through the good offices of that godfather of all writers on Russian music, Gerald Abraham; before long it became evident that, belonging as we did to different generations, our joint work could well be greater than the sum of its separate parts. RT's study of SR's music (supported by still vivid recollections of his performances) extended back to the early 1930s; a study continuing to the present time and more recently supplemented by visits to the Library of Congress, Washington, home of the American Rachmaninoff Archive. GN, with his knowledge of Russian and Russian music is naturally more versed in the later research which has taken place in that country, and for his part has visited the major Rachmaninoff MS collections there. It seemed logical, then, when RT's *Catalogue of the Compositions of Frederick Delius* was completed and published (Delius Trust/Boosey & Hawkes, 1977) that a similar Catalogue of the Compositions of S. Rachmaninoff should be undertaken at once, as a combined operation: the present volume is the result.

Scope and plan of this work

The *oeuvre* of SR forms a classic case of a composer first subjected both to over-exposure and to comparative neglect; to popularity and to ignorance. In the family of the great composers his position is thus not so far from that of Tchaikovsky, the history of whose reputation reveals the same dichotomy of reaction. Different composers bring differing problems to their would-be cataloguers; some from the paucity of the sources available, others from the bewildering diversity of versions, editions or arrangements. In the case of SR let it be stated at the outset, then, that the prospect of cataloguing all editions or publications of the famous Prelude in C sharp minor (which already occupy over six pages in the British Library music catalogue alone) would be daunting to stouter hearts than ours. Professor Tovey once expressed amazement at an arrangement of the *Hallelujah Chorus* for two flutes, in which four-part harmony was represented by acciaccature*: some hardly less strange transcriptions from *The Magic Flute*, made during the Victorian era for similar ensembles, have recently even been reissued. An arrangement of SR's early masterpiece, made by W. H. Reed for unaccompanied violin and published by Boosey & Hawkes in the early 1940s, though it could hardly feel out of place in such company, shall find no further mention in our catalogue; the terms of reference we have set ourselves can briefly be stated as follows:

It has been our aim here to list all of SR's works, in their authentic editions and versions in full detail and in such a way as to render the resulting corpus of information readily accessible to the user of our book. Primarily, this falls into three divisions, as follows:

I. Works published with opus numbers (1–45) by the composer.

II. Works, whether published during the composer's lifetime or posthumously, to which no opus numbers were allocated. For simplicity, these works are numbered in series as under:

Nos.	10 and up:	piano solo, piano 4 & 6 hands, 2 pianos
"	30 "	instrumental chamber music
"	40 "	orchestral music
"	50 "	songs with pianoforte accompaniment
"	60 "	works for chorus
"	70 "	dramatic works and projects
"	80 "	miscellaneous vocal works, settings of Russian songs, etc.

III. Arrangements by SR of works by other composers, here listed in alphabetical order of those composers' names.

Then follow three Appendices, (i) giving the titles of the songs in the 'official' German and French translations; (ii) notes on the dedicatees; and (iii) a schematic chronological conspectus of the compositions; after which the Index gives reference to all names and titles quoted in alphabetical order.

* see Scholes, *The Oxford Companion to Music*, article *Arrangement*, seventh edition p. 49, for a quotation of this version.

Each entry in our catalogue follows the style and layout used in the Delius catalogue mentioned above which has been well received in this respect by its various reviewers. Under each and every item, then, appear the following sections as appropriate:

Title and style of work: in translation also, if appropriate.
Date: with such supporting evidence as is necessary.
Dedication: in the actual words used.
Texts used for songs and vocal works; *libretti* and basis of story for operas.
Key: if appropriate.
Compass: of solo songs (middle c; tenor C; soprano c′).
Details of instrumental and vocal forces called for. Orchestrations are given in the usual abbreviated form; instruments bracketted do not call for separate players, and we assume without comment the interchange of piccolo with third flute.
MSS: the various MS and other sources traced are listed, cross-referenced to previous cataloguers if appropriate, and briefly described.
Publication: dates, original publishers, plate numbers, pages, revisions etc. are given. References to the Collected Editions and details of current availability are also included.
Performance: giving the date and place, if possible, of first and first British performances; in some cases, information on other performances of interest is also included.
Recordings: only those made by SR himself are listed, with cross-reference to the box number concerned of the RCA centenary 'Complete Rachmaninoff'. (Further technical details of these recordings, by Gregor Benko, are to be found in the booklet included with the said boxes; also in Appendix 2, compiled by Philip L. Miller, for the original American edition of S. Bertensson and J. Leyda's biography, see below.) The Ampico piano-roll recordings were re-recorded on disc by Decca in 1978.
Arrangements: in general, only such as were made by the composer himself or (as far as may be assumed) with his co-operation and/or consent are listed. However, a few other arrangements of unusual interest or value are included; though here we cannot and do not pretend to completeness.
Notes: references to articles of outstanding interest concerning the work in question; quotations from letters; information of general interest. Also, in the case of other composers' works arranged by SR, the original source is traced and particulars of any other relevant or similar arrangements are added. Cue numbers are given in bold figures, plus or minus bars therefrom.

Throughout SR's own words are always italicized; and all quotations from his letters have been translated by GN. Here, as in the Delius catalogue, thematic incipits are eschewed, as also are bar-counts and durations.

Sources consulted

The primary sources for our work are of course the composer's MS legacy and his complete published compositions. Firstly, turning to his MSS, the vast majority of these are now to be found divided between two collections. Those of his almost entire output up to the date of his leaving Russia, in December 1917, were left there by him: carefully preserved by Russian scholars, they were then deposited in the State Central Glinka Museum of Musical Culture in Moscow. SR, writing to Boris Asafyev on 13 April 1917, had given a fairly accurate dated list of all the works he wished to preserve up to that time. (This letter is of course included in the published edition of the letters, see below, as no. 488, p. 479.) In 1924, Viktor Belyayev published a pamphlet which included a listing of all these MSS giving their dates. Later, in 1955, Ekaterina Bortnikova issued a reference catalogue of the MSS then in Moscow: we give cross-references to the item numbers allocated in her catalogue, and to the MS numbers, throughout our work.

The second MS deposit, containing almost all the works written or arranged after the composer's departure from Russia, is now to be found in the Rachmaninoff Archive in the Library of Congress, Washington D.C., USA. No actual catalogue of this holding has been published, though a brief listing was given in the Library's accessions journal at the time of its deposit there (see ref. below).

There are very few major or minor works not included in one or other of these two MS collections; any such cases are clearly indicated as they arise. On the other hand, copyists' *Stichvorlagen* of many works, proved by us to exist (e.g. of opp. 40, 41, 43, 44 & 45 and the revised versions of opp. 35 & 36) are not to hand; nor, in most cases, are proof sheets – on to some of which also the composer may have added 'second thoughts'.

Of the published lists of SR's compositions which appeared in the earlier volumes devoted to his life, that in Oskar von Riesemann's *Rachmaninoff's Recollections* is admittedly based almost entirely on Viktor Belyayev's booklet; that in Victor Seroff's biography collates a number of additional and later details; whilst that forming Appendix 1 of the Bertensson/Leyda volume, taking advantage of all available sources up to the time of its first (USA) publication in 1956, remained the most detailed and informative of its kind for another two decades.

As many as possible of the printed editions listed by us have been personally inspected during our research. SR, unlike Scriabin, was evidently a punctilious proof reader: one searches almost in vain for a 'literal' in even the original engravings of his works – at least in those issued by Gutheil: a missing natural sign among the semiquavers at cue 24 in the Second Concerto piano part almost alone springs to mind.

Only a very few original editions have persistently eluded our grasp – the first Russian editions of the instrumental pieces opp. 2 & 6; of the songs opp. 4, 8, 14 & 15; of the second impression of the vocal score of *Aleko*; and some of the Soviet publications of posthumous works, notably Lamm's 1947 song volume.

Occasionally – very occasionally – a slightly different reading may be traced in a recording, which thus becomes a source of text as well as of performance (cf. opp. 10/5, 23/5). Whilst being grateful for the composer's many authentic renderings we are fortunate enough to possess on record, regret must be expressed for those we lack. There are certain of his solo works that SR frequently performed yet never recorded: opp. 23/1–2, 32/8, 39/5, even op. 42, to name but a few. And – while we treasure his incredibly vivid piano accompaniment to Plevitskaya's lively singing of *Powder and Paint*, not to mention his spirited rendering, with his wife Natalya Aleksandrovna, of the *Italian Polka* – what would we not give to have similar recordings, however antique, of his performances with Nezhdanova in the *Vocalise*, Nina Koshetz in *Dreams*, Sobinov in *What wealth of rapture* or Chaliapin in any of those songs written with his voice in mind?

References and abbreviations

RP/A	Z. A. Apetian (ed.): *S. V. Rakhmaninov: pis'ma* [Letters] (Moscow 1955). We have used this edition of the letters, as the three-volume *Literaturnoye naslediye* is still in progress, vol. 1 being dated Moscow 1978 and vol. 2 1980.
VR/A	Z. A. Apetian (ed.): *Vospominaniya o Rakhmaninove*, 2 vols., [Reminiscences ...] (Moscow, 4th. edition 1974; for full details of contents see Norris 200–1.)
EB	Ekaterina Bortnikova: *Avtography S. V. Rakhmaninova v fondakh gosudarstvennovo tsentral'novo muzeya muzykal'noy kul'tury imeni M. I. Glinki: katalog-spravochnik* (Moscow 1955). There is a copy in BL at 2737. ga. 1.
VB	Viktor Belyayev: *S. V. Rakhmaninov* (Moscow 1924). There is a copy in BL at 7903. d. 34.
Culshaw	John Culshaw: *Sergei Rachmaninov*; Dennis Dobson Limited (Contemporary Composers Series), London 1949.
B/L	Sergei Bertensson and Jay Leyda: *Sergei Rachmaninoff: a Lifetime in Music*; New York University Press, 1956; George Allen & Unwin Ltd., London 1965.
Lyle	Watson Lyle: *Rachmaninoff: a biography*; William Reeves Booksellers Ltd., London 1938.
Norris	Geoffrey Norris: *Rakhmaninov*; J. M. Dent & Sons Ltd. (The Master Musicians Series), London 1976, 1978.
OvR	*Rachmaninoff's Recollections* told to Oskar von Riesemann; George Allen & Unwin Ltd., London 1934.
Seroff	Victor I. Seroff: *Rachmaninoff*; Cassell & Company Ltd., London 1951.
Swan	A. J. and K. Swan: 'Rachmaninoff: Personal Reminiscences', in *The Musical Quarterly*, XXX (1944), pp. 1–19, 174–191.

L. of C.	The Library of Congress, Washington D.C., USA. For the note on the original accession of the Rachmaninoff Archive see: *Library of Congress Quarterly Journal of Current Acquisitions*, vol. 9 no. 1, November 1951, pp. 39–42.
BL	The British Library, London.
GMM	The State Central Glinka Museum of Musical Culture, Moscow.

Treatment of Russian names and dates

We cannot defer any longer the answers to questions which inevitably arise when Russian names and dates have to be rendered into English. The decision to retain that spelling of the composer's name used by himself throughout his 'American period' – and indeed on his earlier visits to the West – as recorded also on his passport, this decision is RT's in principle. The same illogical logic should permit our pages to mention Chaliapin, as indeed they must mention Tchaikovsky. At least these transliterations, if unscholarly, are consistent: if scholarly rules are to be followed, should they be those of BS 2979: 1958 or the differing results of ISO/R9? Those of the Department of Printed Books in the British Library, or the modifications crystallized by the editorial board of the new *Grove*? Basically, our decision has been to continue on the lines suggested by GN in the preface to his volume on the composer in the Master Musicians Series, pp. vi–vii. Bibliographical references are transliterated as consistently as possible; names well-known in the West are otherwise referred to in the forms there usually encountered.

To eliminate lengthy, unnecessary and controversial transliterations in song titles and in the names of some other works, we have listed all these in Cyrillic. Here again, the original early publications all included the various letters since eliminated or altered: it seemed better now, however, to use modern Cyrillic spellings (thus differing from Eric Walter White's practice in his *Stravinsky: the composer and his works*). We give the usually-accepted English versions of all such titles, but include a literal translation in the cases of the songs if the 'official' one is too far-fetched.

As regards dates, it is to be noted that all dates as given on MSS and letters in SR's own hand, if before 1/14 February 1918, are to be understood as Old Style. We have, incidentally, standardized all dates into the pattern: Day/Month/Year.

Some general considerations

As our work proceeded, several patterns running through the compositions as a whole have emerged. The general preference for the minor mode has been remarked upon by all commentators: D minor, in particular, almost starts and ends the composer's life. An earlier liking for F sharp minor, also for E minor and major, later recedes; and, apart from such works as the 24 preludes for piano, increasing use of the 'simpler' C minor, G minor and A minor is to be noted.

Only with his complete output before us can we view the *oeuvre* entire – seeing it not only threaded through by the old chant *Dies irae*, but also noting how the First Concerto of 1890–1 was not finally rewritten until 1917 and after; how a rejected piano piece of 1911 reappears in the Fourth Concerto, whose composition spread from 1914 through 1926 to 1942; how part of the central movement of the *Vespers* of 1915 returns to close the last major work, the *Symphonic Dances* of 1940; how the elusive introductory bars of that early six-hand piano Romance of 1891 underpin the whole slow movement of the Second Concerto written a decade later ...

Before embarking on the Catalogue proper, however, four short essays bearing on certain general topics of importance will be presented: their introduction here will obviate a certain amount of repetition when we later come to list the details of each individual work.

(i) Rachmaninoff's sketches; and some reflections on his processes of composition

B/L 403, introducing their Appendix 1 (which lists SR's works), state that they have not fully itemised therein 'The composer's sketchbooks, in the L. of C.'. They also state 'There may also be uncatalogued sketchbooks in the other large collection of SR MSS in ... Moscow'. Indeed, EB's list of the SR MSS there includes many sets of sketches for specific works, listed thereafter; but she does not refer separately to any more general sketchbooks as such. In his original description of the setting up of the SR Archive in the L. of C. (see *Quarterly Journal of current acquisitions*, vol. 9 no. 1, Nov. 1951, pp. 39–42), Edward N. Waters speaks of 'a large quantity of very important sketches' among the autograph MSS in section one of that Archive. On visiting the latter again in 1979, it was clear to RT that the 'thorough analytical treatment and description' envisaged by Mr. Waters is still awaited. Meanwhile, a number of hitherto unidentified sketches could be and were named on the spot; the resulting new information is carried into our catalogue at the appropriate places.

The limited amount of musical effects in SR's luggage when he left Russia was noted by several commentators: B/L 207 refer to the first act of *Monna Vanna* and 'sketchbooks containing the new [Nov. 1917] piano pieces'. It is now possible to amplify this statement somewhat. In the first place, the material relating to *Monna Vanna* also apparently included the original libretto and drafts plus two gatherings of pencil sketches, in addition to the complete fair copy of the vocal score of Act 1 (see entry below, p. 181). Next, as we shall also see below (item II/19), the Nov. 1917 piano pieces (then untitled) were in fact taken away in the form of separate fair copies, carefully written out and dated. Most valuable and interesting in this context, however, are several books of MS paper (Breitkopf & Härtel 4E) all originally with the publisher's light blue paper wrappers, some of which latter still survive. All these books have been used to a greater or lesser extent: some are completely full, others more than half empty. All doubtless accompanied the composer from Russia; indeed, some contain notes for works completed (or published) before then. The more interesting, then, is it to trace the faint but clear pencillings inscribed therein and to recognize not only extensive drafts for the Fourth Concerto but fragments used in other works completed in America much later still. We now give a brief note of the contents of these four fascinating sketchbooks:

(a). Contains pencil sketches on 4 staves for most of the first movement of the Fourth Concerto; however, the opening thematic statement appears towards the end of this 32-page book.

(b). Contains a pencil sketch of the setting from St. John (written in February 1915, according to the facsimile dating on the first published edition); also sketches of the latter part of the first movement of the Fourth Concerto (as above), and for the third movement: extending from after the soloist's 'small note flourish' (after the D flat section) until the coda.

(c). This similar book has now shed its wrapper, but traces of the characteristic original Breitkopf light blue paper still adhere to the stitches. It contains pencil sketches of portions of the A minor Etude-Tableau op. 39 no. 2 (of which the final MS appears to be undated, but publication is known to be 1917), and also fragments of the Etude-Tableau op. 39 no. 3 (final MS dated Oct. 1916). Then comes a line of melody, accompanied by gusli-like chords marked *Arpe & Piano*, which is readily identified as the opening of the middle movement of the Third Symphony (though here in a different key), a work only to be taken up and completed in the late 1930s. The rest of this book is unused (pp. 40).

(d). This book, formerly part of the Siloti collection, bears the inscription on the original Breitkopf wrapper, in an unidentified hand:

Сергей Васильевич Рахманинов/1920–21 гг./Америка. It contains a pencilled memorandum of the C minor chords later used at cue 1 at the start of the Symphonic Dance, op. 45 no. 1. Next come sketches for parts of the Fourth Concerto similar to those already noted in books (a) and (b), viz. the transition section to the second theme in the first movement; a fragment of the high violin line used in the D flat section of the last movement; the latter part of the last movement (similar to book (b) above)(pp. 32).

In addition to these four genuine 'sketchbooks', quantities of drafts and some sketches exist for opp. 42, 43, 44 and 45 (but not, apparently, for op. 41), usually in the form of gatherings of paper, some spirex bound. These are probably, though not necessarily certainly, of a date nearer to the established dates of composition of these scores; and as such are listed in our catalogue under the works concerned. From an examination of all this material, one salient point emerges: all these drafts and sketches for orchestral works are in the form of a (usually 4-stave) particell, and nowhere do we find any drafted pages of full score. We have already drawn attention above to the completion – in vocal score – of the first act of *Monna Vanna*: all these features indicate that the actual orchestral setting appears to have been, for SR, the last link in the chain. The case of the Capriccio op. 12, deliberately written first for piano duet and subsequently orchestrated, gives independent corroboration to this assumption, as does similar work on the Second Symphony documented by letters to Morozov (RP/A, 13 April, 2 August 1907; B/L 136, 141). True, minor structural or orchestral changes were sometimes subsequently made, before and/or after publication – the material of the Third Symphony described below shows examples of each. (This had already been known from examination of the MS of the Third Concerto and from the correspondence referring, for example, to *The Isle of the Dead*.)

It follows therefore that a closer study of the MSS of opp. 1–29 and 31–39 than we have been able to give may in some cases reveal minor alterations in the text, previous to its use as a *Stichvorlage*, or even minor differences between MS and first edition only explicable by intermediary overworking at the proof stage (our commentaries below on opp. 30 and 40–45 are relevant in this context). A comment, albeit a somewhat extreme one, by SR's close friend and conductor-colleague, Leopold Stokowski, may perhaps also be fittingly recalled here: 'Everything he wrote he would send to me. We would rehearse it, he would listen, and then later he would want to change the orchestration. But unfortunately his music was already printed. He suffered very much from that. Many things he wanted to change, but couldn't because he printed them too fast.' (v. Music and Musicians, vol. 19 no. 11, July 1971, p. 23: *Stokowski looks back* by Edward Johnson.)

Meanwhile, the 'thorough analytical treatment and description' of SR's sketches foreseen by Edward Waters, their first custodian in the L. of C., is thus seen to be a project still awaiting the closer attention of students. May we hope that a sympathetic and dedicated scholar will take up this subject before too long, amplify the hints we have given above, and gather together all the considerable mass of information still surviving: surely much valuable light will then be thrown on the life and work of SR the composer.

(ii) A note on the allocation of the early opus numbers

The four very early posthumously-published piano pieces listed below as II/12 are numbered on the MSS opus 1 nos. 1–4 in the composer's hand; but the MSS of the first piano pieces actually to be published (op. 3 nos. 1–5) have their opus numbers apparently added by the engraver. Again, the first printed edition of the First Concerto, the 'official' opus 1, bears no such number at all (though apparently the MS, EB 32, is thus numbered); only later was 'op. 1' retrospectively added to the printed editions. If plate numbers are any guide, the two cello pieces now known as op. 2 and the opera *Aleko* (vocal score) predated the publication of the First Concerto. *Aleko*, strangely enough for such a major score, never received an opus number at all; and, as we have so far been unable to consult a first edition of the cello pieces (whose MS, too, is unlocated), to establish whether their numbering coincided with first publication is not at present possible for us.

It is known that the *Capriccio bohémien*, later published as op. 12, was written first in the form of a piano duet and later orchestrated (see entry below). According to the editor of SR's letters, in a footnote to the letter documenting this, the MS of the 4-hand piano arrangement was marked *op. 4.* (Meanwhile, to the MS of the 5 Morceaux de fantaisie was allocated the number 3.) To complete the list of alterations, it must be noted that a partial draft score of the orchestral Fantaisie since published as op. 7 bears the number *op. 6.* An original allocation of numbers in fairly strict chronological sequence seems thus to have been early established; the curious features which remain are the failures of *Aleko* and the first publication of the Concerto to attract opus numbers at all. To summarize:

op. 1 nos. 1–4 Four piano pieces (only published posthumously, without numbers)
? 2 Two pieces for cello and piano
0 *Aleko*, opera
– First Concerto (published first without number; later as op. 1)
4 Capriccio bohémien for piano duet; later published, when orchestrated, as op. 12; the number 4 going to six songs
6 Fantaisie for orchestra; published as op. 7, the number 6 going to two pieces for violin and piano.

(iii) Rachmaninoff's publishers

The firm of A. Gutheil, Moscow, was SR's first publisher. Founded by Aleksandr Bogdanovich Gutheil (1818–82) in 1859, it was continued after his death by his son Karl Aleksandrovich, who was responsible for engaging SR. The works published by this house up to the turn of the century (i.e. opp. 1–6, 8–12, 14) were engraved in Moscow by G. Grosse and were apparently not copyrighted outside Russia (except in France): hence the amazing proliferation of foreign editions of the more popular early songs and piano pieces. Subsequently, until the death of K. A. Gutheil, International Copyright was obtained by the use of the joint A. Gutheil/Breitkopf & Härtel imprint for opp. 17–30 & 32–36, as also for subsequent reissues of the earlier works which were now all re-engraved by Breitkopf & Härtel in Leipzig. Of the 'missing' numbers above, op. 13 had been withdrawn from Gutheil before publication whilst opp. 7 and 15–16 were first issued by P. Jurgenson, Moscow. The excellent Gutheil, however generous in other ways, appeared extremely tight-lipped when it came to dating his publications of SR's music, hardly any of which bears the year of its issue. He was sometimes equally parsimonious in respect of plate numbers: using the same number for later editions of the same work, whether re-engraved (cf. op. 5 for example) or even, in some cases, recomposed (e.g. op. 9).

On the death of Gutheil in 1914 his firm was purchased by Serge Koussevitzky, and later issues of all the above Gutheil publications subsequently appeared over the imprint of A. Gutheil (S. et N. Koussevitzky)/Breitkopf & Härtel, some war-time issues bearing the legend 'Copyright by J. & W. Chester Ltd., London, W. &

Brighton'. Meanwhile opp. 37–39 were published by Koussevitzky's own firm, Édition Russe de Musique (Russischer Musikverlag) and were first engraved by V. Grosse of Moscow, opp. 38–9 being re-engraved after the war by Röder of Leipzig.

After SR's emigration to the USA, his next publications (with one exception: *Fragments*) were issued by Carl Fischer Inc. of New York; until with the return to large-scale original work the publishing house of TAIR (set up in 1925 and named after the composer's daughters Tatyana and Irina) took over the European publication and distribution of opp. 40–2 and some transcriptions, with plate numbers reaching from 1 to 11. Opp. 40–1 were engraved, printed and published in Paris and copies were sent to Washington D.C. to register the copyright there also (v. SR to Somov, 17 June 1928; B/L 254; referring to op. 41). Op. 42 and the transcriptions of Bach (Prelude), Mendelssohn and Schubert were first engraved in America and printed and published by Édition TAIR Paris and Carl Fischer, simultaneously in the case of the first three; the Schubert work was re-engraved in Paris for TAIR's slightly later edition. Retaining the TAIR imprint (but not the separate if simultaneous European issues), op. 43 appeared from Carl Fischer; opp. 44–5, together with the last transcriptions and the reworkings of earlier pieces (including the Fourth Concerto), were actually published by Charles Foley, already for many years SR's concert agent and now his publisher as well: in this capacity he also took over all those works previously issued by Carl Fischer.

To save unnecessary duplication of details, the principal original publishers concerned are referred to in our catalogue by the shortened titles given below. To the right of each one stands the more detailed imprint and engraver's name to be found on the printed copies.

Gutheil: Moscou chez A. Gutheil
St. Pétersbourg chez A. Iohansen
Kieff chez L. Idzikowski
Varsovie chez Gebethner & Wolff
'Gravé et impr. chez G. Grosse à Moscou, Mylnicoff per. prop. maison.'

Gutheil/Breitkopf: as above, adding
Breitkopf & Härtel, Leipzig [Bruxelles, Londres, New York etc.]
'Gravure et impression de Breitkopf & Härtel à Leipzig.'

Gutheil/Koussevitzky: A. Gutheil (S. et N. Koussevitzky)
Breitkopf & Härtel, Leipzig etc.
'Gravure et impression de Breitkopf & Härtel à Leipzig.'

Jurgenson: Moscou chez P. Jurgenson
St. Pétersbourg chez J. Jurgenson
Varsovie chez G. Sennewald
'Gravé et impr. chez P. Jurgenson à Moscou.'

ERM (RMV): Édition Russe de Musique
(Russischer Musikverlag GmbH)
Berlin, Moscou, St. Pétersbourg, Leipzig, Londres, New

York, Bruxelles, Breitkopf & Härtel/Max Eschig, Paris
'Stich und Druck von C. G. Röder GmbH, Leipzig.'
(Some publications during the first war were originally engraved by V. Grosse, Moscow).

Fischer: Carl Fischer, Inc., [62] Cooper Square,
New York, N.Y.
(engraver not stated).

TAIR: Édition 'TAIR' Paris (ТАИР) *
Dépôt pour l'Europe et ses Colonies: S. A. des Grandes Éditions Musicales, 22 Rue d'Anjou, Paris
'Imp. Delanchy-Dupré, Paris-Asnières, Grandjean Grav.'
Selling Agents for the USA, Canada and Mexico:
Carl Fischer Inc., Cooper Square, New York, N.Y.

Foley: Charles Foley, Music Publisher, 4 East 46 Street,
(later 67 West 44 Street), New York City.
(engraver not stated, but apparently the same as used by Carl Fischer).

After the composer's death in 1943 almost all the hitherto-unpublished early works were issued by the Music Section of the State Publishing House in Moscow (MUZGIZ) under the principal editorship of Pavel A. Lamm. Later, a Collected Edition of the piano works, under the same editorship, also appeared from this publisher with the following make-up:

1948, *Vol. I*: opp. 3, 10, 16, 22, 23, 28; including early and revised versions, together with some hitherto unpublished pieces antedating the above, M 18453 Г pp. 303.
1948, *Vol. II*: opp. 32, 33, 36 (second version), 39, 42, Oriental Sketch, M 19224 Г pp. 218.
1950, *Vol. III/1*: further previously-unpublished pieces, transcriptions and op. 36 (first version), M 20114 Г pp. 179.
1950, *Vol. III/2*: op. 11 and other works for 4 and 6 hands, M 20114ª Г pp. 109.
1950, *Vol. III/3*: op. 13 arranged for piano duet by the composer, M 20589 Г pp. 134.
1951, *Vol. IV/1*: Russian Rhapsody and op. 5, for 2 pianos, M 20886 Г pp. 143.
1951, *Vol. IV/2*: op. 17 and op. 45 (arranged by the composer) for 2 pianos, M 20886ª Г pp. 214.

(Our catalogue gives the necessary cross-references to this 'Coll. Ed.' where appropriate.)

Meanwhile a volume of 'Vocal Works not published by the composer' [Posthumous vocal works] had also been edited by Lamm and this was issued in 1947; a complete edition of the songs, edited by Z. Apetian, appeared in 1957. After Lamm's death in 1951, scholarly work on SR's music has continued

* The spelling 'TAÏR' only appears in the copyright line and plate number of Paris issues.

by other editors, principally G. Kirkor and I. Iordan, who have reissued a number of scores accordingly.

The Koussevitzky catalogue, including all the Gutheil and Édition Russe publications of SR's works, was transferred in 1947 to Boosey & Hawkes Inc., now Boosey & Hawkes Music Publishers Limited; by them, the items in question are being kept in regular circulation. Likewise, the 'American' works passed to Belwin Mills Music Ltd. in the early 1970s, and they promptly marked the Centennial year, 1973, with a number of valuable reissues.

It should be noted that the transfers of works from one publisher to another, and the conflicting claims of different houses involved with arrangers and arrangements, together with the differences of copyright laws between different countries, mean that the full publishing history is in some cases even more involved than would appear from our entries. As already stated above, when specifying our terms of reference, we have basically contented ourselves with recording details of the original editions and current availability, together with any revised versions by the composer, re-engravings or inclusion of any new editorial matter. It is perhaps natural, too, that our perspective, being that of two Londoners, should thus reveal itself in our treatment of, for example, the English translations of the songs.

(iv) The publications of the songs

For reasons which have already been explained above, the first editions of the early songs issued as opp. 4, 8 & 14 by A. Gutheil, Moscow lacked International Copyright. Originally published at the time of composition with Russian words only, apparently, their export was then, to say the least, limited and we have failed to locate a single copy in a general collection in England. With the composer's increasing fame, translations – presumably 'authorized' – were later issued by the original publishers or their representatives, Breitkopf & Härtel in Leipzig and J. & W. Chester in England (amongst others). During World War I, for example, the latter firm issued a number of the songs (with 'Edition Gutheil' included in the imprint), with English words by Rosa Newmarch and later by M. C. H. Collet, French words by G. Jean-Aubry, of which we note examples under the appropriate entries below.

Meanwhile (if plate numbers are to be believed) A. Gutheil/Breitkopf issued the op. 21 songs in 1902 with Russian and German words („Romanzen für Gesang"), the latter translated by Lina Esbeer, copyrighted accordingly; they then proceeded to re-engrave and reissue op. 4 nos. 1–5 similarly. In 1906–7 it was the turn of op. 4 no. 6, opp. 8 & 14, followed immediately by the first publication of op. 26; op. 34 (nos. 1–13 only) followed likewise in 1913. Almost all these publications appeared in high, medium and low keys, each key bearing a different plate number; these numbers, in the cases of opp. 21, 26 & 34 being apparently allocated by a system more easily understood in our present Bingo-conscious age. Unable to unravel the pattern completely in view of the insufficient evidence presently available, we have regretfully refrained from attempting to give a chart of all the numbers involved. (Gutheil's catalogues do not give the plate numbers; the whereabouts, indeed the survival, of his plate book is presently undetermined.)

The stage was thus set for the further issue by Gutheil/Koussevitzky (in 1921–2) of all these 65 songs with English versions by Edward Agate and Rosa Newmarch (only the original key of each song being available with English text), a portrait on the covers, and the plate numbers being distinguished by the addition of a superscript ª suffix. These versions, together with the remaining six songs (op. 38, now reissued with multilingual words) were also published as 'Seventy-one Songs with Pianoforte accompaniment ... complete in two volumes' by Gutheil/Koussevitzky in 1921–2, pp. 127, 141. It is the details of these definitive issues of the Russian/English editions which we have entered in our listing. We have also identified some similar separate issues with English and French words (traduction française de M. D. Calvocoressi) dating from 1921 (and printed on paper obviously of that date ...); these bear a new run of plate numbers in the 9000 series (however, one exemplar examined of a Russian/French issue had the same plate number and suffix as the corresponding Russian/English copy!).

In 1947, Boosey & Hawkes took over the Gutheil/Koussevitzky catalogue, and in 1949 they published a volume of [12] 'Selected songs/Mélodies choisies/Ausgewählte Lieder – new edition with English, French, German and Russian texts' to their numbers 16600–1 (high/medium), pp. 47. Containing opp. 4/1–3–5; 14/2–8–11; 21/5–12; 26/6–7–10 and 34/14, titles in Russian and French and words underlaid in Russian, Fr., Eng. and Ger., this issue is marked 'Copyright by Edition A. Gutheil for all countries, assigned 1947 to Boosey & Hawkes Inc. New York USA'. The original plates are quite obviously French-engraved (though we are unable to trace any earlier French issue) with the exception of op. 34/14, taken from the original German plates 'reprinted in England by special arrangement with S. & N. Koussevitzky, proprietors of Edition A. Gutheil'. (The medium key of this song – the Vocalise – incidentally, is here A minor.) In 1973, Boosey & Hawkes reissued the two volumes of Gutheil's 1921–2 edition, original keys only, Russian and English words, to their overall numbers 20174–5, quoting the following copyright dates: opp. 4 & 8, 1922; op. 14, 1906/1922; op. 21, 1902; op. 26, 1907; op. 34, 1913; op. 38, 1922. (Many numbers have also been made available in separate issues.)

After SR's settling in America, a 'new edition of Russian music revised and edited by the Composer', republished by Carl Fischer, Inc. in the 1920s, had included eleven separate songs. Details of these are entered in the appropriate places below. (This evidently supplanted any earlier editions, such as the album of Six Songs by SR with English texts by C. Engel (edited by H. Clough-Leighter) published by the Boston Music Co. in 1919.*) Finally, after the composer's death, Pavel Lamm's 1947 volume of 'Vocal works not published by the Composer' [Posthumous vocal works] (which even included a copy in SR's hand of a song by N. Ladyzhensky, EB 128 (MS 143)!) at last made possible the publication of a true complete edition of the songs now totalling 83. Issued by

* No. 225a/b, BM Co. 6063 (complete) 6064–9 (separate), pp. 27; containing op. 4 nos. 2 and 3; op. 14 nos. 2 and 11; op. 21 no. 5 and op. 26 no. 10.

the State Music Publishers, Moscow, in one volume in 1957 under the editorship of Z. Apetian, based on Lamm's earlier work, and subsequently reissued a number of times, first in one and later in two volumes, this edition (which contains the original keys and Russian words only) may be considered the definitive text (С.Р. – Романсы – Полное Собрание М 26012 Г pp. 326). Not only is each song dated, but a valuable list giving brief biographical details of the dedicatees gathers much useful information otherwise not easily located, in addition to the editor's general preface. We cross-refer to this 'Coll. Ed.' by giving the item number therein of the song in question; also, under 'Current editions', we give page references to the later 2-volume edition from Muzyka, Moscow.

Acknowledgments

Although the collection and collation of the information involved in volumes such as ours remains entirely the choice and responsibility of its authors, the willing co-operation of all those to whom we have often had to turn for information and assistance, many of whom have been bombarded with letters or verbal enquiries concerning often trivial-seeming, but intricate, detail, has been a necessary prerequisite to the successful completion of our task. (In this context passing reference must be made to the fact that, writing as we are after the demise of both Gabriel Païchadze and Charles Foley, some of our conclusions are bound to be the results of deduction rather than of information: some areas which still remain obscure to us would doubtless have been clear to them.) At times the fear has begun to form that, by the end of our task, we would have few friends left – such is the neglect to which some have been subjected by our work-in-progress, coupled with the excess of attention devoted to others. Be this as it may, it is now an extremely pleasant duty to list forthwith the names of those persons and bodies to whom we feel most indebted.

Edward N. Waters has been a most valued correspondent for well over twenty years, during much of which time he was Chief, Reference Department, Music Division, The Library of Congress, Washington D.C., USA. Since his retirement, assistance has also been given by Wayne D. Shirley and William C. Parsons, Reference Librarians in the same institution. Oliver Neighbour, Music Librarian, Reference Division and Miss Pamela Willetts, Deputy Keeper, Department of Manuscripts, The British Library, have likewise given their personal aid to answering our queries in their respective areas. The libraries and staffs of the Royal Academy of Music, London; the BBC Music Library; the Senate House, London University; the Oxford Faculty of Music; the City Library, Liverpool and the Music Library, University of Liverpool have all given valuable help as well.

Next, we must chronicle the assistance we have received from SR's current publishers. The copyright departments of Boosey & Hawkes Music Publishers Ltd. (Miss Muriel James and Miss Celia Springate), Carl Fischer Inc. (John Brummet), Rob. Forberg/P. Jurgenson (Joachim v. Roebel) and Belwin Mills Music Limited (Mrs. Maggie Barton) have willingly helped by searching their records for us. So many other members of the staff of Boosey & Hawkes Ltd. have helped over so long a period that it is not possible to name them all; but no terms can be too warm for the thanks we owe to J. Malcolm Smith and his staff, the patient, efficient and untiring team in their Hire Library.

Permission to use a number of quotations from *Rachmaninoff's Recollections told to Oskar von Riesemann* and from *Sergei Rachmaninoff: a Lifetime in Music* by Sergei Bertensson and Jay Leyda was willingly granted by the publishers of the volumes in question, Messrs. George Allen & Unwin (Publishers) Ltd. Permission to include reproductions of the material used for our illustrations has been given by copyright holders and/or owners as follows:

Plate 1: The Library of the Royal Academy of Music, London.

2: Novosti Press Agency; also Boosey & Hawkes Music Publishers Limited (owners of the copyright of the music).

3–4: Boosey & Hawkes Music Publishers Limited (owners of the copyright of the music).

5–6: ditto.

7–8: J. & W. Chester/Edition Wilhelm Hansen London Limited; The British Library (Department of Manuscripts); also Boosey & Hawkes Music Publishers Limited (owners of the copyright of the music).

9–10: The British Library Photographic Service.

11: Messrs. George Allen & Unwin (Publishers) Ltd.

12: Reprinted by kind permission of Belwin-Mills Music Ltd., 250 Purley Way, Croydon, Surrey, CR9 4QD (owners of the copyright of the music); also Boosey & Hawkes Music Publishers Limited.

14–15: The British Library Photographic Service.

To all the above, we extend our special thanks for their willing co-operation.

ROBERT THRELFALL
GEOFFREY NORRIS
London, Christmas 1980

Postscript: While this book has been in the press, a new edition of Bortnikova's catalogue of the SR autographs in GMM has been published (Moscow 1980, ed. M. G. Rytsareva). This incorporates several more recently received items and hence alters the numbers of the original listing; the actual MS numbers, however, remain unchanged. In addition to a quantity of proof sheets and printed copies with MS corrections and annotations, the following items are now also to be found in the GMM collection:

1. Sketch book [1916], MS 1292, ff 18; ff 8–11 are for the Three Russian Songs.
2. Sketches for the Fourth Concerto and the Three Russian Songs, in a small notebook given to Evgeny and Elena Somov in 1922, MS 1424, ff 30.
3. The MS of the Valse for piano six hands, MS 2127, ff 18.
4. The MSS of the songs op. 4 no. 3, II/50 (1–2) and II/52 (1–2), numbered 1135, ff 15. Also included with these MSS is that of II/53 (3) dated *16–17 July 1891*: this song should therefore be catalogued as II/52 (3) and the entry transferred from p. 168 to p. 167, references being amended accordingly.

ПАМЯТИ С. В. РАХМАНИНОВА

What is music!? How can one define it?

Music is a calm moonlit night, a rustling of summer foliage.
Music is the distant peal of bells at eventide!
Music is born only in the heart, and it appeals only to the heart; it is Love!
The sister of Music is Poesy, and its mother is Sorrow!

(SR to Walter E. Koons, 1932)

Music is enough for a whole lifetime – but a lifetime is not enough for music.

(SR, reported by W. G. King, in
New York *Sun*, 13 October 1937)

EDITION GUTHEIL

À

Monsieur A. Ziloti.

CONCERTO

pour le Piano

AVEC ACCOMPAGNEMENT D' ORCHESTRE

(ou d'un second Piano)

COMPOSÉ PAR

S. Rachmaninoff.

Partie de Piano ...... 4 Rbl.
Pour 2 Pianos (2 Ex.) 8 "

PROPRIÉTÉ DE L' ÉDITEUR

MOSCOU chez A. GUTHEIL

Fournisseur de la cour IMPERIALE
et commissionnaire des Theatres IMPERIAUX
au Pont des Morechaux maison Junker No 10.
St PETERSBOURG chez A. IOHANSEN Perspective de Nevsky No 44.
KIEFF. chez L. IDZIKOWSKI.
Lith. W. Grosse à Moscou Miljnikorr per. prop Maison.

Plate 1: First Concerto: titlepage of first edition (1892)

I. Works with opus numbers

CONCERTO pour le Piano avec accompagnement d'Orchestre (ou d'un second Piano) composé par S. Rachmaninoff [op. 1] [ORIGINAL VERSION]

1. Vivace – Moderato	F sharp minor
2. Andante cantabile	D major
3. Allegro scherzando	F sharp minor – major

Date: 1890–1. (First movement 1890 [cf. Asafyev]; work completed 6 July 1891, Ivanovka [SR to Slonov 20 July 1891, RP/A; B/L 36]). Also SR to Natalya Skalon, 26 March 1891: *Two movements are already written, the last movement is composed but not written down* (RP/A; B/L 32).

Dedication: *À Monsieur A. Ziloti.*

Orchestra: 2. 2. 2. 2 – 4. 2. 3. 1 – Timp. – Strings.

MS: GMM; (a) *Full score*, earliest version, with red ink corrections by the composer and A. Siloti and with pencilled alterations; *Vivace/Andante/Finale. Allegro moderato*, EB 34 (MS 31), ff 41. (Although EB 34 gives the date of these alterations as '1917', it is evident from Iordan and Kirkor's preface to their subsequent first publication of the full score in 1971, v. inf., that this date is inapplicable.)

(b) *Full score*, EB 32 (MS 32), ff 36. 'Opus 1'. This MS lacks the solo part, but is basically the text established by (a) above, as altered (Letter to GN from Mme. E. N. Alekseyeva, 1 Nov. 1973).

(c) Arrangement for two pianos, EB 33 (MS 33), ff 40.

(d) Sketch of the earliest version of the first movement (*Allegro moderato*) dated *8 June* [1890], for two pianos, EB 35 (MS 34), ff 8, unfinished.

Publication: [1892–3], A. Gutheil, Moscow, A 6395 G, pp. 92 [arrangement for 2 pianos]. 'Partie de Piano 4 Rbl. Pour 2 Pianos (2 Ex.) 8 Rbl.' (OvR 103–4 gives an anecdote concerning this price). According to later Gutheil back covers (v. plate 10), 'Partitur und Stimmen in Abschrift'. Few first editions of their composer's putative 'opus 1' can have surpassed this imposing tall folio of 92 pages, of which a fine copy may be seen in BL h. 3984. n. (There is another copy in the Henry Wood Library, RAM, into which Wood has pencilled details of the orchestration.) The wrapper is printed in black on gray paper; the titlepage, bearing the identical wording (in French) is also printed in black with a panel of buff tint within the border. Nowhere does this first edition bear the number 'op. 1'. *See plate 1.*

1966, Muzyka, Moscow, 2775, pp. 82. Arrangement for 2 pianos, edited by L. Roizman.

1971, Muzyka, Moscow, 6489, pp. 167. First publication of the orchestral score, with preface and 'prepared for publication by I. Iordan and G. Kirkor'.

Current edition: IMC 2320 (following the 1966 Muzyka edition, for 2 pianos, ed. Roizman).

Performance: 17 March 1892, Small Hall of Nobility, Moscow Conservatoire, SR and student orchestra cond. V. I. Safonov; first movement only.
4 October 1900, London (Queen's Hall), Evelyn Suart and Queen's Hall Orchestra cond. Henry J. Wood.

Arrangement: Andante cantabile aus dem Klavier-Konzert Fis moll, bearbeitet für Violoncell mit Klavierbegleitung von F. Schertel.

Publ: A. Gutheil/Breitkopf A 9649 G, pp. 7, [1]. This arrangement follows this original version (not the revised one).

Notes: Despite the statement made by Iordan and Kirkor in the preface to their first publication of the score, this work was not performed by the composer on the occasion of his London début in Queen's Hall on 7 April 1899, at which he played solos and conducted (see opp. 3 and 7 inf.). Invited to return the following year and play his First Concerto, SR 'promised to compose a second and better one for London' (B/L 87).

Writing to Morozov on 12 April 1908, SR said *I have three pieces that frighten me: the First Concerto, the Capriccio* [op. 12] *and the First Symphony. I should very much like to see all these in a corrected, decent form* (RP/A; B/L 145). Another nine years were to pass, however, before the opportunity to rework the First Concerto was taken; the other two works remained as they were originally written.

The revision and reissue of the present work are in every way so substantial that it is necessary to make separate entries in this catalogue for the two versions.

1er Concert pour Piano avec accompagnement d'Orchestre [Nouvelle édition] op. 1 [REVISED VERSION]

1. Vivace – Moderato F sharp minor
2. Andante D major
3. Allegro vivace F sharp minor – major

Date: completion of revision dated *10 November 1917* [Moscow] *Composed 1890–91.*

Dedication: *Mr. A. Siloti.*

Orchestra: 2. 2. 2. 2 – 4. 2. 3 (3 = bass). 0 – Timp. (in 3 only: Triang. Piatti) – Strings.

MS: GMM; (a) *Full score*, dated 10 November 1917, EB 36 (MS 35), ff 68. It appears that the piano arrangement of the orchestral accompaniment is not included at the foot of this score: its whereabouts is not known.

(b) Sketches in pencil, EB 37 (MS 36), ff 16.
See also *Notes* below.

Fascimile: of first page of orchestral score, Norris (between pp. 52 & 53); *plate 2*; see also *Notes* below.

Publication: 1920, full score, State Music Publishers, Moscow, ГМ 162 ИМ pp. 145. (There is a fine copy in BL h. 3984. q.). (Muzyka's republication to no. 1313 as late as 1965 follows the same text though an entirely different engraving. Pp. 146, it commences on p. 3 instead of on p. 2.) Neither printing has a tempo indication at the start of the second movement; in the BL copy, *Andante cantabile* has been added in ink. This is an earlier state than the following (v. inf.).

[March 1921] (according to B/L and the publisher's records; the work is not entered in Hofmeister), full score, A. Gutheil/Breitkopf (no mention of Koussevitzky – an omission rectified on later printings), A 10300 G, pp. 94, gray wrappers. Stich und Druck von Breitkopf und Härtel in Leipzig. Titlepage in French and Russian. The opus number now appears. 'Copyright 1919 by S. Rachmaninoff, New York'. The BL copy is on very indifferent paper; so bad, in fact, that each leaf has had to be separately laminated.

[?1922] (the BL accession date cropped by the binder, but probably early 1922), arrangement for 2 pianos 4 hands by the composer, A. Gutheil/ Breitkopf, A 10301 G, pp. 46, ditto ditto. Also on bad (mechanical) paper. (Later reprints included the Koussevitzky imprint, and made handsome amends by exceptionally clear printing on very fine white paper.)
For differences between these editions, see below.

Current edition: Boosey & Hawkes 16425 (score – also available in miniature format, HPS 19), 16351 (2 pianos), following the text of the Gutheil editions; (Schirmer, Leeds Music).

Plate 2: First Concerto: first page of MS of revised score (1917)

Performance: 29 January 1919, New York, Russian Symphony Society Orchestra, SR cond. Modest Altschuler.

Recording: SR and the Philadelphia Orchestra, cond. Eugene Ormandy (1939–40), V.

A projected recording with the LPO in London in September 1937 – as a 'bribe' towards the proposed parallel recording of the Third Symphony (v. SR to Wilshaw, 7 June 1937, B/L 330–1) – was abandoned. So too, in consequence, was the inclusion of the work in the orchestral concert given with Sir Thomas Beecham on 2 April 1938. The programme as given on that date, consisting of Beethoven's First Concerto and SR's Paganini Rhapsody, to which Sir Thomas added two of his own favourites – Haydn's Symphony no. 102 and Sibelius's *Tapiola* – still remained a memorable occasion. (Sir Thomas, only just recovered from an attack of gout, broke a baton in the first *tutti* of the Beethoven finale.)

Notes: *I have rewritten my First Concerto; it is really good now. All the youthful freshness is there, and yet it plays itself so much more easily* (SR to Alfred Swan, *Musical Quarterly*, Jan., April 1944; B/L 277).

The changes in this revised version are the most far-reaching of any of SR's large-scale rewritings. 'The new setting has left little more of the old Concerto than a few of the most beautiful themes, which have, however, retained all the charm and freshness of their youth' (OvR 235). Structurally, the central *tutti* of the first movement from **7** + 6 until **14** is newly composed on the main material and much extended; the whole first half of the cadenza, up to the change into D flat at *Allegro Moderato* is newly composed and thematically more organized; the soloist's introductory cadenza in the slow movement and the whole middle section (from **31** to the reprise) likewise being strengthened by organic development. In the finale, however, recasting is carried to a higher power. There, the principal section is greatly extended by recomposition; the middle episode is shifted from the D major, already used for the Andante, into E flat – a key quite new in this context; and a newly-composed coda of increasing brilliance is substituted for the original Maestoso final return of that middle episode. Here, the piano writing and, to some degree, the orchestration now anticipate the Fourth Concerto completed nine years later rather than recall the Third of eight years before.

We have not been able to determine conclusively the exact chronology and sequence of events, as far as this work is concerned, between SR's signing the revised MS on 10 November 1917 and publication by A. Gutheil/ Breitkopf in March 1921. Unless and until the full details of the business workings of Koussevitzky's publishing affairs in Russia and Germany during this momentous period* are chronicled, some uncertainty is bound to remain. At all events, the revision appears to have been more of a continuing process

* (which saw the October Revolution in 1917, the cessation of hostilities between Russia and Germany and the Treaty of Brest-Litovsk in early 1918 and the armistice and Treaty of Versailles concluding World War I in 1918–19).

Plates 3–4: First Concerto: the last two pages of the second movement (Muzyka, 1965, edition)

Fl.
Ob.
Cl.
Fag.
poco sforz.
Cor.
Tr-be
Tr-ni
Timp
suivez.
rit.
dim.
pp
P-no
dim.
p
Archi
pp
ppp

1313

Plate 4

than has hitherto been assumed; just as it seems likely that the revised version first performed in New York early in 1919 had not yet reached the final state now familiar from current publications.

No MS material relating to the revisions of this work is to be found in the L. of C., and the survival in GMM of the revised – though indeed not fully and finally revised – MS 35 makes it likely that this MS never left Moscow, where it was presumably used by the State Music Publishers when engraving their edition issued in 1920, their engraver's note 'ГМИ 162' appearing at the foot of the first page. Despite the upheavals of the time, the score might conceivably have been first engraved for Koussevitzky by V. Grosse (as other wartime scores had already been, cf. opp. 34/14, 37, 38 & 39 inf.). SR might then have received plate pulls to check on his travels, (but if so, unless a copy of the MS of some sort accompanied them, what did he read them against?), and he could well have used a set of the same for both study and performance. On these as a basis, either before or (more likely) after the New York première in January 1919, his final thoughts could have been overwritten; and the resultant revised copy would then have formed the basis for Koussevitzky to have re-engraving carried out in Leipzig for his own 'Gutheil' publication of 1921 (as was done for opp. 38–9). On the other hand if Koussevitzky's edition was first engraved in Leipzig, this could presumably not have taken place until late 1918, then leaving little time for SR to check proofs, register the copyright at the L. of C. and perform the work by very early 1919. Furthermore, if this had been the sequence of events, the MS would have left Moscow, and this under circumstances which make it difficult to explain how it should ever have returned there. At any rate, the 'Gutheil' printings show no sign of their present plates having ever been altered.

Strangely enough, the later Muzgiz edition of the two-piano version, e.g. that issued in 1946 (no pl. no.) is an exact photolithographic reproduction of the Gutheil/Breitkopf edition, A 10301 G.

The first to draw attention to the many differences of detail between the two above-listed early editions of the full score was GN (v. inf.). Those differences, though admittedly more noticeable to the performer than to the listener, and all concerning minor details of pianistic layout or of orchestration, are nevertheless too numerous to be listed here in full (see Norris 110–115, where an example of the rewriting of the solo part is discussed; also cf. our plates 3–4 which give the close of the second movement from the Muzyka edition to facilitate comparison with the readily-available Boosey HPS 19).

The reproduction of the first page of the MS full score (Norris pp. 52–3; our plate 2) also reveals other and earlier changes: the opening fanfare, on horns and bassoons in the original version, was now given to (horns), first trumpet and first trombone. The latter parts were then removed with a knife (and restored to the clarinets, horns and bassoons in bars 1–2); in bars 9–12 the full brass orchestration was retained.

See: G. Norris: R's Second Thoughts (*Musical Times*, April 1973, pp. 364–8). Norris 110–115.

Prélude et Danse orientale op. 2
pour violoncelle avec accompagnement de piano

1. *Prélude*	Comodo	F major
2. *Danse orientale*	Andante cantabile	A minor

Date: 1892 (VB); 1891 (Asafyev).

Dedication: *Dedié à Monsieur A. Brandoukoff.*

MS: at present untraced (Asafyev); not listed in EB.

Publication: [1892] A. Gutheil, Moscow, A 6339–6340 G [not seen]. Later printings re-engraved by Breitkopf and published by A. Gutheil/Koussevitzky are pp. 7, [1]; 7, 2. (same pl. no.)

Current editions: Boosey & Hawkes (no. 2 only) 16342; IMC 1659, 1819.

Performance: 30 January 1892, Moscow, Vostryakov Hall, A. A. Brandukov and SR (Prelude only).

Notes: The first of these two pieces is an arrangement for piano and violoncello of the prelude in F major composed for piano solo at Ivanovka six months earlier, q. v. II/15 inf. For the programme of the concert at which the first performance took place, see B/L 41–2.

[5] Morceaux de Fantaisie pour piano — op. 3

1. *Elégie*	Moderato	E flat minor
2. *Prélude*	Lento	C sharp minor
3. *Mélodie*	Adagio sostenuto	E major
4. *Polichinelle*	Allegro vivace	F sharp minor
5. *Sérénade*	Sostenuto – Tempo di Valse	B flat minor

Date: Autumn 1892.

Dedication: *A Monsieur A. Arensky.*

MS: (a) GMM; EB 48 (MSS 80–84), ff 13. (The opus number appears to have been added to this MS by another hand, in preparation for the engraver.) See also under *Facsimile* below.

(b) L. of C., parts of ML 30. 55a. R3:
no. 2 (Two piano arrangement by the Composer), pp. 10, in ink. No signature or date. With the engraver's annotations for staves and pages.

no. 3 (revised version), pp. 9 (= 3–11 of a 12-page sewn section), in pencil. Titlepage *Melodie / op. 3 / S. Rachmaninoff*; at end *26 February 1940 / New York / S. R.*

no. 5 (revised version). First MS, unfinished, pp. 7 of a 12-page section, in ink. *Sérénade op. 3 no. 5 / (revised version) / S. Rachmaninoff.* This is a slightly earlier state than the following definitive MS, and it is abandoned about 30 bars before the end. Undated.
Second MS, pp. 9 (= pp. 3–11 of a 12-page section), in ink; with engraver's annotations; undated. Titlepage *Sérénade / S. Rachmaninoff.* This is evidently the *Stichvorlage* for the revised edition as published in 1940.
Another MS, pp. 5, in a copyist's hand, received in the L. of C. from the Siloti collection, is an earlier state approximating to that recorded in 1922–3. Also, pencil drafts for the final version (i.e. as published) now in L. of C. too, were among those 'found after [the composer's] death on the shelf near his Piano in New York'.

Facsimile: nos. 1 and 2 only, complete, Muzyka 1977, pp. 7, 5. With preface by Yu. Keldysh. (This proves these MSS were the *Stichvorlagen.*)
no. 2, two piano arrangement; first page only in L. of C. Quarterly Journal, Vol. 9 no. 1, November 1951, opposite p. 41.

Publication: [1893], A. Gutheil, Moscow, A 6515–9 G (separate numbers), pp. 7, 5, 5, 9, 5. Titlepage (in French only) in black within a red ornamental border (reproduced in RP/A, opposite p. 112). A single copy – that of no. 4 – may be seen in BL h. 3984. r. (4). A later (undated) edition, A. Gutheil/ Breitkopf, 'Compositions pour Piano', B & H cartouche at end of each item, retains the number 6516 for the Prélude but allocates A 9719ª. – 9722ª. G to the other four items. Editions of nos. 2 and 5 'revue et doigtée par A. Siloti' (nos. 2ª. and 5ª.) and of no. 2 'simplifiée par R. Hill' (no. 2ᵇ.) were also later issued by Gutheil.

Perhaps the (undated) French edition of Ed. Hamelle fils (Paris, J. Hamelle, Editeur, Anc^{ne} M^{on} J. Maho) should be mentioned here, since it bears the legend 'Cette édition est seule autorisée en France et Belgique' and the further caution that 'Toute autre édition que la présente est rigoureusement interdite en France et Belgique'. This edition contains all five numbers of op. 3 of which the last (the only one examined) carries the plate number E 129 H and the note 'J. Guidez Grav. 86 rue Lepic'. Nos. 1, 3 and 5 also appear 'pour Violon ou Violoncelle et Piano' and no. 2 also 'pour 2 pianos'. (France and Russia had a reciprocity agreement.)

1940, nos. 3 & 5 only, 'Revised and as played by the Composer'. 'Copyright 1940 by Charles Foley, New York', TAIR, Edition Charles Foley nos. 2013, 2043; pl. nos. R 15–6, R 12–6, pp. 7, 7, in the gray silurian wrappers ubiquitous for this publisher's editions of SR. The reworking in both cases is considerable: the *Melodie*, now marked *Andante con moto*, is slightly cut (one bar from before the climax, four bars from the coda) and completely recast in texture and harmony; the *Sérénade*, though also considerably revised and elaborated in detail, is basically unaltered in outline and structure: evidently the end-product of an ongoing process of revision, as witness the MSS above, and see under *Recordings* below.

Coll. Ed. I/3–29, 1948 (including the revised versions of nos. 3 & 5; the originals appear separately at pp. 280–7).

Current editions: Boosey & Hawkes (nos. 1–2), 17464, 17405. Revised versions of nos. 3 & 5, Belwin Mills ('A Commemorative Collection' contains nos. 3 [and 4] but not no. 5). Bosworth (Album), nos. 1–5 (original versions).

Performance: no. 2 only: 26 September 1892, Moscow, Electrical Exposition, SR. Complete: 28 December 1892, Kharkov, Gorodsky Dom Hall, SR. No. 2 was first played in England and USA in autumn 1898 by Aleksandr Siloti; nos. 1 and 2 were played by SR on 19 April 1899 at a Royal Philharmonic Society's concert in Queen's Hall, London.

Recording: no. 1 (Allegro – Royale LP, ?transferred from a player-piano roll, cf. B/L 438).
no. 2 (1919, 1921), I; (1928), II; also Ampico roll.
no. 3 (original version), Ampico roll; (revised version) (1940), II.
no. 4 (1923), I; also Ampico roll.
no. 5 (1922), I; (1936), II; also Ampico roll, dated 1923. Not only the first recording on disc, but also the Ampico roll dated as early as 1923, clearly point to the revision of this piece: though basically following the original version, from halfway through many of the rewritings are included.

Arrangements: no. 2, *Prélude*. Our attitude to the incredible multiplicity of publications and arrangements of this most famous of all SR's works was given in the preface: we ask indulgence for the consequent evasion of our musicological responsibilities here and in some other like instances. However, certain adaptations are sufficiently authentic to demand inclusion, viz.

'Pour 2 Pianos à 4 mains, arrangé par Richard Lange', [1911], Gutheil/ Breitkopf, A 9094 G, pp. 13. This in turn must now make way for:

'Two piano arrangement by the composer', Carl Fischer Inc. pp. 9, 'Copyright 1938 by Charles Foley, New York'. Included in Foley's *Album* for two pianos; current edition, Belwin Mills.

Orchestral arrangement by Lucien Calliet (originally handled by Charles Foley); 3. 3. 4. 3 – 4. 3. 3. 1 – Timp. Perc. – Harp – Strings. An earlier orchestral arrangement (with piano conductor) by Adolf Schmid, dated 1908, transposed into C minor, was published by Hawkes and Co. London, 4296; one by Henry J. Wood was published by Novello in 1914, 14032, pp. 12.

no. 3, *Mélodie.* Reverie (Melodie), vocal arrangement and words by Geraldine Farrar; 1937, Carl Fischer Inc., New York, V 1366, Fa 3–7, pp. 9.

no. 5, *Sérénade.* Transcrit par J. Nasaroff et M. Zawadsky pour violon et piano; 1911, A. Gutheil/Breitkopf, A 9605 G, pp. 7, [1]. Transposed down into A minor.

ditto, Concert Transcriptions for Violin and Piano by Mischa Elman, no. 3; 1917, Carl Fischer, New York, 20600–9, pp. 7, 3. 'To Fritz Kreisler'. Transposed up into D minor.

ditto, Transcription pour Violon et Piano par Michel Press; 1918, A. Gutheil/ Koussevitzky (Copyright by J. & W. Chester), A 10107 G, pp. 7, 2 (not transposed). 'Imprimerie de Breitkopf & Härtel à Leipzig.'

Notes: see 'My Prelude in C-sharp Minor' by SR, *Delineator*, Vol. 75, February 1910; reprinted in Seroff, 45–6.

1. О нет, молю, не уходи!
(Oh no, I beg you, forsake me not; first published Eng. trans. Oh stay, my love, forsake me not.) A 8388ª G, mezzo-soprano or baritone.
Con allegro [sic], D minor (m). (B – f′)
[EB gives key of MS as C♯ min; VB gives E minor].
Date: 26 February 1892 [VB: 1890; Asafyev 1891].
Text: Dmitry Merezhkovsky (1865–1941).
Dedication: A. A. Lodyzhenskaya.

2. Утро.
(Morning.) A 8392ª G, contralto or bass.
Moderato, F major (l). (A – c′♯)
Date: 1892 [Asafyev 1891].
Text: Mariya Yanova (1840–1875).
Dedication: Yu. S. Sakhnovsky.

3. В молчаньи ночи тайной.
(In the silence of the secret night; first published Eng. trans. In the silent night.) A 8394ª G, mezzo-soprano or baritone.
Lento, D major (m). (B – f′♯)
Date: 17 October 1890 [VB: 1889; Asafyev ditto].
Text: Afanasy Fet (pseudonym of Afanasy Shenshin, 1820–1892).
Dedication: V. D. Skalon.

4. Не пой, красавица.
(Sing not to me, beautiful maiden; first published Eng. trans. Oh, never sing to me again [Georgian Song].) A 8395ª G, soprano or tenor.
Allegretto, A minor (h). (e – a′)
Date: 1892 [Asafyev: summer 1893].
Text: Aleksandr Pushkin (1799–1837).
Dedication: N. A. Satina.

5. Уж ты, нива моя.
(Oh thou, my field; first published Eng. trans. The Harvest of Sorrow.) A 8398ª G, soprano or tenor.
Lento, D minor (h). (g – b′♭)
Date: 1893, Lebedin.
Text: A. K. Tolstoy (1817–1875).
Dedication: E. N. Lysikova.

6. Давно ль, мой друг.
(How long, my friend; first published Eng. trans. So many hours, so many fancies.) A 8801ª G, soprano or tenor.
Andante tranquillo, G minor – major (h). (d – b′)
Date: 1893, Lebedin.
Text: A. A. Golenishchev-Kutuzov (1848–1913).
Dedication: Countess O. A. Golenishcheva-Kutuzova.

MS: GMM; EB 110 (nos. 1, 5 & 6 only; MSS 119, 122, 123), ff 6. The MS of no. 5 is marked op. 4 no. 6; that of no. 6 op. 4 no. 5.

Publication: [1892–] 1893, (according to EB), A. Gutheil, Moscow (separate numbers), Russian only; 2 keys of each (3 of no. 2). A copy of this Gutheil edition of 1893, inscribed to the composer's paternal grandmother, is preserved in GMM no. 369 (EB V/A/1). Re-engraved 1902–6 by A. Gutheil/ Breitkopf, Russian and German words (German by Lina Esbeer); in high, medium and low keys (except no. 3 – h. m. only) with plate nos. in range 8387–8400 and 8801–3. The Russian/English edition appeared in 1921, 'original keys only', pl. nos. as under individual items above, including the superscript [a] (Eng. trans. by Edward Agate, nos. 1–4, 6 and Rosa Newmarch, no. 5).

Earlier, in 1916–7, J. & W. Chester, London and Brighton/Edition Gutheil had issued some items, certainly nos. 3 (JWC 3734) and 5 (JWC 3737) with Eng. trans. by Rosa Newmarch (later by M. C. H. Collet) and French trans. by G. Jean-Aubry.

1922, Carl Fischer, New York, no. 5 'Oh thou waving field of golden grain', V 782, 22597–4, pp. 5. Russian text; English version by Geraldine Farrar (h. only).

1923, Carl Fischer, New York, no. 2, V 805, 22868–4, pp. 5. Russian text; English version by Geraldine Farrar, Ger. by Lina Esbeer (h. m. & l.).

Coll. Ed. 10–15.

Current edition: Boosey & Hawkes, Songs, vol. 1, pp. 3–24; Muzyka, Romansy, vol. 1, pp. 46–68.

Performance:

Arrangements: of the many and varied arrangements (especially of no. 3) we list the following as evidently having SR's approval:

no. 3, 'When night descends in silence', with violin obbligato by Fritz Kreisler, 1930 Carl Fischer Inc., New York, V 1107, 25439–6, pp. 7, [1]. Russian text; Eng. version by Edwin Schneider, Ger. by Lina Esbeer, (h. only). 'As sung by John McCormack.'

no. 4, 'Oh, cease thy singing, maiden fair', with violin obbligato by Fritz Kreisler, 1922 Carl Fischer, New York, V 784, 22580–8, pp. 7, 3. Russian text; Eng. version by John McCormack (h. only).

no. 4, Chanson Géorgienne. Mélodie pour chant avec accompagnement ... instrumentée par Leonidas Leonardi.

Orch: 2. 2. CA. 2. 2 – 4. 3. 3. 1 – Timp. Cym. Trgl. T de B. BD – Harp – Strings (16. 14. 10. 10. 8)

Publ: 1922, A. Gutheil/Breitkopf, A 10320 G, pp. 13.

Note: an [earlier?] arrangement by Leonardi for salon orchestra is also listed; also one for violin, cello and harmonium or piano by A. Dischkewitsch (Gutheil).

Notes: Pushkin's *Song of Georgia* had also been set for voice and piano in 1863 by M. Balakirev; he later orchestrated his accompaniment too (Edition A. Gutheil).

For details of other songs composed during the same period as this opus, but not issued by the composer, see below, pp. 166–8.

For German and French titles, see Appendix (i).

Fantaisie (Tableaux) pour deux Pianos op. 5

1. *Barcarolle*	Allegretto	G minor
2. *La nuit ... l'amour*	Adagio sostenuto	D major
3. *Les larmes*	Largo di molto	G minor
4. *Pâques*	Allegro maestoso	G minor

(for the epigraphs appended to each movement, see *Notes* below)

Date: Summer 1893, Lebedin.

Dedication: *A Monsieur P. Tschaïkowsky*. (Tchaikovsky died before hearing this work.)

MS: GMM; EB 73 (MS 110), ff 16.

Publication: [?1894 – EB offers 1897], A. Gutheil, Moscow, A 6723 G, pp. 75, in score. The part for the first piano, on the upper two lines of each 4-stave system, is engraved throughout in larger size than that for the second piano. (Even Gutheil's generosity does not appear to have extended to the logical stage, of engraving a companion score in which the second piano part was the larger of the two.) In gray wrappers with wording in Russian; titlepage in French (there is a copy in BL h. 2020. n. (4).).

This original edition – as spacious as that of the First Concerto, though a little less firmly printed – was later re-engraved more sharply by Breitkopf & Härtel to the same plate no. but now slightly condensed and occupying only 69 pages (dark blue titlepage wording in French), the part for the first piano still being larger than that for the second.

Coll. Ed. IV (i)/53–141, in score (but here, both players read from equal-sized systems). Two pages of variant readings (one passage from each of the first two movements) in the second piano part are given in an appendix, from a copy in the possession of A. Goldenweiser.

Current editions: Boosey & Hawkes; IMC 522 (both in score). Boosey & Hawkes, who had reproduced the re-engraved Gutheil/Breitkopf edition exactly to their plate no. 16340 in 1948, reissued the entire work again in a 'Re-engraved Edition 1979', B. & H. 20339, pp. 70. In this, not only were both piano parts engraved to the same size (as was also done by IMC for their edition), but preliminary consultation of the above volume of Lamm's Coll. Ed. was made to clarify various other minor textual discrepancies.

Performance: 30 November 1893, Moscow, SR and Pavel Pabst.

Notes: Epigraphs, originally in Russian only, appear above the four movements, as under:

1. from Lermontov
2. from Byron (Parisina, I)
3. from Tyutchev
4. from Khomyakov

Both the currently available editions translate these lines. SR to Natalya Skalon, 5 June 1893 ... *I am occupied with a fantasy for 2 pianos, which consists of a series of musical pictures* (RP/A; B/L 57). SR also told Sophia Satina that the third movement was inspired by the bells tolling during a funeral at the Novgorod monastery (B/L 58 f. n.). The last movement introduces the chant 'Christ is risen' as a counter-theme to the insistent Easter bell motif. For Rimsky-Korsakov's comments on this procedure see B/L 61 (Rimsky would have preferred the chant to be stated first alone, but SR refused to alter it, as *in reality it always comes together with the bells*).

A curious textual problem occurs in the second piano part at bar 6 of the last movement. In the first edition, a bass clef was given at the end of bar 4 of the R.H. part; in the later Gutheil/Breitkopf one a bass clef was supplied at the same place for the L.H. also. At the end of the next bar (5) a treble clef was added in the R.H. in this later edition (it did not appear before). Bar 6 commenced a new page in both these editions, with a *treble* clef in the R.H. It is this last that gives rise to the query, especially as it is omitted in Lamm's usually very reliable Coll. Ed. The open chord CGCG is in keeping with the previous two bars, yet the Mussorgsky-like CGAE flat appears again as soon as the second half of bar 9, and thereafter *passim*.

[2] Morceaux de Salon pour Violon et Piano op. 6

1. *Romance*	Andante ma non troppo	D minor
2. *Danse hongroise*	Vivace	D minor

Date: Summer 1893, Lebedin.

Dedication: [Dedié à Monsieur Julius Conus], according to EB; (no dedication on later reprint, v. inf.).

MS: GMM; EB 77 (MS 114), ff 8.

Publication: [?1894–5], A. Gutheil, Moscow.
The later Gutheil/Breitkopf printing (cf. copy in BL.), pp. 8, 3; 12, 5, has neither plate number nor dedication.

Current edition: E. Kalmus 4348 (Belwin Mills) (no. 2 only).

Performance:

Arrangement: (no. 2) Danses Tziganes. Revu et edité (pour violon et piano) par S. Dushkin. Transcription de Concert no. 2, 1924, B. Schotts Söhne, Mainz, 31079, pp. 11, 4.
(Dushkin's changes concern the violin part only.)

Notes:

Fantaisie pour orchestre op. 7
[Утёс] [The Rock (The Crag)] (E major)

Date: Summer 1893, Lebedin.

Dedication: none on published score; but a copy inscribed to Nikolay Rimsky-Korsakov (see illus. in RP/A opp. p. 128) expresses SR's gratitude for the first performance in St. Petersburg of the *Aleko* 'Gypsy Girls' dance', given by the former on 17 December 1894 at a Russian Symphony Concert.

Orchestra: Picc. 2. 2. 2. 2 – 4. 2. 3 (3 = bass). 1 – Timp. Triang. Tambno. Piatti. Cassa. Tamt. – Harp – Strings.

MS: GMM; (a) *Full score* EB 17 (MS 38), ff 45. A note refers to the inscription to appear on the flyleaf.

(b) partial draft score EB 18 (MS 39), ff 3, marked *opus 6.*

(c) arrangement for piano 4 hands EB 19 (MS 40), ff 12.

Publication: 1894, full score, P. Jurgenson, Moscow, 19163, pp. 69. (The first full score of any of SR's orchestral compositions to appear in print.) Wrapper in Russian (cf. RP/A, facing p. 113); titlepage in Russian (ibid., facing p. 128). A copy (smaller folio) in BL RM. 16. a. 5. (6) (? a later impression) has the titlepage in French.

[1894], Arrangement à 4 mains par l'auteur, ditto, 19165, pp. 35 (primo and secundo on opposite pages). Gray silurian wrappers with wording in Russian printed in blue-black; titlepage in French. (There is a copy in BL h. 3984. g. (2).)

On the flyleaf is printed (in Russian):

This fantasy is written under the influence of Lermontov's poem 'The Rock'. *The composer has chosen the opening lines of the poem as epigraph for this composition:*

A little golden cloud slept
On the breast of the giant rock

See also *Notes* below.

1955, Muzgiz, Moscow, 24845, pp. 72 ('Утёс') (a re-engraved, but exact, reprint).

Current edition: Material: C. F. Peters hire library; miniature score and piano duet version: Robert Forberg / P. Jurgenson, Bad Godesberg.

Performance: 20 March 1894, Moscow, Russian Music Society cond. Vasily Safonov.
20 January 1896, St. Petersburg, Russian Symphony Concerts, cond. Aleksandr Glazunov.
19 April 1899, London (Queen's Hall), Philharmonic Society, cond. SR ('Fantaisie in E major').
Tchaikovsky's untimely death in 1893 came as he was planning to perform

this work during his European tour the following year; he had set the Lermontov poem for mixed voices *a cappella* in 1887.

Notes: A copy of the printed score, given by SR to A. P. Chekhov, is inscribed: *To dear and highly respected Anton Pavlovich Chekhov, author of the story 'Along the Road', the plot of which, with the same epigraph, served as a programme for this musical composition. S. Rachmaninoff, 9 November 1898.* Herein lies the real, 'private', programme of the work, as distinct from the 'official' one given above. See also B/L 58–62; the flyleaf with the inscription is reproduced in RP/A, opp. p. 129. Chekhov's short story was published in *Novoye vremya* in 1886.

[Six songs] op. 8
(to translations of German and Ukrainian texts)

1. Речная лилея.
(The Water Lily.) A 8804ª G, mezzo soprano.
Vivo, G major (m). (B – g′)
Date: October 1893, Lebedin.
Text: Heinrich Heine (1799–1856); original „Die schlanke Wasserlilie“ (Neue Gedichte, *Neuer Frühling*, no. 15).
Dedication: A. A. Yaroshevsky.

2. Дитя! Как цветок, ты прекрасна.
(Child, thou art as beautiful as a flower; first published Eng. trans. Like blossom dew-freshen'd to gladness.) A 8806ª G, mezzo or baritone.
Andante, E flat major (m). (d – f′)
Date: October 1893, Lebedin.
Text: Heinrich Heine; original „Du bist wie eine Blume“ (Buch der Lieder, *Die Heimkehr*, no. 49).
Dedication: M. A. Slonov.

3. Дума.
(Brooding.) A 8807ª G, mezzo or baritone.
Moderato, D minor (m). (c♯ – g′)
Date: October 1893, Lebedin.
Text: Taras Shevchenko (1814–61); original Минають дни, минають ночі (1845).
Dedication: L. G. Yakovlev.

4. Полюбила я на печаль свою.
(I have grown fond of sorrow; first published Eng. trans. The soldier's wife.) A 8810ª G, mezzo soprano.
Adagio sostenuto, G minor (m). (f♯ – g′)
Date: October 1893, Lebedin.
Text: Taras Shevchenko.
Dedication: M. V. Olferyeva.

5. Сон.
(The Dream.) A 8812ª G, soprano or tenor.
Allegretto, E flat major (h). (e♭ – g′)
Date: October 1893, Lebedin.
Text: Heinrich Heine; original „Ich hatte einst ein schönes Vaterland“ (Neue Gedichte, *In der Fremde*, no. 3).
Dedication: N. D. Skalon.

6. Молитва.
(A Prayer.) A 8815ª G, soprano.
Moderato, C minor (h). (c – a′)

Date: October 1893, Lebedin.
Text: J. G. von Goethe (1749–1832).
Dedication: M. A. Deysha-Sionitskaya.

The above texts were translated into Russian from the German and Ukrainian respectively by A. N. Pleshcheyev (1825–1893).

MS: GMM; no. 2 only. EB 111 (MS 124), ff 1.

Publication: 1894, A. Gutheil, Moscow (separate numbers). Russian only. Re-engraved 1906 by A. Gutheil/Breitkopf, Russian and German words (German by Lina Esbeer); in keys as follows: no. 1 m. only; no. 2 h. m. only; no. 3 m. l. only; nos. 4–5 h. m. l.; no. 6 h. m. only. Plate nos. 8804–8816. The Russian/English edition appeared in 1921, original keys only, pl. nos. as under individual items above, including the superscript [a] (Eng. trans. by Edward Agate).

Earlier, in 1915, J. & W. Chester, London & Brighton/Edition Gutheil had issued some items, certainly no. 4 (JWC 3702) with Eng. trans. by Rosa Newmarch (later by M. C. H. Collet).

1924, Carl Fischer, New York, no. 5, V 825, 22925–3, pp. 5. Russian text; English version by Geraldine Farrar, Ger. by Lina Esbeer (h. only). An *ossia* marked '(2nd. Version)' appears in each verse, preceding the pause; of which the second extends the upwards compass to a'♭.

Coll. Ed. 16–21.

Current edition: Boosey & Hawkes, Songs, vol. 1, pp. 25–40; Muzyka, Romansy, vol. 1, pp. 69–85.

Performance:

Arrangements: no. 2, Romance transcrite pour piano par A. Siloti.
Publ: A. Gutheil, Moscow, A 7796 G, pp. 3.

no. 4, arranged for salon orchestra by L. Leonardi.
Publ: A. Gutheil.

Notes: For German and French titles, see Appendix (i).

Trio élégiaque pour Piano, Violon et Violoncelle op. 9
(Seconde partie avec accompagnement d'Harmonium)
[1st edition only]

1. Moderato – Allegro vivace D minor
2. *Quasi Variazione* F major
   Andante [1st edn Harmonium (peut être remplacer par le piano); 2nd edn Piano solo]
   Allegro [1st edn Allegro moderato]
   Lento [piano solo]
   Allegro scherzando [1st edn Vivace]
   Moderato
   L'istesso tempo [1st edn Allegro scherzando]
   Allegro vivace (B flat) [1st edn piano solo, F major, differs]
   Andante (D minor)
   Moderato (D flat major – F major)
3. Allegro risoluto – Moderato D minor

Date: *25 October – 15 December 1893.*

Dedication: [1st edn] (on flyleaf, black with green laurel wreath surround) Памяти великого художника [P. I. Tchaikovsky] [2nd edn] *A la mémoire d'un grand artiste*, and as 1st edn.

MS: GMM; (original version) (a) EB 41 (MS 60), ff 36, dated.
(b) Extract from the first movement, not appearing in the published work, EB 42 (MS 61), ff 1.
The whereabouts of the altered score doubtless forming the 'copy' for the revised version is at present unknown.

Publication: [1894] A. Gutheil, Moscow, A 6784 G/a/b, pp. 79, 15, 15. Title-page in black with gray-green shadowing. (There are copies in the Central Music Library (Reserve 024622), RAM and Cambridge University Library.)

[1907] *Nouvelle édition, revue par l'auteur.* (This edition eliminates the harmonium. For further details of the cuts and alterations also involved, v. inf. *Notes.*) A. Gutheil/Breitkopf, A 6784 G, pp. 64, 12, 12. (According to Goldenweiser, not published until 1915.)

1950, Muzgiz, Moscow, M 20346 Г, pp. 100, 12, 12. Edited from the copy marked by SR for the violinist Mogilevsky in 1917, and with introduction by A. Goldenweiser. For details of the further cuts here applied, see below.

Current edition: Boosey & Hawkes 17308 (1907 version); IMC.

Performance: 31 January 1894, Moscow.
SR, Julius Conus, Anatoly Brandukov. (According to OvR 93, the violinist was Barzevich.)
Revised version: 12 February 1907, Moscow, Kerzin Music Circle, A. Goldenweiser, K. Grigorovich, A. Brandukov.

Notes: SR to Natalia Skalon, 17 December 1893: *While working on it, all my thoughts, feelings and energy were devoted to it ... All the time I was tormented and worried ...* (RP/A; B/L 63).

In form, this work was modelled closely on Tchaikovsky's own Trio in A minor (op. 50) written in 1882, itself 'in memory of a great artist' – Nikolay Rubinstein. Indeed, the first eight notes of the theme of the variations in SR's trio coincide with the first seven in Tchaikovsky's, to which a passing note was added after the third note; also the melody is changed by commencing with an upbeat instead of an accented note. The keys differ only by a semitone, Tchaikovsky's movement being in E major, SR's in F.

Revived by the Moscow Trio (David Schor, Kreyn, Ehrlich) in 1903; SR then made 'cuts and changes, and there are even five bars written in by you (an introduction after the third variation – not usually played)'. (David Schor to SR, 29 July 1929, cf. B/L 100.) SR was reading the proofs of the new edition in 1907 (SR to Morozov, 11 February 1907, RP/A, B/L 134).

The principal differences made in this 'nouvelle édition' of 1907 are as follows (all cue numbers and MM marks were added; also some dynamics were supplemented or refined):

1st. movement. Violin and cello have exchanged parts at **2**–5.
At *Allegro vivace*, some slight amendments to the piano L.H.
At *Meno mosso*, 10 bars replace 16 similar bars, then marked *Moderato.*
Before the *Allegro moderato* a whole section (in F major, 3/4) of 22 bars (during which the cello was silent) has been omitted.
At *Maestoso*, the piano part is thinned in the L.H.; the string parts are rewritten; 2 + 2½ bars are cut. The violin's last 3 bars originally stood (slightly different) in the cello part.
At *Meno mosso* the piano L.H. part is slightly improved.
The 6 bars before **11**, by internal repetitions, were originally 12; the 4 after **11** were likewise 6.
The 3 bars before the *Moderato (Tempo I)* were originally 5; the mutes only appear in the revision.
The *Meno mosso* section here remains unaltered, except for a slight harmonic simplification; but again 22 bars (during which the violin is silent this time) are cut.
The same changes as before are made in the *Maestoso.*

2nd. movement. Originally, the Harmonium made its début at the outset, in the statement of the theme. Some slight harmonic improvements, careful phrasing marks, and the option of omitting the repeat – here and elsewhere – mark the revision, which hands the whole paragraph back to the pianist.

Allegro (orig. *A. Moderato*): 2 bars are omitted before the last bar of the first part; some minor pianistic and harmonic changes improve the second part. (The piano's solo *Lento* recitative is unaltered.)
In the *Allegro scherzando* (orig. *Vivace*), the piano first part originally ran along in all-too-Tchaikovsky-like open octaves, and the string chords

were off the beat with more rhythmic complexity than now. The string parts are added from the double-bar to **22**, as is the subsequent improvement of the piano part. (The *Mod*.[to] is unaltered.)

At *L'istesso tempo* (orig. *Allegro scherzando*) the mutes are added in the revision; the violin and (later) piano tremolo has been speeded up from semiquaver sextoles, and the pianist's chromatic figure at **24**, originally staccato chords, has been simplified. The final harmonic is new!

The *Allegro vivace* is entirely newly written; and it replaces a vigorous piano solo (in F major).

The *Andante* has had the anacrusis figure altered into a descending one, with all consequent modifications.

Eight bars have been cut before **29**. The piano's 8 solo bars after **30** replace 13 with a change of time to C, which continued to the end of the movement; except that the two phrases now given to the strings were originally played by the harmonium.

3rd movement. The diminuendo against the string tenuti after **31** is compressed by half.

At *Tempo rubato*, 3 bars of duplication are cut; as are 3 at **33**.

At *Moderato* the piano figuration was improved; the string parts at *Più vivo* were added, and 2 bars cut from the build-up to the climax.

The piano part in the last 7 bars is thinned-out a little.

In a note to SR's letter of 29 December 1906 to Mme. Kerzin, RP/A, no. 281, the editors state 'However this latter (1907) edition did not satisfy R. because in 1917, before a performance of this Trio with Mogilevsky and Brandukov, R. made a considerable number of changes. This version also appeared in a new publication in 1950 issued by Muzgiz under the editorship of Goldenweiser.' (Incidentally, this may be the place to mention that, after Rachmaninoff's death in 1943, Goldenweiser in turn paid tribute to him with a 'Trio in memory of SR, op. 31.').

The cuts in this 'final version' are as follows: (ref. to score of 1907 edition) p. 9, bars 4–7; p. 20, bars 7–8; p. 24, bars 3–4 and 7–8; p. 27, last 4 bars; p. 31, repeat deleted; p. 49, all string entries advanced 1 bar; p. 50, bars 10–13 deleted; p. 57, last 2 bars compressed to one; p. 60, bars 8–9 deleted.

[7] Morceaux de Salon pour piano op. 10

1. *Nocturne*	Andante espressivo	A minor
2. *Valse*	Allegro assai	A major
3. *Barcarolle*	Moderato	G minor
4. *Mélodie*	Allegretto	E minor – major
5. *Humoreske*	Allegro vivace	G major
6. *Romance*	Andante doloroso	F minor
7. *Mazurka*	Tempo di Mazurka	D flat major

Date: December 1893 – January 1894.

Dedication: *A Monsieur Paul Pabst.*

MS: (a) GMM; nos. 1, 2, 3 & 5 only, EB 49 (MSS 85–88), ff 11; nos. 4, 6 & 7 missing.

(b) L. of C., no. 5 only (revised version), part of ML 30. 55a. R3: pp. 13 (= pp. 3–15 of a 16-page sewn section), in pencil. With engraver's marks and queries. Titlepage *Humoresque / op. 10 / S. Rachmaninoff*; at end *3 March 1940 / New York / S.R.* See also under *Notes* below.

Publication: [1894], A. Gutheil, Moscow, A 6794–6800 G, (separate numbers), pp. 5, 9, 11, ..., 9, 3, ... Titlepage (in French only) in black; wide ornamental border panel in black reversed out of pink background. A later (undated) edition, A. Gutheil/Breitkopf, 'Compositions pour Piano', B & H cartouche at end of each item, only includes nos. 1, 3, 5 & 6 as A 9723ª–9726ª G, pp. 5, 11, 9, 3. The titlepage lists all the items but nos. 2, 4 & 7 are unpriced and were evidently not included. If the case of op. 33 (q. v.) is anything to go by, these exclusions were presumably at SR's insistence. The Hamelle edition, described at some length under op. 3 above, also contains nos. 2, 3 & 5 from the present opus.

1940, no. 5 only, 'Revised and as played by the Composer'. 'Copyright 1940 by Charles Foley, New York', TAIR, edition no. 2008, pl. no. R14–9, pp. 11. The rewriting is considerable (for further notes on revised readings, v. inf. *Recordings* and *Notes*).

Coll. Ed. I/30–73, 1948 (including the revised version of no. 5; the original version appears separately at pp. 288–294).

Current editions: Revised version of no. 5, Belwin Mills ('A Commemorative Collection'). Bosworth (Album) nos. 2, 4 & 5 (original versions).

Performance: 31 January 1894, Moscow, SR. Nos. 4, 5, 6 & 7 only.

Recording: no. 3 (1919), I; also Ampico roll (slightly edited).
no. 5 (1940), II, (revised version); also Ampico roll dated 1920 (original version, slightly edited).

Notes: The above-listed Ampico recordings on player-piano rolls are interesting in that they reveal slight 'retouchings' – unusual in SR's performances of his own compositions (his fidelity to the printed texts was usually so scrupulous that one can hardly recall any other alteration or addition – save the slight pianistic strengthening towards the end of the final cadenza of the Second Concerto, just audible on the recording. Radically revised and rewritten versions, 'as played by the composer' are, of course, a different thing). In view of the scarcity of these Ampico rolls, we add a few notes on the principal variants.

no. 3 (Barcarolle). At bar 5 and similar places, the second quaver in the L.H. figure is often omitted; in the middle section, bars 9–12 before the *Presto*, the melody notes (except the initial B flat) are doubled in the upper octave; most surprising of all, the diminished seventh chord in the penultimate bar is played *tremolando*!

no. 5 (Humoreske). In the *Andante* middle section, the sixth and 28th bars make a quintole of the melody by inserting a C sharp between the 2nd and 3rd notes (C and D); at the 14th bar, the bass note is lowered from G to F natural.

Among the loose pencilled sheets of MS, now in L. of C., 'found ... on the shelf near his Piano ...' is one on which SR had noted the RH melody of the Valse, no. 2: perhaps he contemplated rewriting this too at the period (in 1940) when he issued revisions of other works from his earlier collections (see above, and op. 3).

Six Morceaux pour le Piano à quatre mains op. 11

1. *Barcarolle*	Moderato	G minor
2. *Scherzo*	Allegro	D major
3. *Thème russe*	Andantino cantabile	B minor
4. *Valse*	Tempo di valse	A major
5. *Romance*	Andante con anima	C minor
6. *Slava*	Allegro moderato	C major

Date: *April 1894.*

Dedication: none.

MS: GMM; EB 70 (MS 106), ff 28.

Publication: [1894?], A. Gutheil, Moscow, A 6851–6 G, separate numbers, pp. 13, 13, 7, 11, 7, 15 (opposite pages). The titlepage (in Russian and French) has a red or blue ornamental border surrounding the black text (copies may be seen in BL h. 3984. a. (1)). The later edition, A. Gutheil/ Breitkopf, was re-engraved and printed by Breitkopf, using the same plate numbers.

Coll. Ed. III (ii)/3–69 (1950), in score (i.e. not on facing pages).

Current edition: Boosey & Hawkes, reprinted to no. 20288 complete in one volume (on opposite pages); previously separate numbers 18604, 18605, 18606, 17558, 18607, 18608; IMC 1343.

Performance:

Notes: nos. 3 & 6 comprise two of the very few uses by SR in instrumental guise of 'Russian Themes' (see also opp. 12 & 13). The use of the *Slava* theme in no. 6 recalls the coronation scene of *Boris Godunov* rather than the *maggiore* of Beethoven's second Razumovsky (E minor) quartet, op. 59 no. 2, third movement (Allegretto). The *Thème russe*, the basis of no. 3, unidentified by SR, remains unidentified by any of his subsequent biographers. It does not occur in the standard collections by Balakirev, Rimsky-Korsakov, or Tchaikovsky – but then, nor do the themes of the later Trois Chansons Russes, op. 41, q. v.

КАПРИЧЧИО НА ЦЫГАНСКИЕ ТЕМЫ — op. 12

Capriccio bohémien pour grand orchestre

E minor – major

Date: Summer 1892 in piano duet form; orchestration completed by September 1894.

Dedication: *A Monsieur P. Lodijensky.*

Orchestra: Picc. 2. 2. 2. 2 – 4. 2. 3. 1 – Timp. Triang. Tamburino. Tamburo. Piatti. Cassa – Harp – Strings.

MS: (a) *Full score*, present whereabouts unknown.

(b) Arrangement for piano 4 hands by the composer, GMM; EB 20 (MS 41), ff 17. Marked by the composer *opus 4* acc. to editor's footnote to letter from SR to M. Slonov, 2 August 1892 (RP/A, and v. inf. *Notes*).

Publication: [1896], full score, A. Gutheil, Moscow, A 7312 G, pp. 61. Title-page in Russian; 'Gravure et impression de Breitkopf & Härtel à Leipzig'.

[1895], Arrangement pour piano à 4 mains par l'auteur, A. Gutheil, Moscow, A 7136 G; later edition printed (?re-engraved) by Breitkopf & Härtel, pp. 39 (opposite pages).

1966, Muzyka, Moscow, 3363, pp. 70 (a re-engraved, but otherwise exact, reprint of the full score).

Material: Boosey & Hawkes hire library.

Performance: 22 November 1895, Moscow, cond. SR.
20 January 1896, St. Petersburg, Russian Symphony Concerts, cond. Aleksandr Glazunov.

Notes: SR to M. Slonov, 2 August 1892: *I am now writing a capriccio for orchestra, not on Spanish themes, like Rimsky-Korsakov, nor Italian themes, like Tchaikovsky, but on gypsy themes. I shall finish it in four days. For the time being I think I shall write it for four hands and orchestrate it later.* Here again, then, we see the use of 'nationalistic' themes, this time in an orchestral work. SR to Morozov, 12 April 1908: *I have three pieces that frighten me: the First Concerto, the Capriccio and the First Symphony. I should very much like to see all these in a corrected, decent form.* (RP/A; B/L 145.) Only the first of these 'three pieces' was ever revised by the critical and perhaps ultra-scrupulous composer, whose much quoted sentences may have militated against more frequent performance of the present colourful work.

A quotation from *Aleko*, which was being read in proof simultaneously with the composition of the present work, may be noted: at the *con moto* after cue **13**, the motif of Aleko himself appears.

FIRST SYMPHONY op. 13

1. Grave – Allegro ma non troppo — D minor
2. Allegro animato — F major
3. Larghetto — B flat major
4. Allegro con fuoco — D major

Date: *January* – [30] *August 1895* (Asafyev).

Dedication: *A. L.* [Anna Aleksandrovna Lodyzhenskaya].

Orchestra: 3 (Picc). 2. 2. 2 – 4. 3. 3. 1 – [4] Timp. Triang (not in 1, 3). Tamburo Mil. (in 4). Tamburino (in 4). Piatti (not in 3). Gr. Cassa (not in 2, 3). Tamt. (in 4) – Strings.

MS: (a) The complete original full score, though it is at present unlocated, possibly still survives somewhere despite the composer's anathema (SR to Asafyev loc. cit. *I won't show the symphony to anyone and in my will I shall make sure nobody looks at it*).

(b) The following fragmentary pages are in GMM: EB 22 (MS 43), ff 2 of variants from the first movement (5th page) and fourth movement (8th page); EB 23 (MS 44), extracts from the first movement not included in the score published in 1947 (v. inf.), ff 6;

(c) Pencil sketches, EB 24–5 (MSS 45–6), ff 14, 3.

(d) Orchestral parts in a copyist's hand, Leningrad Conservatoire (it was from these parts that the score published in 1947 was reconstructed).

(e) Arrangement for piano 4 hands by the composer, GMM; EB 21 (MS 42), ff 34, *1895 Ivanovka* acc. to EB and Coll. Ed. [Acc. to B/L 74 without other evidence this arrangement was in fact made in 1898].

Publication: 1947, full score, State Music Publishers, Moscow & Leningrad, M 18693 Г, pp. 245, thick paper wrapper printed in maroon with buff panel. Wording in Russian and English. Reconstructed from the MS parts (d) above by B. G. Shalman under the direction of B. S. Asafyev and A. V. Gauk. Preface by Aleksandr Gauk (trans. in Culshaw, 55–6).

1950, arrangement for piano 4 hands by the composer, Coll. Ed. III (iii), M 20589 Г, pp. 3–134, in score. At end, two pages of notes by P. Lamm. (Footnotes to the text refer to the author's pencilling in the MS and other variant readings, see above.)

The 1947 full score was reprinted (ca. 1972) by Rare Music Edition / British & Continental, London.

Orchestral material currently on hire from Boosey & Hawkes.

Further study of all the above source material by the two Russian musicologists responsible for a number of critical editions and reissues of SR's scores has recently led to the following important publication:

1977, full score, Muzyka, Moscow, 9326; new edition edited by I. Iordan and

G. Kirkor. Preface, pp. 3–5; score, pp. 7–249 (but newly engraved, and in part differently laid out, from the 1947 edition); appendix, pp. 253–285. Differences between the 1947 score and the parts are footnoted; and in particular the more elaborate original percussion parts are now included. Describing the 'changes and additions' they found in the MS orchestral parts, the editors state 'it is evident that all these changes in the orchestration of the symphony were made on the instruction of A. K. Glazunov'. The appendix contains the following:

(1st movement) 1a (pp. 253–4): passage rejected from the 'second subject', four-hand piano version.
1b (255–6): part of same, rejected from MS orchestral score.
2 (257–8): another rejected leaf from the same.
3 (259–263) } rejected leaves of the original scoring of the start of the
4 (264–8) } development.
5 (269–270): rejected original scoring of link to reprise.
6 (271–3): rejected passage leading to return of 'second subject'.
7 (274–7): rejected leaf from 'second subject'.

(3rd. movement) 8 (278–282): rejected original scoring of coda.

(Finale) 9 (283–5): rejected original scoring of end of work.

Performance: 15 March 1897, St. Petersburg Conservatoire, Russian Symphony Concert, cond. A. K. Glazunov.
17 October 1945, Moscow, Great Hall of the Conservatoire, USSR State Symphony Orchestra cond. A. V. Gauk.
19 March 1948, Philadelphia Orch., Academy of Music, cond. Eugene Ormandy.
2 January 1964, London, Royal Festival Hall, Polyphonia Symphony Orchestra, cond. Bryan Fairfax.

Notes: Whereas the themes of the preceding opus were drawn from gypsy sources, those of the symphony are based on traditional chants of the Russian Orthodox Church taken from the *Oktoekhos* (OvR 98; B/L 67). The *Dies irae* motif also can clearly be heard in the closing trombone chords.

According to B/L 68 (with the authority of Sophia Satina, VR/A, vol. 1, p. 28) the score bears an epigraph, the same as that placed by Tolstoy above *Anna Karenina:* 'Vengeance is mine; I will repay, saith the Lord' (Romans, xii, 19). This is also noted at the end of one of the orchestral parts (v. preface to 1977 edition). It does not appear in the Muzgiz first publication of 1947.

SR writing to Slonov, 2 September 1895, refers to his continuing work on the first movement: *Several places will have to be worked over again, at the same time I will make it a little shorter.* The rejected and altered pages are probably those listed under MS (b) above and referred to by Lamm in his publication of the 4-hand piano arrangement, which thus establishes the definitive form of the work.

1. Я жду тебя.
   (I wait for thee.) A 8819ª G, soprano.
   Largo, F major (h), [E♭ major, VB & EB]. (c – b′♭)
   Date: 1894.
   Text: Mariya Davidova.
   Dedication: L. D. Skalon.

2. Островок.
   (The little island.) A 8822ª G, soprano or tenor.
   Lento, G major (h), [D major, VB & EB]. (e♭ – g′)
   Date: 1896.
   Text: Konstantin Balmont (1867–1942), after *The Isle* (1822) by Percy Bysshe Shelley (1792–1822).
   Dedication: S. A. Satina.

3. Давно в любви.
   (For long [there has been little consolation] in love; first published Eng. trans. How few the joys.) A 8826ª G, contralto or bass.
   Allegro, F sharp minor (l). (G♯ – f′♯)
   Date: October 1896.
   Text: Afanasy Fet (pseudonym of Afanasy Shenshin, 1820–1892).
   Dedication: Z. A. Pribytkova.

4. Я был у ней.
   (I came to her.) A 8828ª G, mezzo soprano or baritone.
   Vivente, E flat major (m), [F major, VB & EB]. (B♭ – g′)
   Date: October 1896.
   Text: Aleksey Koltsov (1809–1842).
   Dedication: Yu. S. Sakhnovsky.

5. Эти летние ночи.
   (These summer nights; first published Eng. trans. Midsummer nights.) A 8830ª G, soprano or tenor.
   Allegro, E major (h). (d♯ – b′)
   Date: October 1896.
   Text: Daniil Rathaus (1869–1937).
   Dedication: M. I. Gutheil.

6. Тебя так любят все.
   (How everyone loves thee; first published Eng. trans. The world would see thee smile.) A 8832ª G, mezzo soprano or baritone.
   Moderato, G minor (m). (d – g′(e′))
   Date: 1896.
   Text: A. K. Tolstoy (1817–1875).
   Dedication: A. N. Ivanovsky.

7. Не верь мне, друг!
(Believe it not, [friend].) A 8834ª G, soprano or tenor.
Allegro moderato, C major (h). (e – b′♭)
Date: 1896.
Text: A. K. Tolstoy.
Dedication: A. G. Klokachova.

8. О, не грусти.
(O, do not grieve!) A 8838ª G, mezzo soprano or baritone.
Andante, F minor (m). (B♭ – a′♭)
Date: 1896.
Text: Aleksey Apukhtin (1841–1893).
Dedication: N. A. Aleksandrova.

9. Она, как полдень, хороша.
(She is lovely as the noon; first published Eng. trans. As fair as day in blaze of noon.) A 8840ª G, mezzo soprano or baritone.
Lento, E flat major (m). (B♭ – g′♭)
Date: 1896.
Text: N. Minsky (pseudonym of Nikolay Maksimovich Vilenkin, 1855–1937).
Dedication: E. A. Lavrovskaya.

10. В моей душе.
(In my soul; first published Eng. trans. Love's flame.) A 8842ª G, contralto or bass.
Lento, D major (l). (A – d′)
Date: 1896.
Text: N. Minsky (see above).
Dedication: E. A. Lavrovskaya.

11. Весенние воды.
(Spring waters.) A 8843ª G, soprano or tenor.
Allegro vivace, E flat major (h), [D flat major, VB & EB].
(e♭ [B♭] – b′♭)
Date: 1896.
Text: Fyodor Tyutchev (1803–1873).
Dedication: A. D. Ornatskaya.

12. Пора!
('Tis time!) A 8848ª G, contralto or bass.
Allegro appassionato, E flat minor (l), [D minor, VB & EB].
(B♭ – f′)
Date: 1896.
Text: Semyon Nadson (1862–1887).
Dedication: none.

MS: GMM; autographs of the complete set, EB 112 (MS 125), ff 17.

Publication: 1896, A. Gutheil, Moscow (separate numbers), Russian only; nos. 8 & 11, also German words. Re-engraved 1906 by A. Gutheil/Breitkopf, Russian and German words (German by Lina Esbeer); in keys as follows: nos. 1, 2, 4, 7, 11, 12 h. m. l; nos. 3, 6 m. l; nos. 5, 8, 9 h. m; no. 10 h. l only. Plate numbers 8819–8848. The Russian/English edition appeared in 1921, 'original keys only' (but note discrepancies from keys of the MSS of nos. 1, 2, 4, 11, 12 supra), plate nos. as under individual items above, including the superscript ª (Eng. trans. by Rosa Newmarch, nos. 8 & 11; the remainder by Edward Agate).

Earlier, in 1916, J. & W. Chester, London & Brighton/Edition Gutheil had issued some items, certainly no. 11 (JWC 3736) with Eng. trans. by Rosa Newmarch (later by M. C. H. Collet).

The English/French edition (Fr. trans. by M. D. Calvocoressi) also bears the copyright date 1921, and its plate numbers run in the 90.. and 96.. series.

1922, Carl Fischer, New York, nos. 2 ('The Mirage') and 11 ('Ecstasy of Spring'); V 779, 778; 22591–2, 22595–6, pp. 3, 7. Russian text; English versions by Geraldine Farrar (h. only).

Coll. Ed. 22–33.

Current edition: Boosey & Hawkes, Songs, vol. 1, pp. 41–80; Muzyka, Romansy, vol. 1, pp. 86–125.

Performance:

Arrangement: no. 2, arranged for salon orchestra by L. Leonardi.

Publ: A. Gutheil

Many and varied are the different arrangements to be found of no. 11 – another of SR's popular items.

Notes: Tchaikovsky's settings of two of the above texts may be mentioned: that of no. 5 in 1893, as his op. 73 no. 3, and of no. 7 in 1869, as his op. 6 no. 1.

For German and French titles, see Appendix (i).

ШЕСТЬ ХОРОВ для женских (или детских) голосов с сопровождением ф – п. op. 15

[Six choruses for women's or children's voices with piano accompaniment]

1. Славься (Be praised), Lentamente, G minor
   Text: Nikolay Nekrasov (1821–1878).
2. Ночка (The night), Lento molto, F major
   Text: Vladimir Ladyzhensky (1859–1939).
3. Сосна (The pine tree), Andante, A minor – major
   Text: Mikhail Lermontov (1814–1841).
4. Задремали волны (Dreaming waves), Moderato, D major
   Text: K(onstantin) R(omanov) (1858–1916) [Grand Duke Konstantin Konstantinovich].
5. Неволя (Captivity), Non troppo allegro, F major
   Text: Nikolay Tsyganov (1797–1831).
6. Ангел (The angel), Non troppo allegro, E major
   Text: Mikhail Lermontov.

Date: 1895–6.

Dedication: none.

Voices: womens or childrens choir, S.A. (and piano).

MS: GMM; (a) EB 91 (MS 64), nos. 1, 2 & 6 autograph, ff 6; no. 6 *1896.*

(b) ditto, nos. 3, 4 & 5 proofs, ff 6.

(c) another version of no. 1 (Слава Александру II) [unpubl.], EB 92 (MS 65), ff 1.

(d) no. 5, EB 93 (MS 66), ff 1, dated *15 October 1895.*

Publication: 1895, nos. 1, 2, 3 & 4 in Детское чтение, 1895 nos. 1, 3, 6 & 10; 1896, no. 5 in the same, 1896 no. 1. (B/L 408 states 'First published in a magazine, probably *Pedagogichesky Listok*'.)

1896, complete, P. Jurgenson, Moscow; scores 20748–53, parts 20754–59.

1913, The Boston Music Co., Boston, Mass. 3312–7; complete as 3318, pp. 31. In this edition, the titles are as follows (and the sequence is changed):

1. Night
2. The lonely Pine
3. Sleeping Waves
4. The Captive
5. The Angel
6. Glorious forever

'From the Russian of ... by Nathan Haskell Dole. Edited by H. Clough-Leighter.'

1933, no. 4 only ['Now the Waves are dying'], Galaxy Music Corporation, (The Swarthmore Choral Series edited by Alfred J. Swan), GM 597, pp. 6. 'The words by K.R. (The Grand Duke Konstantin Konstantinovich). English version by Alfred J. Swan.'

1946, no. 3 only ['Northern Dream'], Edward B. Marks Music Corporation, New York (Choral Masterpieces of Russia, Series 1), pp. 5. 'English translation by Wladimir Lakond, English adaptation by Olga Paul.'

1976, complete, Muzyka, Moscow, 9252, pp. 2–26, in Хоровые Произведения ... ed. A. P. Aleksandrov. In this edition, no. 1 appears as Слава Народу! (Copy in BL. G. 936. qq. (3).)

Performance:

Notes: SR commented, after completing the work, that these choruses were so difficult that no child would ever be able to sing them (Norris 24: letter to Zatayevich, 7 December 1896).

6 Moments musicaux pour Piano op. 16

1. Andantino	B flat minor
2. Allegretto	E flat minor
3. Andante cantabile	B minor
4. Presto	E minor
5. Adagio sostenuto	D flat major
6. Maestoso	C major

Date: October–December *1896.*

Dedication: *A Monsieur A. Zatayévitch.*

MS: (a) GMM; EB 50 (MS 89), ff 18. Dated *1896.*

(b) L. of C., no. 2 only (revised version), part of ML 30. 55a. R3: pp. 9. Titlepage: *Moment musical / op. 16 / S. Rachmaninoff*; in pencil; dated *5 February 1940.*

Publication: 1896, P. Jurgenson, Moscow [/Leipzig], 20796–20801, complete, pp. 43, and in separate numbers, pp. 9, 11, 5, 9, 6, 11. The titlepage of this edition has a blue border with corner ornaments surrounding the black text (a slightly later copy may be seen in BL. h. 3984. a. (2)). Later prints with a different (monochrome) titlepage, also those separate issues with the imprint 'P. Jurgenson / Rob. Forberg / Leipzig' to nos. PJ 1021–6 are in musical content identical.

1925, Anton J. Benjamin, Leipzig, reprinted in separate numbers (AJB –, 8281, 8328, 8282, 8283, 8300) in Series 2 of their 'Modern Russian Masters' (Neu-Russische Meister). The highly ornamental wrappers, printed in black, red and gold, were some compensation for the subsequent lowering of the original standard set by Jurgenson in this respect; on the other hand the re-engraving by Geidel of Leipzig, (though sharply printed) 'Rev. M. Frey' not only failed to revise, but introduced spurious 'slurrings' and allowed a number of errors to gain currency (though nothing like so many as in the later Scriabin works also republished – and 'revised' – by the same hands).

1940, no. 2 only, 'Revised and as played by the composer', now marked *Allegro*, 'Copyright 1940 by Charles Foley, New York', TAIR, edition no. 2020, pl. no. R16–11, pp. 13. The revisions, apart from a slight tightening of the structure immediately preceding the climactic chord, are concerned with a number of minor (though helpful) pianistic improvements, plus the addition of fingerings.

Coll. Ed. I/74–113 (1948) (including the revised version of no. 2; the original version there is given separately at pp. 295–303).

Current edition: Richard Schauer (Anton J. Benjamin) EE 3170; IMC 512.

Performance:

Recording: no. 2 (1940), II.

Arrangement: no. 3. Transcribed for string orchestra by Alexander Reisman. *Publ:* Western International Music Co., Los Angeles, pp. 10.

Notes: The original edition only included fingerings in no. 4. This number also included pedalling – almost the only case of SR systematically indicating such in one of his piano works, except for a few special effects, such as the closes of op. 33 no. 2, op. 39 no. 8 and the Bach *Preludio*, and on p. 13 of the score of the Fourth Concerto (1928 edition) (cf. Lamm's scrupulously edited Coll. Ed., where all such are preserved).

The revision of no. 2 possibly antedates its 1940 writing-out and publication: this item was fairly frequently performed in recital by the composer in later years, and it is likely that the pianistic refinements to what was already a most effective – and most characteristic – piece date from such occasions.

2me Suite pour deux pianos op. 17

1. *Introduction*	Alla Marcia	C major
2. *Valse*	Presto	G major
3. *Romance*	Andantino	A flat major
4. *Tarantella*	Presto	C minor

Date: December 1900 – April *1901, Moscow.*

Dedication: *A Monsieur A. Goldenweiser.*

MS: GMM; (a) EB 74 (MS 111), ff 38, dated *1901, Moscow.*

(b) Sketches in pencil, EB 75 (MS 112), ff 12.

(c) Corrected proof sheets, EB 76 (MS 113), pp. 39.

Publication: [October 1901], A. Gutheil/Breitkopf & Härtel, A 8101 G. Two separate individual piano parts, pp. 39, 37, not in score. The titlepage of the first player's part was gorgeously lithoed (by Breitkopf & Härtel, Leipzig) in black, red, blue, green, yellow and gold; the composite wrapper to the second part being printed in black only on the usual gray silurian paper (as the old catalogues would have said „mit originalem Umschlag und farbigem Titelblatt"). French wording only.

Coll. Ed. IV (ii)/3–108, 1951; in score, as are later Muzyka prints (though these were re-engraved to occupy 83 pages only, instead of the Coll. Ed's 108).

Current editions: Boosey & Hawkes 16370, in two separate parts; (IMC 508 – in score, pp. 55; previously in separate parts. Nos. 2–3 only included in an Album formerly issued by Charles Foley).

Performance: 24 November 1901, Moscow (Philharmonic Society); SR and Aleksandr Siloti.

Arrangement: for piano and orchestra, by Lee Hoiby.
Orch: 2. 2. 2. 2 – 4. 2. 2. 1 – Timp. Perc. – Strings.
Publ: (material) B. & H. Inc. Hire Library.

Notes: In the last movement, at the 22nd bar, the following footnote appears:
Thême principal est emprunté du receuil des chansons italiennes.

Second-Concerto pour le Piano avec Orchestre ou un 2^d Piano op. 18

1. Moderato C minor
2. Adagio sostenuto E major
3. Allegro scherzando C minor – major

Date: The composition of the second and third movements in Autumn 1900 preceded that of the first movement (v. inf.). The work was finished on 21 April *1901, Moscow.*

Dedication: *A Monsieur N. Dahl.* For Dr. Nikolay Dahl's successful treatment of the composer, see B/L 89–90. Dr. Dahl was at least once associated in performance with this very work, see B/L 96 f. n.

Orchestra: 2. 2. 2. 2 – 4. 2. 3. 1 – Timp. (G. C. & Ptti in finale only) – Strings.

MS: GMM; (a) *Full score* EB 38 (MS 47), ff 89, dated.

(b) Sketches in pencil for first movement and finale, EB 39 (MS 48), ff 13.

Publication: [October 1901], full score, A. Gutheil/Breitkopf, A 8102 G, pp. 116. Titlepage lithoed (by Breitkopf & Härtel) in black, red, green, gray, buff and gold (a copy may be seen in BL. h. 3984).

Ditto, arrangement for 2 pianos 4 hands by the composer, A 8104 G, pp. 63, gray wrappers (with wording in Russian and French); titlepage, French only.

A miniature edition of the full score was later issued to pl. no. A 8102^A G, printed by Imp. Delanchy-Dupré, Paris, Asnières.

Current editions: Boosey & Hawkes 15209 (miniature score also available, HPS 17), 16674 (2 pianos); (IMC ['Our larger size edition facilitates the reading of this score'], Schirmer, Leeds Music, Broude Bros; also included in an Album formerly issued by Charles Foley).

The first editions again exhibit the gorgeous multicolour titlepages noted already for op. 17, in the case of the full score and of the two piano reduction, where two separate copies were included. Whether this treatment, which certainly reappeared in op. 30, was continued for any of the intervening works seems unlikely. Later editions of op. 18 (after the Koussevitzky purchase of Gutheil) retained the black plate only for the titlepage, with the ordinary gray wrapper.

Performance: (2nd and 3rd movements only)
2 December 1900, Moscow, Nobility Hall, SR cond. A. Siloti. Reproduction of the programme in RP/A opp. p. 209.
(complete work)
27 October 1901, Moscow Philharmonic Society, SR cond. A. Siloti.
29 May 1902, London (Queen's Hall), Philharmonic Society, Basil Sapellnikoff, cond. Frederic H. Cowen. Siloti's performances in Birmingham and Manchester preceded this London première.

26 May 1908, London Symphony Orchestra (Queen's Hall), SR cond. S. Koussevitzky.
8 November 1909, Philadelphia, Boston Symphony Orch., SR cond. Max Fiedler.

Recording: SR and the Philadelphia Orchestra cond. Leopold Stokowski (1924, I; 1929, V).

Arrangements: (We pass over the many settings of lyrics to the justly famous melodies of this work, even its use – with other compositions from the same source – in a once-popular musical; but list the following attractive adaptation by a friend and musical associate of many years' standing): *Preghiera* – Prayer from the Piano Concerto no. 2 of Rachmaninoff; for Violin and Piano in collaboration with the Composer [by] Fritz Kreisler.

Publ: 1940, Charles Foley, 1164, K19–10, pp. 9, 3. This condensed version of the slow movement is transposed into C major.

Notes: Notwithstanding the case of William Walton's [First] Symphony, whose first three movements were performed in public before the finale was composed, the case of SR's Second Concerto must surely take pride of place for unusual modern premières; the second and third movements being completed and publicly performed before the composition of the first. (It seems only at one remove from such previous cases as the première of Chopin's F minor Concerto, when the earlier movements had been separated by a horn solo or a set of solo violin variations.)

The principal motif of the first movement is often stated to have been extracted from the finale, where indeed it appears to occur at the 3/2 passage between cues **29** and **30**; also see the transitional passage at **38** – which reveals the thematic kinship of the principal themes of both movements. The 'harmonic fluctuation' (as Hindemith would call it) preceding the entry of the finale's principal theme at cue **28** is basically the same as that of the soloist's chord progression which opens the first movement; likewise the telescoped progression that concludes the first movement is repeated at once, quite transformed in character, as the transitional phrase introducing the E major of the Adagio, see *plates 5–6.* (It would be most interesting to learn if these four bars stood before the entry of the soloist as early as that first incomplete performance. 'Strokes of genius', such as this, often have a severely practical basis: e.g. the equivalent link from the first movement in Mendelssohn's Violin Concerto to the melody of the Andante is revealed, from an inspection of the MS, to have been a means of using up the rest of a sheet of paper.)

Another interesting point concerns the elusive 4 x 3 = 3 x 4 figuration of the Adagio: not only this, but the actual outline of the four solo bars which precede the entry of the melody first occurred in the corresponding passage of the early Romance for piano trio, composed a decade earlier for the six hands of the Skalon sisters (see II/22 inf.). Then, however, the pregnant possibilities of the rhythm had lain unexplored and a comparatively ordinary

Plate 5: Second Concerto: last page of the first movement

Plate 6: Second Concerto: first page of the second movement

theme in triple time followed, crushing its accompaniment to agree and eliminating its mystery in the process.

According to Seroff 69, Leonid Sabaneyev told him that 'the second theme in the last movement came from Nikita Morozov. [SR] is said to have heard this melody which Morozov composed, and remarked: 'Oh, that is a melody I should have composed.' Morozov ... said ... 'Well, why don't you take it?' '

Sonate pour Piano et Violoncelle op. 19

1. Lento – Allegro moderato	G minor
2. Allegro scherzando	C minor
3. Andante	E flat major
4. Allegro mosso	G major

Date: [Summer –] *12 December 1901, Moscow.*

Dedication: *A Monsieur A. Brandoukoff.*

MS: GMM; (a) EB 80 (MS 115), ff 38, dated.
(b) Sketches, EB 81 (MS 116), ff 10.

Publication: [March 1902], A. Gutheil/Breitkopf, A 8164 G, pp. 49, 13.
Current edition: Boosey & Hawkes 16338.

Performance: 2 December 1901, Moscow, Anatoly Brandukov and SR.

Notes:

ВЕСНА [Spring] op. 20

КА́НТАТА; баритон-solo, хор и оркестр.
(Текст Некрасова)
Der Frühling ... Nach dem russischen Text von N. Nekrassoff.
Deutsche Umdichtung von Wladimir Czumikov.

(E major)

Date: January – February *1902, Moscow.*

Dedication: *Herrn N. S. Morosoff.*

Text: N. A. Nekrasov (1821–1878): Zelyony shum ('The verdant noise').

Orchestra: 3 (Picc). 2. CA. 2. BsCl. 2 – 4. 2. 3. 1 – Timp. Triang. Ptti & Cassa. Tamt. – Harp – Strings.

Voices: Chorus S. A. T. B. – Baritone solo.

MS: GMM; (a) *Full score*, EB 82 (MS 7), ff 33, dated at the end *Moscow 1902* (the Ger. words entered in the hand of N. S. Morozov).

(b) Corrected proof sheets, EB 83 (MS 911), pp. 69.

(c) *Vocal score*, EB 84 (MS 8, ff 1–14), ff 14.

(d) Sketches in pencil, EB 85 (MS 9), ff 10, dated at end *Moscow 1902.*

Publication: [1902; (March 1903, B/L)], full score, A. Gutheil/Breitkopf, A 8322 G, pp. 69.

Ditto, vocal score, ditto, A 8323 G, pp. 35. Gray wrappers, printed in Russian; titlepage in German.

Material: Boosey & Hawkes Hire Library.

Current edition: The full score was reprinted unedited by Muzyka, Moscow, pl. no. 21, in 1964, pp. 102 & 2 pp. words.

Performance: 11 March 1902, Moscow Philharmonic Society, A. V. Smirnov (baritone), cond. A. Siloti.
8 January 1905, St. Petersburg; soloist: F. Chaliapin.

Notes: cf. OvR 144: *How I would like to touch up the orchestration of my Cantata today ... No, I would alter the whole instrumentation* was SR's comment on recalling Rimsky-Korsakov's remark (after the performance in Paris in 1906): 'The music is good, but, what a pity! There is no sign of spring in the orchestra.'

At the final choral setting of the words Идет гудет (Der Frühling kommt) the motif C, E, B, E occurs, in equal quavers. An almost identical motif, D, G, E, G, with broken rhythm, is introduced by Medtner in the Finale (Rondo) of his Sonata no. 2, op. 44, for violin and piano, composed in 1926. Here, the motif, on its first appearance in the piano part, is underlaid with the words Весна идет, and a footnote states: 'motto from a poem by Tyutchev' – the same as set by SR in his op. 14 no. 11 ('Spring Waters').

[Twelve Songs] op. 21

1. Судьба.
   (Fate.) Allegro moderato
   C minor (l) in Coll. Ed. (bass). (AA♭ – e)
   D minor (m) in Gutheil, A 8325ª G (baritone).
   Date: 18 February 1900.
   Text: Aleksey Apukhtin (1841–1893).
   Dedication: F. I. Chaliapin.
   MS: GMM; EB 115 (MS 126), ff 4, inscribed: *Dedicated to Fyodr Ivanovich Chaliapin by his sincere admirer S. Rachmaninoff, 21 February 1900.* Also, another copy in the hand of M. A. Slonov, dedicated to F. I. Chaliapin in SR's hand, and with his pencilled annotations. Key of C minor.
   Publication: 1900, A. Gutheil, Moscow. Also see below.
   Performance:
   Notes: As a note on the published score explains, the recurring motif of the song is taken from the opening of Beethoven's Fifth Symphony.

2. Над свежей могилой.
   (By the grave.) A 8303ª G, contralto or bass.
   Largo, E minor (l), [EB – A minor, but VB – E minor]. (C – e)
   Date: April 1902.
   Text: Semyon Nadson (1862–1887).
   Dedication: none.

3. Сумерки.
   (Twilight.) A 8304ª G, soprano or tenor.
   Lento, E minor (h). (c – g'♯)
   Date: April 1902.
   Text: Jean-Marie Guyot (1854–1888), translated by M. Tkhorzhevsky (see VR/A, vol. 2, p. 503; 'M. Guyot' in Gutheil).
   Dedication: N. I. Vrubel.

4. Они отвечали.
   (They answered; first published Eng. trans. The answer.) A 8305ª G, soprano or tenor.
   Allegro vivace, D flat major (h). (e♭ – b'♭)
   Date: April 1902.
   Text: Victor Hugo (1802–1885), translated by Lev Mey (1822–1862); original: Autre guitarre ('Comment, disaient-ils'), from *Les Rayons et les Ombres* (1840), no. 23.
   Dedication: E. Kreutzer.

5. Сирень.
   (Lilacs.) A 8306ª G, soprano.
   Allegretto, A flat major (h). (e♭ – g')
   Date: April 1902.
   Text: Ekaterina Beketova (1855–1892).

Dedication: None on MS or standard Gutheil edition; Muzgiz 1957 volume gives 'A. N. Strekalov', but this does not appear in the 1973 2-vol. reissue.

6. Отрывок из А. Мюссе.
   (Fragment from de Musset; first published Eng. trans. Loneliness.) A 8307ª G, soprano.
   Allegro non tanto, F sharp minor (h). (c♯ – a′)
   Date: April 1902.
   Text: Alfred de Musset (1810–1857), translated by Aleksey Apukhtin (1841–1893); original, La nuit de mai (stanza 4: 'Pourquoi mon coeur bat-il si vite?'), from *Poésies nouvelles* (1835).
   Dedication: A. A. Liven.

7. Здесь хорошо.
   (How fair this spot.) A 8308ª G, soprano.
   Moderato, A major (h). (d – b′)
   Date: April 1902.
   Text: G. Galina (pseudonym of the Countess Adolfovna Einerling, 1873–1942).
   Dedication: Dedicated to N[atalya Rachmaninova].

8. На смерть чижика.
   (On the death of a linnet.) A 8309 G, soprano or tenor; though Gutheil has A 8379ª G, mezzo soprano or baritone, in vol. 1.
   Allegretto, C minor (m), [VB & EB, D minor]. (c – f′)
   Date: April 1902.
   Text: Vasily Zhukovsky (1783–1852).
   Dedication: O. A. Trubnikova.

9. Мелодия.
   (Melody.) A 8310ª G, soprano or tenor.
   Non allegro, B flat major (h). (B♭ – b′♭)
   Date: April 1902.
   Text: Semyon Nadson.
   Dedication: N. N. Lanting.

10. Пред иконой.
    (Before the image.) A 8311ª G, mezzo soprano.
    Adagio, E flat minor (m). (B♭ – f′)
    Date: April 1902.
    Text: Arseny Golenishchev-Kutuzov (1848–1913).
    Dedication: M. A. Ivanova.

11. Я не пророк.
    (No prophet I.) A 8312ª G, soprano.
    Moderato, E flat major (h). (e♭ – a′♭)
    Date: April 1902.
    Text: Aleksandr Kruglov (1853–1915).
    Dedication: none.

12.Как мне больно.

(How painful for me; first published Eng. trans. Sorrow in springtime.)
A 8313[a] G, soprano.
Allegro mosso, G minor (h). (d – b′♭)
Date: April 1902.
Text: G. Galina (see above).
Dedication: V. A. Satin.

MS: GMM: of no. 1, see above.
of nos. 2–12, EB 116 (MS 8, ff 15–39), ff 25; dated at the end *April 1902.*

Publication: of no. 1 only, see above.

1902, complete, A. Gutheil/Breitkopf, Russian and German words (German by Lina Esbeer); all in h. m. and l. keys except nos. 3, 8, 9, 10 h. m. only. Plate numbers of nos. 2–12 (original keys) 8303–8313; of other keys in range 8360–8386. The Russian/English edition appeared in 1921, original keys only, plate nos. as under individual items above, including the superscript [a] (Eng. trans. by Rosa Newmarch, nos. 1, 2, 5, 7, 12; Edward Agate, nos. 3, 4, 6, 8, 9, 10, 11).

Earlier, in 1916, J. & W. Chester, London & Brighton/Edition Gutheil had issued some items, certainly no. 5 (JWC 3735) with Eng. trans. by Rosa Newmarch.

The English/French edition (Fr. trans. by M. D. Calvocoressi) also bears the copyright date 1921, and its plate numbers run in the 96.. series.

1922, Carl Fischer, New York, nos. 5 ('The Tryst') and 7 ('Here beauty dwells'); V 781, 780; 22592–3 and 22594–3, pp. 5, 5. Russian texts; English versions by Geraldine Farrar (h. only).

Coll. Ed. 34–45.

Current edition: Boosey & Hawkes, Songs, Vol. 1 pp. 81–127; Muzyka, Romansy, Vol. 1 pp. 126–173.

Performance:

Arrangements: no. 5

(a) Le Lilas/Сирень/Flieder/The Lilacs – Romance transcrite pour le piano par l'Auteur.
Date: December 1914 (Asafyev); B/L gives 1913.
MS: ?
Publ: [?1919, acc. B/L 411; but 1914 if pl. no. is to be believed], A. Gutheil, A 9685 G, pp. 5.
Perf: 6 May 1922, London (Queen's Hall), SR.
Recording: (1923), I; also Ampico player roll.

(b) Lilacs 'Revised and Transcribed for the piano by the Composer'.
Date:
MS: ? The *Stichvorlage* for this revised version would doubtless have been a paste-over on a copy of the earlier edition.
Publ: TAIR, Copyright 1941 by Charles Foley New York, R–2058, pp. 5.
Coll. Ed. III (i)/76–80, 1950. The revision only concerns bars 46–51, foot-noted (from the earlier edition) on p. 80.
Recording: (1942), II.

(c) arranged for salon orchestra by L. Leonardi.
Publ: A. Gutheil.

(d) arranged for piano, violin and violoncello by A. Schaefer.
Publ: A. Gutheil.

no. 7

(a) violin obbligato by Fritz Kreisler (cf. B/L 426, referring to a recording by John McCormack, DA 680). Apparently unpublished.

(b) 'It's peaceful here'; arranged for violin and piano (22.9.1965) by Jascha Heifetz. Transposed up into B major.
Publ: 1968, Carl Fischer Inc., New York, B 3376, N 4918, pp. 3, [1].

no. 9

'Melody'; arranged for violin and piano (15.10.1956) by Jascha Heifetz.
Publ: 1958, Carl Fischer Inc., New York, B 3341, 31222–8, pp. 7, 3.

no. 12

Arranged for salon orchestra by L. Leonardi.
Publ: A. Gutheil.

Notes: SR, having written the song *Fate* (op. 21 no. 1) in 1900, during the largely unproductive period that followed the première of the First Symphony, completed the op. 21 songs at the Hôtel Sonnenberg near Lucerne, where he and his wife were spending their honeymoon. Hence the dedication of 'How fair this spot', one of the loveliest of all SR's songs, to 'N' – Natalya, his wife.

For German and French titles, see Appendix (i).

Variations pour le Piano sur un thème de F. Chopin op. 22

Thème	Largo	C minor
Var. 1	Moderato	”
2	Allegro	”
3	[L'istesso tempo]	”
4	[L'istesso tempo]	”
5	Meno mosso	”
6	Meno mosso	”
* 7	Allegro	”
8	[L'istesso tempo]	”
9	[L'istesso tempo]	”
* 10	Più vivo	”
11	Lento	E flat major
* 12	Moderato	C minor
13	Largo	”
14	Moderato	”
15	Allegro scherzando	F minor
16	Lento	”
17	Grave	B flat minor
18	Più mosso	”
19	Allegro vivace	A major
20	Presto	C sharp minor
21	Andante	D flat major
–	Più vivo	–
22	Maestoso – Meno mosso – Presto*	C major

* [see under *Notes* below]

Date: August 1902 – February 1903 (acc. to Asafyev; MS *1902*, altered to 1903 in an unknown hand).

Dedicated: *A Monsieur Th. Leschetizky.*

MS: GMM; (a) EB 53 (MS 8, ff 40–58 [see also op. 20]), ff 19, 1st version.

(b) Sketches, EB 54 (MS 93), ff 14.

(c) Corrected proof sheets, EB 55 (MS 94), ff 18.

Publication: [1903; (February 1904, B/L)], A. Gutheil/Breitkopf A 8330 G, pp. 35, gray wrappers; monochrome titlepage, title in French on wrapper and titlepage.

Coll. Ed. I/114–151, 1948.

Current edition: Boosey & Hawkes (currently reprinting); (IMC).

Performance: 10 February 1903, Moscow, SR.

Notes: The theme is Chopin's C minor prelude, op. 28 no. 20 (played without the repeat of the second stanza). Variations 7, 10 & 12 and the final Presto page (marked * above) are footnoted for optional omission, and the addition of an extra chord to variation 9 and to the penultimate Meno mosso in such case. The close 'family resemblance' of all the works of this period cannot better be seen than by a comparison of the first, second and seventh variations of this work with the contemporary prelude in the same key, op. 23 no. 7.

The comment on the work by OvR (224) anent the 'great impressiveness of the theme rather defeating the ... effect of the ... variations' leads to a rather daring thought: to try, if just once, the effect of carrying his suggestion to its literal conclusion: starting 'quasi improvisando' with Var. 1 (omitting the theme), and reserving Chopin's text to substitute for the final Meno mosso, so to conclude the work.

In his letter to Asafyev of 13 April 1917, SR writes: *I played the op. 22 variations in a shortened & altered form. I intend to include these corrections in a new edition.* Nothing further is known of this project, but see also Swan op. cit. *I have also changed the Variations on a theme of Chopin.*

Ferruccio Busoni's op. 22 also consists of 'Variationen und Fuge in freier Form über F. Chopin's C moll – Präludium' (1884). A later recension of this work, also separately published as 'Zehn Variationen über ein Präludium von Chopin' is included in the *Klavierübung* of 1922, and in Book VIII ('Neun Variationen ...') of the complete edition thereof published posthumously in 1925.

10 Préludes pour Piano op. 23

1.	Largo	F sharp minor
2.	Maestoso	B flat major
3.	Tempo di minuetto	D minor
4.	Andante cantabile	D major
5.	Alla marcia	G minor
6.	Andante	E flat major
7.	Allegro	C minor
8.	Allegro vivace	A flat major
9.	Presto	E flat minor
10.	Largo	G flat major

Dates: no. 5, *1901*; the remainder, 1903. The individual dates of composition appear to be unrecorded, unlike the cases of the later sets of shorter piano pieces, opp. 32, 33 & 39.

Dedication: *A Monsieur A. Siloti.*

MS: GMM; (a) EB 56 (MS 8, ff 59–84 [see also op. 20]), ff 23 (and 3 blank leaves).

(b) Corrected proof sheets, EB 57 (MS 95), ff 17.

Publication: [1903; (February 1904, B/L)], A. Gutheil/Breitkopf, complete, pp. 49, gray wrappers, and in separate numbers, A 8338–8347 G. Also issued later together with op. 3 no. 2 and op. 32 as '24 Préludes pour piano' in one volume, pp. 108. Editions of nos. 4ª 'revu…' and 5ª 'revu et simplifié par A. Siloti' were also issued by Gutheil.

Coll. Ed. I/152–199, 1948.

Current edition: Boosey & Hawkes (complete 15793, separate 16431–40); (IMC, Schirmer).

Performance: 10 February 1903, Moscow, SR, nos. 1, 2 & 5 (acc. to keys quoted in editorial footnote to letter postmarked 3 January 1903 to Goldenweiser, v. RP/A) but nos. 1, 4 & 10 acc. to B/L 100, following Yury Engel's review. Maybe the sequence was altered before publication?

Recording: no. 5 (1920), I (with a couple of added notes at the end!). Also Ampico roll (1920).
no. 10 (1940), II.

Arrangements: no. 5, transcribed for violin and piano by Fritz Kreisler, *publ.* 1946, Charles Foley 1028, pp. 9, [3].

no. 5, orchestral arrangement by Lucien Calliet (originally handled by Charles Foley).

no. 5, orchestrated by Edmund Rubbra, *publ.* 1940, Boosey & Hawkes 8303; 2. 2. 2. 2 – 4. 2. 3. 1 – Timp. SD. – Harp – Strings – Piano conductor (or 1. 1. 1. 1 – 2. 2. 3. 0 and no harp).

no. 9 transcribed for violin and piano (12.1.1935) by Jascha Heifetz, *publ.* 1937, Carl Fischer B 2423, CC 27914–9, pp. 7, 5.

no. 10ª, arrangé pour Violoncelle et piano par A. Brandoukoff, (transposed into G major), *publ.* A. Gutheil [1904], A 8349 G, pp. 5, 1.

Notes: This set of 10 preludes has its own internal logic of tonalities, the G flat major no. 10 balancing the F sharp minor opening number and the remaining ones following in natural sequence.

СКУПОЙ РЫЦАРЬ [The Miserly Knight] op. 24

Опера в трех картинах

Der geizige Ritter. Oper in 3 Bildern

Libretto: An almost word-for-word setting of Pushkin's 'little tragedy' of the same name (1830). Deutsche Umdichtung von Friedrich Fiedler.

Date: August 1903 – June 1905, and see below.

1. Introduction. Scene with Albert and the servant: *19 May 1905.*
2. In the vaults; the Baron's monologue: *30 May 1905.*
3. At the court: *7 June 1905, Ivanovka.*

Dedication: none.

Cast:

The Baron	*Baritone*
Albert (his son)	*Tenor*
The Count	*Baritone*
Jewish Moneylender	*Tenor*
Servant	*Bass*

Orchestra: 3 (Picc). 2. CA. 2. BsCl. 2 – 4. 3. 3. 1 – Timp. Triang. Tamburo. Piatti. Cassa. Tamtam – Harp – Strings.

MS: GMM; (a) *Full score*, EB 6 (MS 10), ff 152. Dated as above.
(b) *Vocal score*, EB 7 (MS 11), ff 65, *28 February 1904;*
(c) corrected proof sheets, EB 8 (MS 12), ff 62, *June–August 1904.*
(d) Sketches in pencil, EB 9 (MS 13), ff 34, *August 1903.*

Publication: 1904, vocal score by the composer, A. Gutheil, Moscow, A 8350 G, pp. XIV [libretto], 118, small folio. Imprimerie de Breitkopf et Härtel. Russian and German words.
1905, full score, A. Gutheil/Breitkopf, A 8817 G, pp. 248, yellow paper-covered boards, black cloth back; lithographed by Breitkopf & Härtel. Russian and German words. (SR to Morozov, 2 July 1904: *Gutheil ... will send it abroad for printing.*)
1972, full score, Muzyka, Moscow, 6820, pp. 268, cloth boards. Engraved (Leipziger Druckhaus); Russian and German words.
Material: Boosey & Hawkes Opera Library.

Performance: 11 January 1906, Moscow, Bolshoy Theatre; Georgy Baklanov (Baron), Anton Bonachich (Albert), Ivan Gryzunov (Count), S. Barsukov (Jewish Moneylender), cond. SR.
3 February 1907, St. Petersburg, Hall of Nobility, Scene 2 only, F. Chaliapin, cond. A. Siloti.

Notes: Pushkin's other 'little tragedies' had already been set as operas by famous Russian composers as follows:

The Stone Guest:	Dargomyzhsky (1866–9)
Mozart and Salieri:	Rimsky-Korsakov (1897)
A Feast in Time of Plague:	Cui (1900).

FRANCESKA DA RIMINI op. 25

Dramatische Episode aus dem V. Liede Dantes „Die Hölle" entnommen. Oper in zwei Bildern mit Prolog und Epilog

Libretto: M. I. Tchaikovsky (Deutsche Umdichtung von Lina Esbeer). Based on Dante Alighieri: Divina Commedia, Inferno, Canto V.

Date: Summer 1904 – August 1905; except for the duet of Paolo and Francesca, composed in 1900. See below also.

1. Prologue, *20 June 1905.*
2. Scene 1, *9 July 1905.*
3. Scene 2, undated in MS score.
4. Epilogue, *25 June – 22 July 1905.*

Dedication: none.

Cast:

Ghost of Virgil	*Baritone*
Dante	*Tenor*
Lanceotto Malatesta	*Baritone*
Francesca	*Soprano*
Paolo	*Tenor*
Cardinal	(non-singing role)

Spectres of Hell; retinue of Malatesta and of the Cardinal.

Orchestra: 3 (Picc). 2. CA. 2. BsCl. 2 – 4. 3. 3. 1 – Timp. Piatti. Cassa. Tamtam – Harp – Strings.
On stage: 4 horns, 2 trumpets.

MS: GMM; (a) *Full score*, EB 10 (MS 14), ff 197. Dated as above.

(b) *Vocal score*, EB 11 (MS 15), ff 76, *25 May – 30 July 1904, Ivanovka* [except for the duet of Paolo and Francesca, composed in July 1900].

(c) corrected proof sheets, EB 12 (MS 16), ff 136.

(d) Sketches in pencil, EB 13 (MS 17), ff 34.

Facsimile: of a page from the MS vocal score, in RP/A opp. p. 273.

Publication: 1904, vocal score by the composer, A. Gutheil, Moscow, A 8355 G, pp. XIII [libretto], 161, small folio. Russian and German words. For inclusion of the libretto in this publication, see also *Notes* below.

1905, full score, A. Gutheil/Breitkopf, A 8818 G, pp. 269, paper-covered boards, black cloth back; lithographed by Breitkopf & Härtel. Russian and German words.

1974, full score, Muzyka, Moscow, 7689, pp. 362, cloth boards. Engraved (Röderdruck, Leipzig); Russian and German words.

Material: Boosey & Hawkes Opera Library.

Performance: 11 January 1906, Moscow, Bolshoy Theatre; Georgy Baklanov (Lanceotto Malatesta), Nadezhda Salina (Francesca), Anton Bonachich (Paolo), cond. SR.
3 February 1907, St. Petersburg, Hall of Nobility, Scene 2, Ivanova and Chaliapin, cond. A. Siloti.

Notes: To judge from the correspondence between SR and his librettist Modest Tchaikovsky, the composition of *Francesca* caused him more frustration than any of his other works. SR wrote to Modest on 28 July 1898 asking if he would write him a libretto *on that Shakesperian subject you suggested to me last Spring.* There is no evidence as to what this subject was, but in any case Modest replied not with a Shakesperian subject but with an idea for an opera based on Canto V of Dante's *Inferno.* His letter (preserved at the Tchaikovsky House Museum, Klin) says that in two months he could 'prepare not only the scenario but also part of the libretto'. SR replied (28 August 1898) with various suggestions and questions; but during his largely barren years towards the end of the century no more was said of the project.

In the summer of 1900, however, Modest wrote to SR asking whether he intended to continue with the opera, because, it seems, somebody else was interested in the libretto. SR replied from Varazza, Italy on 27 June: *I received your letter today, and I am replying quickly. Two years have passed since I was with you at Klin, and in those two years I have not written a single note apart from one song* [Fate, op. 21 no. 1] ... *Speaking sincerely, I want to try again this summer to write* Francesca *and I hope that now perhaps something will come of it ...*' Modest agreed to give SR more time, and in July 1900 SR composed the bulk of the Love Duet for Paolo and Francesca (Scene 2). He then put the opera aside until 1904, when he took up the threads again in the hope that he could introduce both *Francesca* and *The Miserly Knight* during his season as conductor at the Bolshoy Theatre in Moscow. But he began to notice flaws in Modest's libretto, and wrote to him on 26 March 1904:

I want to ask you to alter your libretto for Francesca. *With alterations the libretto looks like this:*

1. The prologue and epilogue remain without changes.

2. The first two scenes are omitted.

3. The last two scenes remain, but with the following changes: in the second I would ask you first of all to replace 16 lines of poetry with others, and secondly to add some completely new lines before the epilogue to give more space to the Love Duet. In the first scene the episode with the cardinal must be cut out, and in its place I want Lanceotto to tell the audience first about the trick he planned in order to attract Francesca, also about the part Paolo played in it, and finally about himself in relation to these two characters. After the monologue he addresses his servant (as in your version) with the order 'summon my wife' and the scene continues and ends (without changes) as in your version ... if at all possible will you agree to undertake this work now? (I need it by the middle of May). Modest agreed to the alterations, and SR completed the short score on 30 July. On 3 August he wrote to Modest: *alterations to your text, and in one place, forgive me, I have written two lines, for which I blush. But these two lines were essential, and, as I had no others, I was forced into it ... Now that I have finished, I can tell you that, while I was working, I suffered above all because of the shortage of text. This is felt most of all in the second scene, where there is a build-up to the Love Duet and a conclusion to the Love Duet but there is no actual duet. This shortage of words was all the more apparent because I do not allow myself to repeat words. But in* Francesca *I had to allow it because there were just too few words. The second scene and epilogue last 21 minutes. This is terribly little. The whole opera lasts little more than an hour ...* On the following day he wrote to his friend Nikita Morozov ... *The last scene proved to be too short. Although* [Modest] *Tchaikovsky added some words for me (very banal ones by the way) there were not enough ...*

Once he had completed the short score SR sent a copy of the libretto for Modest to check; and, when he received it back, he discovered that Modest had made a *mass of changes.* He wrote to Modest on 7 September 1904: *If you insist on* [these changes] *then I shall have to make fundamental alterations* [to the music] *in many places. In your final version some words are replaced by others, and with different stresses; there is one place where unnecessary words have been added; finally there is one place where you have crossed out two phrases and it's now absolutely impossible to alter it. Further on I note that, whereas before you had 'Galego' you now have 'Galeotto'* [in the score SR retained 'Galego']. *In view of the fact that I composed the music to the libretto which you corrected last Spring, and that the text has already been translated into German, I do ask you, respected Modest Ilyich, to let me keep to it ... Could you write for me an aria for Paolo? I am afraid that the second scene will be too short.* SR altered the libretto back to its original form and returned it to Modest. But Modest was adamant; and SR wrote to him on 10 September 1904: *All will be done as you ask, though I regret it very much. I should have preferred to do all the corrections myself, for the sake of correct underlay. I always try to handle the text carefully; I have altered little, and all the alterations are yours. Because of this, I am wondering whether the text, which, as you can see, I do not entirely enjoy, need be printed at the beginning of the score. I should like to put the introductory aria into the duet and not at the beginning. My duet is short. Perhaps you could write some words for the duet? That would be better.*

It seems that the argument was settled with a compromise: in the score the text was printed in the form that SR had used, but Modest's revised version was printed in a brochure attached to the score.

[Fifteen songs] op. 26

1. Есть много звуков.
   (There are many sounds; first published English translation: The Heart's Secret.) A 8867ª G, mezzo.
   Adagio, D flat major (m). (e♭ – f′)
   Date: 14 August 1906, Ivanovka.
   Text: A. K. Tolstoy (1817–1875).

2. Все отнял у меня.
   (He took all from me; first published English translation: All once I gladly owned.) A 8870ª G, mezzo.
   Tempo moderato, F sharp minor (m), [VB – A minor] (f♯ – e′)
   Date: 15 August 1906, Ivanovka.
   Text: Fyodor Tyutchev (1803–1873).

3. Мы отдохнем.
   (Let us rest; first published English translation: Come let us rest.) A 8873ª G, contralto or bass.
   Lento, D minor (m), [EB & VB – G minor]. (A – d′)
   Date: 14 August 1906, Ivanovka.
   Text: from Act 4 of *Uncle Vanya* by A. P. Chekhov (1860–1904).

4. Два прощания (Dialogue).
   (Two partings.) A 8854ª G, soprano & baritone.
   Moderato, C minor. (d – g′; E♭ – d)
   Date: 22 August 1906, Ivanovka.
   Text: Aleksey Koltsov (1809–42).

5. Покинем, милая...
   (Beloved, let us fly.) A 8855ª G, tenor.
   Moderato, A flat major (h). (g – a′♭)
   Date: 22 August 1906, Ivanovka.
   Text: Arseny Golenishchev-Kutuzov (1848–1913).

6. Христос воскрес.
   (Christ is risen.) A 8877ª G, mezzo.
   Moderato, F minor (m). (d – f′)
   Date: 23 August 1906, Ivanovka.
   Text: Dmitry Merezhkovsky (1865–1941).

7. К детям.
   (To the children.) A 8880ª G, mezzo.
   Lento, F major (m). (e – f′)
   Date: 9 September 1906, Ivanovka.
   Text: Aleksey Khomyakov (1804–1860).

8. Пощады я молю!
   (Thy pity I implore.) A 8858ª G, tenor.

Allegro con fuoco, A minor (h). (g♯ – a′)
Date: 25 August 1906, Ivanovka.
Text: Dmitry Merezhkovsky.

9. Я опять одинок.
(Again I am alone; first published English translation: Let me rest here alone.)
A 8859ª G, tenor.
Allegro, D minor (h). (e – a′ (b′♭))
Date: 4 September 1906, Ivanovka.
Text: Ivan Bunin (1870–1904), after Taras Shevchenko (1814–1861).

10. У моего окна.
(Before my window.) A 8860ª G, soprano.
Lento, A major (h). (e – a′ (b′))
Date: 17 September 1906, Ivanovka.
Text: G. Galina (pseudonym of the Countess Einerling, 1873–1942).

11. Фонтан.
(Fountains.) A 8861ª G, tenor.
Maestoso, D major (h). (d – b′♭)
Date: 6 September 1906, Ivanovka.
Text: Fyodor Tyutchev.

12. Ночь печальна.
(Night is mournful.) A 8862ª G, tenor.
Largo, B minor (h). (e – f′♯)
Date: 3 September 1906. Ivanovka.
Text: Ivan Bunin.

13. Вчера мы встретились.
(When yesterday we met.) A 8892ª G, mezzo.
Moderato, D minor (m). (d – e′)
Date: 3 September 1906, Ivanovka.
Text: Yakov Polonsky (1819–1898).

14. Кольцо.
(The ring.) A 8864ª G, mezzo.
Allegro, B minor (m). (B – g′)
Date: 10 September 1906, Ivanovka.
Text: Aleksey Koltsov (1809–1842).

15. Проходит все.
(All things depart.) A 8895ª G, bass.
Adagio, E flat minor (m). (e♭ – f′)
Date: 8 September 1906, Ivanovka.
Text: Daniil Rathaus (1869–1937).

Dedication: M. S. and A. M. Kerzin.

MS: GMM; (a) autograph scores of the complete set, EB 117 (MS 127), ff 36.

(b) Cello part of the composer's arr. of no. 12 for voice, piano and cello, EB 118 (MS 128), ff 1. With SR's note that the bowing was by A. Brandukov and that it would probably sound better played with the mute on.

Publication: [1906; according to Boosey & Hawkes copyright dates, 1907]. A. Gutheil/Breitkopf, Russian and German words (German by Lina Esbeer); in high, medium and low keys (except no. 14 – m. only – and no. 11 – h. m. only) with pl. nos. in range 8854–8896; nos. 1, 2, 6, 7, 13 & 15 also 'for baritone in bass clef'. The Russian/English edition appeared in 1921, original keys only, plate nos. as under individual items above, including the superscript [a] (Eng. trans. by Edward Agate, nos. 1, 2, 3, 4, 5, 8, 9, 11, 14, 15; Rosa Newmarch, nos. 6, 7, 10, 12, 13).

The English/French edition (Fr. trans. by M. D. Calvocoressi) also bears the copyright date 1921 (substantiated by the quality of the paper in contemporary copies ...) and its plate numbers run in the 96.. series.

Earlier, in 1917, J. & W. Chester, London & Brighton/Edition Gutheil had issued some items, certainly no. 6 (JWC 3807), with Eng. words by Rosa Newmarch and French ditto by G. Jean-Aubry.

1923, Carl Fischer, New York:

no. 10 'The Alder Tree', V 783, 22596–3, pp. 5, transposed down into G major. Russian text; English version by Geraldine Farrar.

no. 11 'The Fountain', V 802, 22865–4, pp. 5. Russian text; English version by Geraldine Farrar, German version by Lina Esbeer.

Coll. Ed: 47–61.

Current edition: Boosey & Hawkes, Songs, vol. 2, pp. 3–52; Muzyka, Romansy, vol. 2, pp. 3–60.

Performance: 12 February 1907, Moscow, Ivan Gryzunov (nos. 1, 2, 4, 6, 7, 13, 15), Anna Kiselyovskaya (nos. 3, 4, 9), Aleksandr Bogdanovich (nos. 5, 8, 10, 11, 12) and Elizaveta Azerskaya (no. 14) with Aleksandr Goldenweiser (piano); Kerzin Music Circle Concert.

Arrangements: no. 6, arranged for piano and cello (solo) or salon orchestra – strings (incl. solo cello) and harmonium (ad lib.) by L. Leonardi. *Publ.* 1923 A. Gutheil, A 10357 G, parts only.

no. 10, violin obbligato by Fritz Kreisler (cf. B/L 427, referring to a recording by John McCormack, DA 644). Apparently unpublished.

no. 12, arranged by the composer for voice, piano and cello (cf. MS (b) above). Unpublished.

Notes: B/L 132; RP/A 304–6; Norris 26, 39–40.

For German and French titles, see Appendix (i).

Symphonie [no. 2] E moll op. 27
pour grand Orchestre

1. Largo – Allegro moderato	E minor
2. Allegro molto	A minor
3. Adagio	A major
4. Allegro vivace	E major

Date: October 1906 – April 1907, Dresden. Orchestrated, mid-July 1907, Ivanovka (v. SR to Morozov, 2 August 1907; B/L 141) – mid-January 1908, Dresden.

Dedication: *A Monsieur S. Tanéiew.*

Orchestra: 3 (Picc). 2. CA (Ob). 2. BsCl. 2 – 4. 3. 3. 1 – Timp. Piatti & Gran Cassa (not in 3). Tamburo (in 2). Glsp (in 2 & 4) – Strings.

MS: The MS full score is at present unlocated. In GMM is a copy of the printed Gutheil score corrected by SR (EB 27, MS 49). The printed copy used by SR for conducting, with his cuts etc. marked, is now in L. of C.

Publication: [August 1908], full score, A. Gutheil/Breitkopf, A 8899 G, pp. 230 (plain titlepage).

[April] 1910, Réduction pour Piano à 4 mains par Wladimir Wilshaw, ditto, A 9061 G, pp. 121 (opposite pages).

[c. 1950]. A photographically-reduced study score was issued by Edwin F. Kalmus (orchestral scores no. 141), from the above full score.

1960, full score, Muzgiz, Moscow, 28320, pp. 5–329, edited by G. Kirkor; his claim to have incorporated the corrections made by SR in the printed score (see above) and parts which were not taken up into the Gutheil edition is hardly substantiated by a comparison of the two publications in question. (See also SR to Morozov, 21, 29 June 1908; B/L 146.)

1967, full and miniature scores, Boosey & Hawkes 19577 (HPS 820), pp. 329; photolithographically reproduced from the Muzgiz edition.

Current edition: Boosey & Hawkes.

Performance: 26 January 1908, St. Petersburg, Mariinsky Theatre, cond. SR.
2 February 1908, Moscow, Philharmonic Society, Large Hall of the Conservatoire, cond. SR.
19 May 1910, London, Philharmonic Society, cond. Artur Nikisch.
13 October 1910, Leeds Festival, cond. SR.

Notes: The correspondence between SR and Morozov (v. RP/A: 11 February, 13 April, 2 August 1907; B/L 135–6, 141) here reveals further evidence that SR completed his orchestral works in draft before undertaking the scoring at all (see also op. 12 above, and introduction p. 18).

For some time a number of cuts were regularly made in performances of this work (probably originally stemming from the composer himself – see similar cases in opp. 28, 29 & 30). As in opp. 29 & 30 (but unlike op. 28) the score as first published restores the cuts, and no indication of them is given in the more recent Russian republication. However, we give details of the principal such cuts hereunder, for reference:

1. First 2 bars of *Allegro Moderato*, after **3**.
   4 bars before **10**.
   6 bars at *Tempo I* after **10**.
   14 to **15**.
   8 bars at **19** + 9.
   a tempo after **23** until *Più mosso*; bars 5–8 after *Più mosso*.
   8 bars at **24** + 9.
2. **40** to 17 after **42**.
3. 8 bars at **50**.
   53 to **55**.
4. **61** + 9 until **62** + 9
   7 bars at **69**
   76 until 4 bars before **81**.

[Erste] Sonate für Pianoforte op. 28

1. Allegro moderato D minor
2. Lento F major
3. Allegro molto D minor

Date: January–February 1907; completed *14 May 1907, Dresden.*

Dedication: none.

MS: GMM; EB 58 (MS 96), ff 35, dated. (Evidence of the pre-publication changes mentioned by Igumnov, v. inf., may survive in this MS.) A MS copy of the original version was sent to Igumnov, v. inf.

Publication: [June 1908] A. Gutheil/Breitkopf, A 9030 G, pp. 55, dark gray wrappers.
Coll. Ed. I/200–256, 1948.
Current edition: Boosey & Hawkes 17632; (IMC).

Performance: 17 October 1908, Moscow, Small Hall of the Nobility, Konstantin Nikolayevich Igumnov. (OvR 141 refers to a performance by SR at one of the Conservatoire concerts of the Imperial Russian Music Society in Moscow).

Notes: The literary basis of the sonata – disclosed by the composer to Igumnov, v. inf. – is Goethe's *Faust*: Faust, Gretchen, the flight to the Brocken and Mephistopheles. During the preliminary stages of the composition, SR corresponded on matters concerning the form of the work with K. S. Morozov (SR to Morozov, 10 December 1906; B/L 132–3). He played it privately in Dresden to von Riesemann (v. SR to Morozov, 8 May 1907; B/L 137–8) and later to a group of friends – Catoire, Conus, Medtner and Igumnov – in Wilshaw's apartment in Moscow (B/L 139).

SR's revisions of this work between completion of the draft and publication are referred to in his correspondence with Morozov (8 May 1907; B/L 138) and Igumnov (15 June 1907, 12 April 1908; B/L 139, 145). He sent a MS copy to the latter, inviting comments, and later a first proof; and from this Igumnov noted these changes, some resulting from his own suggestions: 'A considerable part of the recapitulation in the first movement had been recomposed, shortening it by more than 50 bars; some cuts had been made in the finale, mostly in the recapitulation, about 60 bars. Changes of treatment were made only in the finale. The second movement was unchanged.' (Iz arkhiva K. N. Igumnova, *Sovetskaya muzyka*, 1, 1946; B/L 139, 142, 152, 153.) The survival of the MS copy mentioned above is undocumented.

This is probably the only one of SR's solo piano works not to have received its public première at his own hands.

The sonata is absolutely wild and interminable, I think about 45 minutes. I was lured into these dimensions by a programme, i.e. one guiding idea. That is, three contrasting types from a first-rate literary work ... This composition will be played by nobody because of its length and difficulty ... At one time I wished to make this sonata into a symphony ... (SR to Morozov, 8 May 1907; B/L 138).

DIE TOTENINSEL – The Island of the Dead op. 29
Symphonische Dichtung zum Gemälde von A. Böcklin
Symphonic Poem based on Böcklin's famous picture
für grosses Orchester

A minor
(– E flat major)

Date: completed *17 April 1909, Dresden.*

Dedication: *Herrn Nicolas von Struve freundschaftlich gewidmet.* v. OvR 137–8, 139.

Orchestra: 3 (Picc). 2. CA. 2. BsCl. 2. Contra – 6. 3. 3. 1 – Timp. Piatti & Cassa – Harp -- Strings.

MS: GMM; (a) *Full score*, EB 28 (MS 50), ff 37, dated.

(b) 13 leaves of pencil sketches (Spring 1909), EB 29 (MS 51).

Publication: [October 1909], full score, A. Gutheil/Breitkopf, A 9048 G, pp. 71. A photographically reduced miniature score was also issued by Gutheil; copies for England had an English titlepage tipped in.

[May] 1910, für Klavier zu vier Händen bearbeitet von Otto Taubmann, A. Gutheil, A 9081 G, pp. 33 (opposite pages).

1973, Muzyka, Moscow, 7795, pp. 88 (a re-engraved reprint of the text of the original Gutheil score).

Current editions: Boosey & Hawkes 20164 (also photo-reduced from Gutheil's original), HPS 886 (originally 649 was the number allocated); IMC.

Performance: 18 April 1909, Moscow, Philharmonic Society, cond. SR.

Recording: Philadelphia Orchestra, cond. SR, (1929) IV. See notes below for details of cuts and retouchings introduced in this recording of the work.

Notes: A black-and-white reproduction of 'Böcklin's famous picture', seen in Paris, was the inspiration for this composition. The principal melodic motif, developed by the addition of a fourth note at the *Largo* after **14**, is revealed as a version of the *Dies irae* chant, which enters unmistakably in a shuddering tremolo after the pause at **22** + 10.

For quotations from various interviews which refer to this composition's birth, see B/L 156. For references to the revisions the composer made at the proof stage, see B/L 156; also ibid. 158 (SR to Morozov, 6 June 1909): *I made many corrections. I rewrote almost half of it. Changes mainly concerned the orchestration, though I also altered the substance itself; and in one place, for the sake of the scheme of modulation I even made a transposition.* To what extent these changes can be documented by the MS (was it the *Stichvorlage?*) and sketches in GMM is not known.

As in other works of this period – opp. 27, 28 & 30 – SR introduced some cuts, no doubt partly to 'tailor' the work to the three sides of the '78' discs of his own recording in 1929. At least one of his interpreters reopened these cuts, v. L. Stokowski to SR, 18 March 1933 (B/L 292–3). Some other post-publication retouchings dating from the same time are mentioned in B/L 156, but not described in detail; inspection of an old set of marked parts establishes the following:

at **22**, a Fp cresc. is introduced;
in the following *Largo*, the stopped horn notes are marked to be separated crotchets instead of the sustained notes printed;
at **23** + 5 and **23** + 9, 'hairpins' are introduced;
at **25** four bars are rewritten in 3/4 by lengthening the first beats.

Although it is sincerely hoped no-one would now wish to use the cuts referred to above, they are here listed for completeness:

Bars 1–4; 3–6 bars after **3**; 2–3 bars after **4**; from **5** + 5 to **6**; 3rd. bar before **9**; **9** to **10**; 5–10 bars after **11**; 2–3 bars before **12**; 9th bar after **12** to 4th bar after **13**; 8th bar after **14**; 8–9 bars after **26**.

To accommodate these cuts, the clarinet, viola and cello parts were omitted in bars 3–4 after **5**, and a brass chord was added at the *Tranquillo* 5 bars after **13**.

3me – Concerto pour le Piano avec Orchestre ou un 2^{d} Piano op. 30

1. Allegro ma non tanto	D minor
2. INTERMEZZO. Adagio – attacca subito	A – D flat major
3. FINALE. Alla breve	D minor – major

Date: Summer 1909, Ivanovka. *Fine. Moscow, 23 September 1909.*

Dedication: *A Mr. Joseph Hofmann.*
The dedicatee of this major work is believed, however, never to have played it.

Orchestra: 2. 2. 2. 2 – 4. 2. 3. 1 – Timp. Tamburo militare. Gran Cassa & Piatti – Strings. (Trb. Tb. and extra percussion first play at the end of the Intermezzo, at the link to the Finale.)

MS: British Library, London; Loan 75/34. Formerly given by SR to one of his English hosts, this most valuable MS rests now, after various vicissitudes, in the safety of the BL Dept. of Manuscripts.

Lacking a titlepage, the first page of music of this full score is headed *3me Concerto pour Piano / S. Rachmaninoff op. 30*; the MS is then paginated from 1 afresh in each movement, viz.

1. pp. 1–71
2. Intermezzo. pp. 1–44
3. Finale. pp. 1–96

The arrangement of the orchestral accompaniment for Piano II is at the foot of each page of score; the bar lines are not joined on to those of the score. The various *ossias* occurring in the published 2-piano version (but not, except for the alternative cadenza, in the printed full score) appear as follows in this MS:

1. The passage at **4** is shewn thus;
   The *ossia* cadenza, pp. 57–8 of the MS, was in fact the original one; the alternative (now engraved larger) was inserted on a separate leaf numbered 57 bis.
2. The *ossia* at *Più vivo* was also the original reading.
3. The *ossia* before **59** appears thus in the MS; but that before **79** was the original: part of the alternative reading was pinned over.

The engraver's marks throughout prove this MS was in fact the *Stichvorlage.* The plate number A 9086 G (altered to 9088) is pencilled at the foot of the first page, the word *Widmung* at the head.

The MS also has several passages crossed out by the composer in lead pencil and rewritten in ink and some additions to details of bowing and orchestration and remarks to the engraver were added in pencil and red ink. (SR, like many another composer before him, evidently also included a penknife amongst his weapons, and this is often called into use to effect a minor

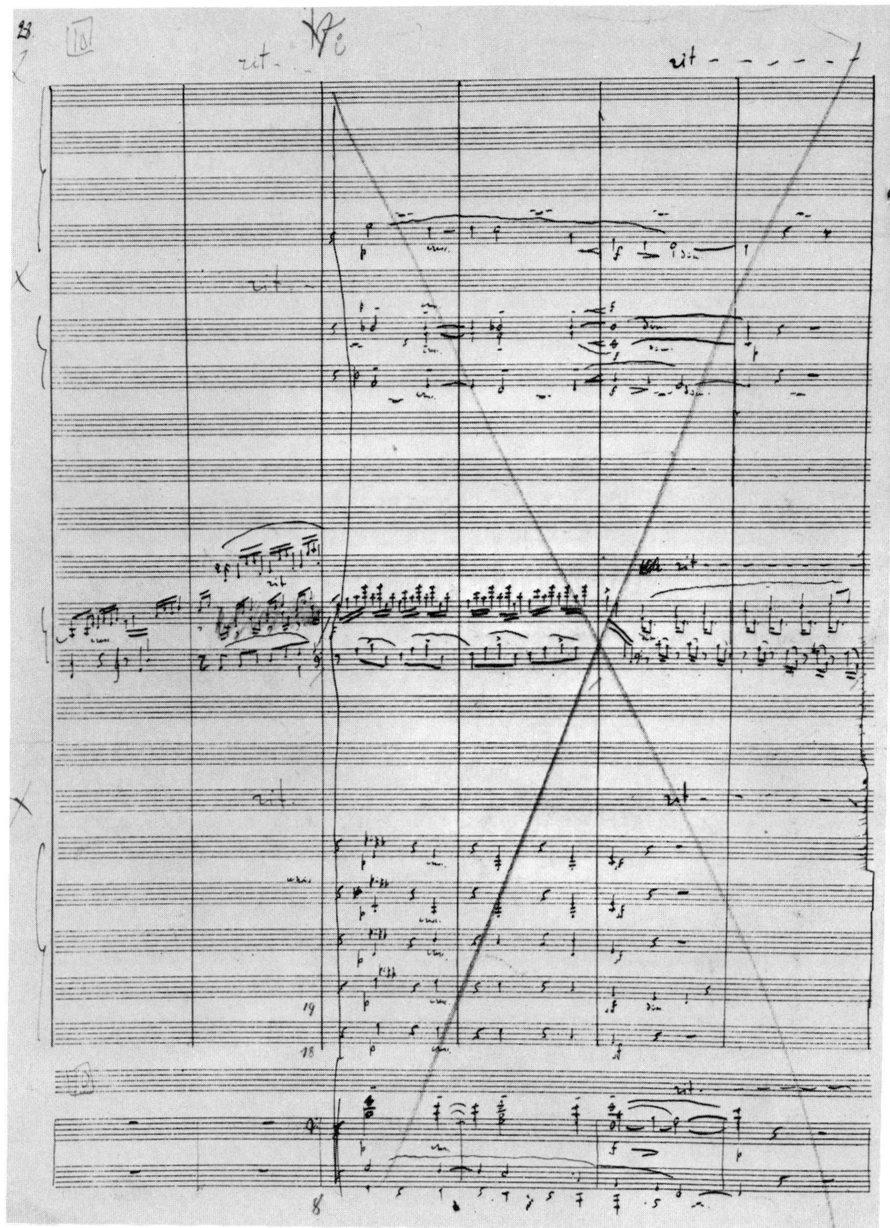

Plate 7: Third Concerto: p. 28 of MS of first movement

deletion. The published score takes all these changes into account.) These different readings in the solo part occur as follows:

1. L. H. strengthened for four bars at **8** + 4;
   the bar at **10** + 2 differed, and four following bars (the first three lightly supported by the orchestra) were cut;
   between **12** and the *più vivo* after **13** there were minimal changes in R. H., made with a knife;
   after **14**, the 4 bars before *Allegro* were at first in a triplet rhythm;
   at **16** & **17** four bars were rewritten each time;
   bars 5–8 before the *Presto* in the cadenza originally differed very slightly.
2. At **26** and **27** (though not at **32**) the layout originally differed slightly;
   the L. H. in the 2 bars after **27** before *più vivo* agreed with the parallel passage after **26**;
   in the whole bar before **39**, the opening figuration continued.
3. The 4 bars before **62** differed slightly in layout;
   at **68**, the hands originally moved independently;
   from **72** to **73** the figuration was quite different;
   after **74**, the 6 bars at *Un poco meno mosso* were at first 4 different bars of 6/4; likewise 10 bars at **75** and 4 bars before **78**;
   at the final *Presto*, originally the R. H. led.

Of changes in the orchestral score, we merely note the following: at **53** for 2 bars, clarinets have replaced horns; at the timpani entry at **59** – 4 a chord is deleted; for 5 bars before **64** the 1st. trumpet part is now made more effective by the double-tonguing being on the beat; and at **69** the 4 bars of string figures were added.

Facsimile: of pp. 43 from the first movement and 91 from the finale (incorrectly captioned) in Culshaw, between 88 and 89;

of the opening page of the Intermezzo in RT's *Rachmaninoff* (Boosey & Hawkes), facing p. 49;

of p. 28 from the first movement, showing a passage later deleted, and p. 66 from the last movement, with conductor's marking ('Trompet') possibly in the hand of Gustav Mahler and composer's notes to the engraver (*Kleine Noten drucken*) in red ink, v. *plates 7–8.*

Publication: 1910, full score, A. Gutheil/Breitkopf, A 9086 G, pp. 138. Titlepage lithoed (by Breitkopf & Härtel) in black, red, green, pink, gray and gold (there is a copy in BL. h. 3984. o.).

1910, arrangement for 2 pianos 4 hands by the composer, ditto, A 9088 G, pp. 79; gray wrappers (with wording in Russian and French) and similarly ornate titlepage. This contains *ossias* at **4**, 7 bars after **27**, 5 bars after **58** and 4 bars before **79**, which do not appear in the full score.

1941, miniature score, Boosey & Hawkes, London 8470 (HPS 18), pp. 140. In this edition, the three pages 36–38 of the original edition containing the

Plate 8: Third Concerto, p. 66 of MS of last movement

cadenza were re-engraved, presumably for legibility, and appear as 35–40; the rest of the work being photographically reduced from the Gutheil score. When Boosey & Hawkes later came to issue a full score to their no. 16855, they rephotoed the original Gutheil layout and used this also for later impressions of HPS 18. (They also reprinted the 2 piano edition to their no. 16326.)

Current editions: Boosey & Hawkes; (IMC ['Our larger size edition facilitates the reading of this score'], Schirmer, Leeds Music).

Performance: 28 November 1909, New York Symphony Orchestra, New Theatre, New York, SR cond. Walter Damrosch.
16 January 1910, New York Philharmonic Orchestra (Carnegie Hall), SR cond. Gustav Mahler.
4 April 1910, Moscow Philharmonic, SR cond. Eugene Plotnikov.
24 October 1911, Liverpool Philharmonic Society, SR cond. Simon Speelman.
7 November 1911, London (Queen's Hall), Royal Philharmonic Society, SR cond. Willem Mengelberg.

Recording: SR and the Philadelphia Orchestra cond. Eugene Ormandy (1939–40), V.

Notes: The composer evidently sanctioned, and himself observed (in his recording and in some performances) a number of cuts in this work, nominally (though not necessarily) to accommodate its bulk to the exigencies of 78 rpm discs. These are as follows:

1. The 8 bars preceding **11**;
   2 bars at the climax of the cadenza, 9–10 before **19**.
2. From *Più vivo* after **27**, 13 bars (containing, in the violins, a reminiscence of the first movement);
   from **36**, 2 or 6 bars or even the whole section **36** to **38** (this cut was not observed by SR in his own recording).
3. From **45** to the tutti at *Allegro molto* 4 bars before **47**;
   from *Meno mosso*, 2 bars after **52** until **54**.

ЛИТУРГИЯ СВЯТОГО ИОАННА ЗЛАТОУСТА op. 31
[Liturgy of Saint John Chrysostom]

For 4-part unaccompanied mixed chorus.

1.	Великая Ектения	The Great Ekteniya
2.	Благослови, душе моя, Господа	Praise the Lord, O my soul
3.	Единородный	The only-begotten
4a.	Во царствии Твоем (двухорное)	In Thy Kingdom (double choir)
4b.	" " " (однохорное)	" " " (one choir)
5.	Приидите, поклонимся	Come, bow
6.	Господи, спаси благочестивыя .... и Святый Боже	Lord, save the faithful, and Holy God
7.	Сугубая и последующия Ектении	The two-fold and following Ektenii
8.	Иже херувимы	Which Cherubim
9.	Просительная Ектения и Отца и Сына ..	The suppliant Ekteniya of the Father and the Son
10.	Верую	I believe (Credo)
11.	Милость мира	The grace at peace
12.	Тебе поем	We sing to thee
13.	Достойно есть и Всех и вся	It is right for all men and all things
14.	Отче наш (двухорное)	Our Father (double choir)
15.	Един Свят	One Church
16.	Хвалите Господа с небес (причастный) ..	Praise God in the Heavens (Communion)
17.	Благословен Грядый и Видехом .... светь истиный	Blessed be the hosts, and We see the true light
18.	Да исполнятся уста наша	And our faith shall show forth
19.	Буди имя Господне (двухорное)	Cry the name of the Lord (double choir)
20.	Слава Отцу и Благочестивейшого	Praise the Father and the Faithful

Date: *Finished, thanks be to God. 30 July 1910, Ivanovka.*

Dedication: none.

Voices: mixed chorus S.A.T.B. divided; double chorus in first version of no. 4, nos. 14 and 19; solo soprano in no. 12.

MS: (a) GMM; EB 100 (MS 67), score with piano arrangement below, ff 35 plus ff 3 variants; dated & signed as above.

(b) British Library, London, Loan 75/35, no. 12 only, pp. 4 in a copyist's hand, entitled 'O salutaris Hostia'; with the words of this Benediction hymn adapted by an anonymous arranger.

Publication: [1910], vocal score with piano reduction underneath, A. Gutheil,

Moscow, A 9079 G, pp. 113. Russian titlepage and text only (engraver not specified). Also separate parts published, and each movement originally available separately (in score or parts). Small folio.

1915, Bayley & Ferguson, London & Glasgow, 6 nos. 'edited and adapted to English words by A. M. Henderson. Accompt. for practice only'.

3.	Glory to God the Father (to end of p. 15 1. 2)	Choral Album no.	1229
8.	Hymn to the Cherubim	do.	1227
12.	To Thee, O Lord, do I lift up my Soul (Ps. XXV, 1–2)	do.	1222
13.	We praise Thee (to end of p. 83 1. 1)	do.	1226
14.	The Lord's Prayer	do.	1224
16.	Praise the Lord from the Heavens (Ps. CXLVIII, 1–2)	do.	1225

1976, Muzyka, no. 12 only (as Тихая мелодия, without words) in Хоровые Произведения . . . ed. A. P. Aleksandrov, 9252, p. 38.

Current edition: Boosey & Hawkes Hire Library.

Performance: 25 November 1910, Moscow, Synodical Choir cond. Nikolay M. Danilin (the treble soloist at this performance was later famous as Sergei Jaroff, conductor of the Don Cossack choir, cf. B/L 171).
10 March 1911, St. Petersburg, ditto.
25 March 1911, St. Petersburg, Siloti matinée concert, Chorus of the Mariinsky Opera cond. SR (12 numbers only).

Arrangement: 'Adapted and arranged for use in the Church of England by Walter S. Vale Mus. Doc.'

1949, Boosey & Hawkes Inc., no pl. no., pp. 26, lithographed. Contains the following movements only:

(i)	Kyrie	= no. 1
(ii)	Credo	= no. 10 (with a small cut, p. 67/2)
(iii)	Sanctus and Benedictus	= no. 11 (with a cut of p. 75 and to middle of p. 76)
(iv)	Agnus Dei	= no. 13 (to bar 2 on p. 83)
(v)	Gloria in excelsis	= nos. 17–18 (to end of first system on p. 107)

Notes: Unlike that of the later *Vespers* op. 37, the musical material of the *Liturgy* appears to be entirely the Composer's original work.

Tchaikovsky's setting of the Liturgy of St. John Chrysostom for 4-part mixed chorus, his op. 41, was composed in 1878.

13 Préludes pour Piano op. 32

1.	Allegro vivace	C major
2.	Allegretto	B flat minor
3.	Allegro vivace	E major
4.	Allegro con brio	E minor
5.	Moderato	G major
6.	Allegro appassionato	F minor
7.	Moderato	F major
8.	Vivo	A minor
9.	Allegro moderato	A major
10.	Lento	B minor
11.	Allegretto	B major
12.	Allegro	G sharp minor
13.	Grave	D flat major

Dates: *1910, Ivanovka*: 1, *30 August*; 2, *2 September*; 3, *3 September*; 4, *28 August*; 5, *23 August*; 6, *25 August*; 7, *24 August*; 8, *24 August*; 9, *26 August*; 10, *6 September*; 11, *23 August*; 12, *23 August*; 13, *10 September* (on MSS).

Dedication: none.

MS: GMM; (a) EB 59 (MS 98), ff 30, dated.
(b) Corrected proof sheets, EB 60 (MS 99), ff 55.

Publication: [1910–11], A. Gutheil/Breitkopf, complete, pp. 56, gray wrappers, and in separate numbers, A 9612–9624 G. Also issued together with op. 3 no. 2 and op. 23 as '24 Préludes pour piano' in one volume, pp. 108. An edition of no. 10ª 'revu par A. Siloti' was also issued by Gutheil.

Coll. Ed. II/3–61, 1948.

Current edition: Boosey & Hawkes (complete 15794, separate 16441–53); (IMC, Schirmer).

Performance: 5 December 1911, St. Petersburg, SR.
13 December 1911, Moscow, SR.

Recording: nos. 3, 6, 7 (1940), II.
no. 5 (1920), I.
no. 12 (1921), I.

Arrangement: no. 5 transcribed for violin and piano (8. 11. 1945) by Jascha Heifetz, *publ.* 1947, Carl Fischer Inc. B 2801, 30246–7, pp. 7, 3. This arrangement is dedicated to Vladimir Horowitz.

no. 5, orchestral arrangement by Lucien Calliet (originally in the catalogue of Charles Foley).

Notes: According to Benno Moiseiwitsch (*The Gramophone*, London, May 1943) the source of no. 10 in B minor was A. Böcklin's painting *The Return* (B/L 296).

On the last page of no. 13 the wheel comes full circle and the cycle of 24 preludes is closed by a transformation in the major of the minor *Urmotiv* from the first prelude, op. 3 no. 2; the characteristic final chord-sequence of that early masterpiece forms the basis of the thrice-interrupted cadence of op. 32 no. 13, which even ends with a D flat major version of the earlier work's last bar. Despite this final logic, the cohesion of the 24 preludes as one unit appears to have evolved during rather than before their completion. A note above to op. 23 refers to the self-contained nature of that earlier cycle at a time when completion of a set of 24 may not yet have been envisaged. Be this as it may, the thought has at times occurred that, just once, a performance of the whole set in the 'cycle of fifths' sequence as used by Chopin, Scriabin and Shostakovich might throw new light on some items in their then new context. The conclusion, with the Tempo di minuetto of op. 23 no. 3, would at least have precedent in the Diabelli variations!

Meanwhile, in the case of op. 32 (unlike op. 23), the dates of composition of the individual pieces are preserved on the MSS.

Plate 9: Etudes-Tableaux, op. 33: titlepage of first edition

[Neuf] Etudes-Tableaux pour Piano op. 33

1. Allegro non troppo	F minor
2. Allegro	C major
3. Grave – Meno mosso	C minor – major
4. Allegro	A minor
5. Moderato	D minor
6. Non allegro – Presto	E flat minor
7. Allegro con fuoco	E flat major
8. Moderato	G minor
9. Grave	C sharp minor

Dates: *1911, Ivanovka*: 1, *11 August*; 2, *16 August*; 3, *18 August*; 4, *8 September*; 5, *11 September*; 6, *23 August*; 7, *17 August*; 8, *15 August*; 9, *13 August* (on MSS).

Dedication: none.

MS: GMM; (a) nos. 1, 2, 6–9: EB 61 (MS 100), ff 13, dated.

(b) no. 3: EB 62 (MS 101), ff 2, dated.

(c) no. 5: EB 63 (MS 102), ff 3, dated.
For no. 4, v. op. 39 no. 6 inf.
Nos. 3–5 must remain in my desk (SR to Asafyev, 17 April 1917).

Publication: [1911–12; August 1914 according to B/L, and see below], A. Gutheil/Breitkopf. Announced complete and in separate numbers; in fact nos. 1, 2, 6–9 only, published separately, A 9686–7 G and A 9691–4 G, pp. 5, 5, 7, 5, 5, 7. *See plate 9.*
(EB gives publisher as RMV despite her date of 1911–12; did Koussevitzky's firm issue a Russian edition over his own company's imprint, on K. Gutheil's death?).

No. 4 originally withdrawn by the composer; later (1916) recasted and reissued as op. 39 no. 6, q.v. See also B/L 173 and f.n.

Nos. 3 & 5 also withdrawn by the composer; first published posthumously, together with all the others except [this original version of] no. 4, in *Coll. Ed.* II/62–94, 1948.

1950, Leeds Music Corporation, New York. 'Etudes-Tableaux op. 33 [and 39] (First complete edition containing two previously unpublished etudes)'. Nos. 3 & 5 also issued separately, pp. 7, 'Two Etudes-Tableaux, published for the first time (from recently discovered manuscripts)'. Edited with special annotations by Alfred Mirovitch. Re-engraved.

1969, Boosey & Hawkes 19662, complete (with the exception of no. 4), pp. 35, re-engraved.

Current editions: Boosey & Hawkes; (IMC, Leeds).

Performance: Oct–Nov 1911, English tour, SR.
5 December 1911, St. Petersburg, SR (after preliminary performance at the Conservatoire there, cf. B/L 174).
13 December 1911, Moscow, SR.

Recording: nos. 2, 7 (1940), II.
no. 8 (1920) (unreleased).

Arrangements: no. 2 transcribed for violin and piano (7. 11. 1945) by Jascha Heifetz, *publ.* 1947 Carl Fischer Inc. B 2800, 30245–6, pp. 7, [1].

no. 7 transcribed for violin and piano (July 1972) by Jascha Heifetz, *publ.* 1974 Carl Fischer Inc. B 3390, N 5726, pp. 5, 3.

no. 7 ('La Foire') orchestrated by Ottorino Respighi, as no. 2 of *Cinq Etudes Tableaux de S.R. Orchestration de Ottorino Respighi*, 1930.

Orchestra: 3 (Picc). 2. CA. 2. BsCl. 2. Contra – 4. 3. 3. 1 – Timp. Triangolo, Tamburo Basco, Piatti – Strings.

MS: Boosey & Hawkes archives, London; pp. 100 (complete), dated *Roma – 30 Settembre 1930.*

Publication: 1931, Edition Russe de Musique, RMV 527, no. 2; 1973, Muzyka, Moscow, 7611, no. 2.

Performance: December 1931,
cond. S. Koussevitzky.

Notes: see also op. 39 inf.

Notes: According to OvR 237 – though the details there given are admittedly somewhat garbled – no. 7 'represents the gay bustle of a Russian fair' and no. 8 was inspired by A. Böcklin's painting *Morning.* For SR's own comments (on no. 7) see SR to Respighi, 2 January 1930 (B/L 263).

The music of the closing page of no. 3, though originally set aside by SR, was used at the close of the Largo of the Fourth Concerto, op. 40 (q. v.) – a work first sketched as early as 1914, completed in its first version in 1926 and finally rewritten as late as 1941–2. The passage in question remained essentially intact through all these changes.

[Thirteen songs] op. 34

1. Муза.
   (The Muse.) A 9635ª G, soprano (or tenor).
   Lento, E minor (h). (e – a′)
   Date: 6 June 1912, Ivanovka.
   Text: Aleksandr Pushkin (1799–1837).
   Dedication: 'R. E.' [Marietta Shaginian].

2. В душе у каждого из нас.
   (In the soul of each of us; first published English translation: The Soul's concealment.) A 9654ª G, bass (or contralto).
   Non allegro, C major (l). (C – e)
   Date: 5 June 1912, Ivanovka.
   Text: Apollon Korinfsky (1868–1937).
   Dedication: F. I. Chaliapin.

3. Буря.
   (The Storm.) A 9637ª G, tenor (or soprano).
   Allegro, E minor (h), [VB gives key as C minor]. (c – a′)
   Date: 7 June 1912, Ivanovka.
   Text: Aleksandr Pushkin.
   Dedication: L. V. Sobinov.

4. Ветер перелетный.
   (The migrant wind; first published English translation: Day to night comparing went the wind her way.) A 9638ª G, tenor (or soprano).
   Andante, A minor – C major (h). (e♭ – g′♯)
   Date: 9 June 1912, Ivanovka.
   Text: Konstantin Balmont (1867–1943).
   Dedication: L. V. Sobinov.

5. Арион.
   (Arion.) A 9639ª G, tenor (or soprano).
   Allegro, D minor (h). (d – b′♭)
   Date: 8 June 1912, Ivanovka.
   Text: Aleksandr Pushkin.
   Dedication: L. V. Sobinov.

6. Воскрешение Лазаря.
   (The raising of Lazarus.) A 9662ª G, bass (or contralto).
   Grave, F minor (l), [E minor (VB)]. (C – f)
   Date: 4 June 1912, Ivanovka.
   Text: Aleksey Khomyakov (1804–1860).
   Dedication: F. I. Chaliapin.

7. Не может быть!
(It cannot be; first published English translation: So dread a fate I'll ne'er believe.) A 9641ª G, mezzo.
Allegro, E flat minor (m). (e♭ – a′♭)
Date: 7 March 1910, Moscow; revised 13 June 1912, Ivanovka.
Text: Apollon Maykov (1821–1897).
Dedication: To the memory of V. F. Komissarzhevskaya.

8. Музыка.
(Music.) A 9642ª G, mezzo.
Andante mosso, E flat minor (m). (B♭ – g′♭)
Date: 12 June 1912, Ivanovka.
Text: Yakov Polonsky (1819–1898).
Dedication: 'P. Ch.' [i.e. P. Tchaikovsky].

9. Ты знал его.
(You knew him; first published English translation: The poet.)
A 9669ª G, baritone (or mezzo).
Marziale, D major (m). (C♯ – f♯)
Date: 12 June 1912, Ivanovka.
Text: Fyodor Tyutchev (1803–1873).
Dedication: F. I. Chaliapin.

10. Сей день я помню.
(I remember that day; first published English translation: The Morn of Life.)
A 9644ª G, tenor (or soprano).
Andante semplice, A flat major (h). (a♭ – b′♭)
Date: 10 June 1912, Ivanovka.
Text: Fyodor Tyutchev.
Dedication: L. V. Sobinov.

11. Оброчник.
(The peasant; first published English translation: With holy banner firmly held.) A 9675ª G, bass (or contralto).
Non allegro, molto marcato, C sharp minor (l). (C♯ – e)
Date: 11 June 1912, Ivanovka.
Text: Afanasy Fet (1820–1892).
Dedication: F. I. Chaliapin.

12. Какое счастье.
(What happiness; first published English translation: What wealth of rapture.)
A 9646ª G, tenor (or soprano).
Allegro con fuoco, A major (h). (c♯ – b′♭)
Date: 19 June 1912, Ivanovka.
Text: Afanasy Fet.
Dedication: L. V. Sobinov.

13. Диссонанс.

(Dissonance.) A 9647[a] G, soprano.

Non allegro, agitato, E flat minor (h). (B♭ – b′)

Date: 17 June 1912, Ivanovka.

Text: Yakov Polonsky.

Dedication: F. Litvin.

(For *Vocalise*, later published as op. 34 no. 14, see separate entry following).

MS: GMM; autograph scores of the complete set, lacking the first page of no. 13, EB 120 (MS 129), ff 37. The earlier, original MS of no. 7, EB 119 (MS 130), ff 2. Pencil sketches of the whole group, EB 121 (MS 131), ff 15.

Publication: 1913, A. Gutheil/Breitkopf, Russian and German words (German by Lina Esbeer); in high, medium and low keys, with pl. nos. in range 9635–9679. The Russian/English edition appeared in 1921–2, original keys only, plate nos. as under individual items above, including the superscript [a] (Eng. trans. by Edward Agate). No. 13 appeared in 4 languages: Eng. above the voice line and Russian, German and French ('adaptation française de May de Rutter') underlaid.

Coll. Ed. 63–75.

Current edition: Boosey & Hawkes, Songs, vol. 2, pp. 53–108; Muzyka, Romansy, vol. 2, pp. 66–128.

Performance:

Notes: Apart from no. 1, dedicated to M. Shaginian (see notes to op. 38 inf.) and nos. 7 & 8 – both memorials – all these songs are dedicated to singers: Chaliapin, Sobinov and Felia Litvin. (The same goes for SR's remaining songs, opp. 34/14 and 38, q. v.).

For German and French titles, see Appendix (i).

VOCALISE op. 34 no. 14
for high voice and piano

Lentamente. Molto cantabile — C sharp minor (c♯ – c″♯)

Date: according to EB and VB, *21 September 1915, Moscow*; Asafyev gives April 1915; while B/L, with no authority quoted, state 'April 1912, revised September 21, 1915'; (they also give publication date as January 1913 – doubtless the publication date of op. 34 nos. 1–13).

Dedication: A. V. Nezhdanova.

Text: (wordless).

MS: GMM; part of EB 120 (MS 129), ff 4; dated as above.

Publication: 'Vocalise: Chant et piano', 1916, 'Edition Russe de Musique', AΓ 9996, 'copyright 1916 for the British Empire and the United States of America by J. & W. Chester, London & Brighton', pp. 5. Directions in Italian and Russian; dedication in Russian. Engraved by V. Grosse, Moscow.

In Gutheil's Vol. 2 this song appears as 'copyright 1919 by S. Rachmaninoff New York' and with plate no. A 9727ª G. (The Boosey reissue of this volume, however, repeats the copyright statement of all the other items in op. 34, viz. 'copyright 1913 ...'.) A later copy of the Russian/German series of this item in BL, bound into a *Konvolut* at H. 3770, has no copyright statement, but also pl. no. A 9727ª G (acc. date 1931), A. Gutheil/Koussevitzky.

Coll. Ed. 76.

Current edition: Boosey & Hawkes, Songs, vol. 2, pp. 109–112; Muzyka, Romansy, vol. 2, pp. 129–132.

Performance: 24 January 1916, Moscow, Koussevitzky concert, A. Nezhdanova and SR (B/L 198).

Arrangements: (a^1) Arranged by the composer 'pour soprano et orchestre' (original key).
Orch: 2. 2. 2. 2 – 2. 0. 0. 0 – Canto – Strings.
MS: GMM; EB 104 (MS 52), ff 7, in pencil.
Publ: 1916, Copyright by J. & W. Chester (Edition Russe de Musique), AΓ 9999, pp. 13. Engraved by V. Grosse.
Perf:
Note: orchestrated at Nikolay Struve's suggestion after the first performance (see above).

(a^2) 'A Song without Words' (Vocalise). Orchestrated by Sir Henry J. Wood (original key).
Orch: 2. 1. CA. 2. 2 – 4. 0. 0. 0 – Bass Drum – Voice – Solo violin, solo viola – Strings (4. 3. 3. 3. 2).
MS: London, RAM (Henry Wood Library).

Notes: A blue-pencilled note on the label of this MS attests that this was the version performed (by Oda Slobodskaya) in August 1938 at a Rachmaninoff Promenade Concert. (Introduced by the prelude to *The Miserly Knight*, the programme continued with the Second Concerto, soloist: Moiseiwitsch, and finished with the Third Symphony.)

(a^3) There also appears to be a version for soprano and orchestra by A. Dubensky, as performed (and recorded) under Leopold Stokowski.

(b) Arranged by the composer for orchestra alone (transposed into E minor).
Orch: 2. 2. CA. 2. 2 – 2. 0. 0. 0 – 16–20 Violini soli – Strings (6. 6. 6. 4. 4).
MS: location not known.
Publ: [1919] A. Gutheil/Breitkopf, no pl. no., pp. 10; lithographed. 'Copyright 1919 by S. Rachmaninoff New York.'
1960, Boosey & Hawkes Inc., DE 102, pp. 10; engraved. (This edition reveals an unauthorized distribution of the violin parts, merely writing Violins I, II & III and ignoring the layout – evidently authentic – shown in the first edition.)
Perf: April 1920, New York Music Festival, cond. W. Damrosch. (B/L 221).
Recording: Philadelphia Orch., cond. SR (1929), IV.

(c) An arrangement for violin and orchestra is listed by ASCAP without specifying the arranger.
Orch: 2. 2. CA. 2. BsCl. 2 – 2. 0. 0. 0 – Strings.

(d) Arranged for string orchestra by Arkady Dubensky.
Publ: Franco Colombo Inc. (Belwin-Mills).

(e) 'Transcription pour Violon avec Piano par Michel Press' (E minor).
MS: ?GMM; EB 78 (MS 117), ff 1 'in an unidentified hand'.
Publ: 1916, A. Gutheil, Imprimerie Breitkopf & Härtel, A 10000 G, pp. 5, 3. Copyright 1916 by J. & W. Chester, London & Brighton.

Current edition: Boosey & Hawkes; IMC ('newly edited by Josef Gingold', 1632, pp. 5, 3), who also publish arrangements for violoncello (by Leonard Rose, 1646) and double bass. An arrangement 'pour violoncelle avec piano, par A. Brandoukoff', Moscow, ГМ 2043 ИМ, 1922.

(f) 'Transcription pour Piano, Violon et Violoncelle par Jules Conus' (transposed into E minor).
MS: L. of C. (uncat.), pp. 4 (pp. 2–5 of an 8-page section), 1, 1. All in ink.
Publ: 1928, A. Gutheil/Koussevitzky, A 10404 G, pp. 5. Imp. Delanchy-Dupré – Asnières – Paris – XXIX.

Current edition: Boosey & Hawkes; IMC.

(g) Transcribed for piano solo by Alan Richardson, 1951 (original key).
Publ: 1956, Boosey & Hawkes 18150, pp. 7.

Notes: B/L 415 incorrectly attributes the arrangements for violin and for cello to the composer, but fails to list the authentic orchestration of the original song accompaniment.

КОЛОКОЛА – Die Glocken – Les Cloches – The Bells op. 35

For Orchestra, Chorus and Solo
Poem by Edgar Poe, translated into Russian by Konstantin Balmont

1. Allegro, ma non tanto	A flat major
2. Lento	D major
3. Presto	F minor
4. Lento lugubre	C sharp minor – D flat major

Date: January–April 1913, Rome; completed 27 July 1913, Ivanovka (v. inf. **MS** for further details). Partial revision of vocal parts of 3rd. movement, 1936 and later.

Dedication: *Meinem Freunde Willem Mengelberg und seinem Concertgebouw-Orchester in Amsterdam gewidmet.*

Text: Edgar Allan Poe (1809–1849), 'The Bells' (The Works of the late Edgar A. Poe ... New York, 1850); Russian translation by Konstantin Balmont (1867–1943).

Orchestra: 1.–3 (Picc). 2. CA. 2. BsCl. 2. Contra – Campanelli, Trgl. Tbno. Tamb. Piatti.
2. – 3. 2. CA. 2. BsCl. 2. Contra – 4 Campane.
3. – Picc. 3. 3. CA. 3. BsCl. 3. Contra – Trgl. Tamb. Mil. Piatti & Cassa, Tamtam.
4. – Picc. 3. 3. CA. 2. BsCl. 2. Contra – Campanelli, Tamb. Piatti & Cassa, Tamtam.
In all movements: 6 Hn. 3 Trp. 3 Trb. & Tb., Timp, Strings; also Pianino (not in 2), Celesta (not in 3), Harp, Organ (ad lib., in 4).

Voices: Chorus S.A.T.B. [divided];
Soli: Tenor in 1, Soprano in 2, Baritone in 4.

MS: GMM; (a) *Full score*, EB 86 (MS 18), ff 70; movements dated:
1. *10–15 June 1913, Ivanovka.*
2. *25–30 June 1913, Ivanovka.*
3. *2–17 July 1913, Ivanovka.*
4. *19–27 July 1913, Ivanovka.*

(b) Draft with instrumentation noted, dated *26 March 1913, Rome*, inscribed *B*[elaya] *S*[iren] * *from S. Rachmaninoff, 1 January 1914*, EB 87 (MS 19), ff 52, in pencil. Also the text, annotated by SR, sent him by Maria Danilova (cf. B/L 187, but account there differs).

(c) Sketches in pencil; for 1st. and 2nd. movements EB 88 (MS 21), ff 19; for 2nd., 3rd. and 4th. movements EB 89 (MS 20), ff 32; for the first movement EB 90 (MS 22), ff 2.

* Belaya Siren, otherwise 'White Lilacs' (Fekla Yakovlevna Rousseau).

(d) The *Stichvorlage* of the 1936 revised vocal score, v. inf. (probably an annotated copy of the earlier vocal score), presumably formerly in the archives of the publisher, is at present untraced.

(e) A pencil draft (½ page) of the post-1936 'spoken' chorus (v. inf.) at **66–8** is to be found in L. of C., part of ML 30. 55a. R 3, among the sketches.

Publication: [1920], full and study scores, A. Gutheil/Koussevitzky, A 9719 G, pp. 117. 'Copyright 1920 by S. Rachmaninoff, New-York City'. Russian, German (trs. from the Russian trans. by Berthold Feiwel), English ('trs. of Balmont's poem' by Fanny S. Copeland).

[1920], vocal score by Aleksandr Goldenweiser, ditto, A 9716 G, pp. 92, ditto ditto. The chorus parts in the full score differ from those in the vocal score in several places in the 3rd. movement, principally at **63–4, 71–3** and particularly from **86** to the *Prestissimo* after **88**. In the first movement the sopranos are an octave higher for 2 bars at **18** in the full score, and in the last movement minor changes occur between **116** and **117**. Gray wrappers, Russian/German.

1936, vocal score ditto, ditto (same plate no.) *Neue, vom Komponisten im Jahre 1936 revidierte Ausgabe.* In this edition, prepared for the performance in English at the Sheffield Triennial Festival in 1936 under Sir Henry J. Wood, the choral portion of the third movement was extensively rewritten. Fresh chorus parts were separately engraved and issued simultaneously with this revised vocal score, which bears the imprint: A. Gutheil, Paris, Copyright 1936 by S. Rachmaninoff, New York (Stich u. Druck von Breitkopf u. Härtel in Leipzig).

At some later stage, possibly connected with SR's own performances in America in his last years, further MS alterations and additions to the 1936 vocal score were made, again in the chorus parts of the third movement. These were pasted over in some copies of the 1936 vocal score now in the Boosey & Hawkes archives. Apart from minor alterations, these changes consist of (a) substitution of a passage of 'spoken' chorus for a passage from **66–8** already rewritten in 1936, and (b) restoration of simplified chorus parts, differing from both vocal and full score versions of 1920, at **87** in a passage completely eliminated from the chorus parts in the 1936 score. NB: none of the above revisions affects the orchestral parts in any way.

A vocal score issued in 1957 by the State Music Publishers, Moscow, 26452, is textually an exact copy of Gutheil's original (1920) edition. See also *Notes* below.

1967, full score, Muzyka, Moscow, 4026, pp. 140, Russian and English words. This score (engraved and printed by Röder of Leipzig and edited by K. Matsyutin) was based on the original full score issued in 1920 by Gutheil, annotated with footnotes establishing the variants in the chorus parts between this and Gutheil's contemporaneous vocal score (see above). Neither this full score nor the vocal score of 1957 refers at all to the composer's revised edition of 1936.

1971 (corrected impression 1973), choral score, Boosey & Hawkes 19946, pp. 63, English and German words. This edition agrees with the chorus parts from the 1920 Gutheil *vocal* score; an appendix gives the revised (1936) version of the third movement, updated by inclusion of the later MS alterations and additions mentioned above.

1979, study score, Boosey & Hawkes 20334 (HPS 898; originally no. 650 allocated), pp. 140, Russian and English words. This publication is photo-lithoed from the 1967 Muzyka re-engraved full score, including the footnotes. 'Text, from the poem of Edgar Allan Poe, by K. Balmont, retranslated into English by Fanny S. Copeland.'

Current edition: Boosey & Hawkes.

Performance: 30 November 1913, St. Petersburg, A. D. Aleksandrov, E. I. Popova, P. Z. Andreyev, Mariinsky Theatre Chorus, cond. SR.
8 February 1914, Moscow, cond. SR.
A performance in Sheffield projected, Autumn 1914, to be conducted by Sir Henry J. Wood, but cancelled.
30 November 1915, Moscow, cond. S. Koussevitzky.
6 February 1920, Philadelphia, cond. L. Stokowski (USA première).
15 March 1921, Liverpool, cond. Sir Henry Wood (UK première).
21 October 1936, Sheffield, London Philharmonic Orchestra, cond. Sir Henry Wood (first perf. of revised version of third movement).
10 February 1937, London, BBC Symphony Orchestra, Parry Jones, Isobel Baillie, Roy Henderson, Philharmonic Choir, cond. Sir Henry Wood.
A performance in Vienna projected for 10 April 1938 to be cond. SR, but abandoned. SR later conducted performances in New York (10 December 1939; Jan Peerce, Susanne Fisher, Mack Harrell, Westminster choir, Philadelphia Orchestra) and in Chicago (1941).

Notes: see Robert Hull: Rachmaninov's 'The Bells', *Monthly Musical Record*, October 1936, pp. 171–2.
Henry J. Wood: *My Life of Music* (London, 1938), 336; also programme note by Sir Henry Wood, quoted in B/L 322–3. For the genesis of this work, see OvR 171; B/L 184, 187 (see also *Pamyati Rakhmaninova*, ed. M. V. Dobuzhinsky, New York 1946; reminiscences by Bukinik).

Although the later Russian editions, as noted above, all ignore the 1936 revision by the composer (perhaps understandably, since this appears to have been prepared primarily for performances in English), one further edition merits mention, viz.

1973, vocal score with piano 4 hands by K. Lebedev, Muzyka, Moscow, 7729, pp. 151, Russian and English text. (The voice parts follow the 1920 vocal score, not the full score.)

SONATE No. 2 für Pianoforte [original edition] op. 36
(Deuxième SONATE pour piano) [2nd. edition]

1. Allegro agitato — B flat minor
2. Non allegro – Lento. Attacca subito — E minor – major
3. L'istesso tempo – Allegro molto — B flat major

(In both editions, the 'attacca' of the third movement is emphasized by not indenting the first system thereof.)

Date: January–August 1913; 1st. movement completed *12 August 1913, Ivanovka*; 2nd. and 3rd. movements *18 September 1913, Moscow.* Revised version, summer 1931.

Dedication: *M. Pressmann.*

MS: (a) (original version), GMM; EB 64 (MS 103), ff 28, dated; a fragment in pencil, EB 65 (MS 56), ff 2.

(b) By analogy with other revisions, the *Stichvorlage* of the revised version probably consisted of a copy of the original version partly 'cannibalized' by SR and partly rewritten. This MS, presumably formerly in the Paris archives of the publisher or engraver, is at present unlocated.

Publication: [June 1914], A. Gutheil/Breitkopf, A 9695 G, pp. 43, dark gray wrappers.

1931, *Nouvelle édition revue et modifiée par l'auteur en 1931*, A. Gutheil/ Koussevitzky, A 10447 G, pp. 31, buff wrappers. Imprimerie Delanchy–Dupré, Paris–Asnières, Grandjean Grav. (most authorities, following OvR, give Tair as the publisher of this version, which is not supported by examination of the printed copy).

Coll. Ed. (original version) III (i)/32–75, 1950.
(revised version) II/95–123, 1948.

Current edition: Boosey & Hawkes 20201; (IMC). Both, revised versions only.

Performance: 3 December 1913, Moscow, SR.
28 January 1914, Manchester, SR.

Notes: *Even in this sonata so many voices are moving simultaneously, and it is too long* (SR to Alfred Swan, *Musical Quarterly,* January, April 1944; B/L 276–7).

My Second Sonata for pianoforte, which I long to revise as I am not satisfied with the setting I gave it at that time (OvR 171).

The revised version is not only considerably cut – see below – but much of the texture (e.g. on the opening page) is 'thinned out' and reworked with a view to increased clarity in performance: in the style of the 'Corelli' variations (of the same year) and the Fourth Concerto rather than that of the Chopin Variations and the Second or Third. Apart from such rewriting, which only the separate study it deserves can clarify, the cut or condensed passages are as follows [references to the original version]:

1. Bars 53–62 are deleted;
   71–81 are condensed to 9 newly-written bars;
   92–97 are condensed to 2 ditto;
   118–119 are omitted;
   125–140 are condensed to a single bar;
   150–163 are condensed to 3 bars;
   166–169 are deleted, and the final passage is slightly condensed.
2. Bars 36–58 are compressed to 13 bars;
   63–79 are slightly condensed.
3. Bars 30–39 are compressed into 2 bars;
   44–47 are slightly condensed;
   83–90 are replaced by 2 new bars;
   117–125 are replaced by 4 ditto;
   116–199 are deleted;
   234–235 are deleted.

KOMPOSITIONEN VON
S. RACHMANINOW

Für Pianoforte zu 2 Händen.

	M.	Pf.	R.	K.
Op. 1. Konzert in Fis moll (mit Begleitung eines 2. Pianoforte	8	50	4	—
Op. 3. Fantasiestücke.				
Nr. 1. Elégie	1	—	—	50
„ 2. Prélude	—	80	—	40
„ 2a. Prélude revue et doigtée par A. Siloti	—	80	—	40
„ 2b. Prélude (erleichtert von Hill)	—	85	—	40
„ 3. Mélodie	—	80	—	40
„ 4. Polichinelle	1	20	—	60
„ 5. Sérénade	—	80	—	40
Op. 10. Sieben Salonstücke.				
Nr. 1. Nocturne	—	80	—	40
„ 2. Valse	1	20	—	60
„ 3. Barcarolle	1	50	—	75
„ 4. Mélodie	—	80	—	40
„ 5. Humoreske	1	20	—	60
„ 6. Romanze	—	60	—	30
„ 7. Mazurka	1	20	—	60
Op. 18. Zweites Konzert in C moll (mit Begleitung eines 2. Pianoforte)	10	—	4	50
Op. 21 Nr. 5. Le Lilas (Flieder). Romance transcrit par l'auteur	1	10	—	50
Op. 22. Variations sur un thème de F. Chopin	4	50	2	—
Op. 23. Zehn Preludien complet	6	—	3	—
Nr. 1. Fis moll	—	80	—	40
„ 2. B dur	1	—	—	50
„ 3. D moll	—	80	—	40
„ 4. D dur	—	80	—	40
„ 4a. D dur (rev. von A. Siloti)	—	80	—	40
„ 5. G moll	1	—	—	50
„ 5a. G moll (revidiert und erleichtert von A. Siloti)	1	—	—	50
„ 6. Es dur	—	80	—	40
„ 7. C moll	1	—	—	50
„ 8. As dur	1	20	—	60
„ 9. Es moll	—	80	—	40
„ 10. Ges dur	—	60	—	30
Op. 28. Sonate in D moll	6	50	3	—
Op. 30. Drittes Konzert (in D moll)	9	—	4	—
Op. 32. 13 Préludes complet	6	60	3	—
Nr. 1. C dur	1	10	—	50
„ 2. B dur	1	30	—	60
„ 3. E dur	1	10	—	50
„ 4. E moll	1	65	—	75
„ 5. G dur	1	10	—	50
„ 6. F moll	1	10	—	50
„ 7. F dur	1	10	—	50
„ 8. A moll	1	10	—	50
„ 9. A dur	1	10	—	50
„ 10. H moll	1	10	—	50
„ 10a. H moll (rev. von A. Siloti)	1	10	—	50
„ 11. H dur	1	10	—	50
„ 12. Gis moll	1	10	—	50
„ 13. Des dur	1	30	—	60
Op. 33. Etudes-Tableaux complet	—	—	—	—
Nr. 1. F moll	1	10	—	50
„ 2. C dur	1	10	—	50
„ 3. C moll	—	—	—	—
„ 4. A moll	—	—	—	—
„ 5. D moll	—	—	—	—
„ 6. Es moll	1	65	—	75
Op. 33. Etudes-Tableaux.				
Nr. 7. Es dur	1	10	—	50
„ 8. G moll	1	10	—	50
„ 9. Cis moll	1	65	—	75
Op. 36. 2e Sonate	—	—	—	—
24 Préludes Op. 3, 23 et 32. complet	11	—	5	—
Aleko, Oper in einem Aufzuge.				
Klavier-Auszug	3	—	1	50
daraus einzeln:				
Männertanz	1	—	—	50
Frauentanz	1	—	—	50
„ (A. Dubuque)	—	80	—	40
Romanze des jungen Zigeuners (A. Dubuque)	—	80	—	40

Für Pianoforte zu 4 Händen.

	M.	Pf.	R.	K.
Op. 11. Sechs Stücke.				
Nr. 1. Barcarolle	1	70	—	85
„ 2. Scherzo	1	70	—	85
„ 3. Thème russe	1	—	—	50
„ 4. Valse	1	50	—	75
„ 5. Romanze	1	—	—	50
„ 6. Slava	2	—	1	—
Op. 12. Capriccio bohémien	4	—	2	—
Op. 27. Symphonie (in E moll)	14	—	6	—
Op. 29. Die Toteninsel. Symphonische Dichtung zum Gemälde von A. Böcklin	4	50	2	—

Für 2 Pianoforte zu 4 Händen.

	M.	Pf.	R.	K.
Op. 1. Konzert in Fis moll	8	50	4	—
Op. 3 Nr. 2. Prélude Cis moll, arrangé par R. Lange	3	30	1	50
Op. 5. Fantasie (Barcarolle — La Nuit... l'amour — Les Larmes — Pâques)	7	50	3	50
Op. 17. Zweite Suite (Introduct. — Valse — Romanze — Tarantelle)	11	—	5	—
Op. 18. Zweites Konzert in C moll	10	—	4	50
Op. 30. Drittes Konzert in D moll	9	—	4	—

Für Violine und Pianoforte.

	M.	Pf.	R.	K.
Op. 3 Nr. 5. Sérénade, arrangé par J. Nasaroff et M. Zawadsky	1	65	—	75
Op. 6 Nr. 1. Romanze	1	50	—	75
„ 2. Ungarischer Tanz	2	—	1	—

Für Violoncell und Pianoforte.

	M.	Pf.	R.	K.
Op. 2 Nr. 1. Prelude	1	20	—	60
„ 2. Orientalischer Tanz	1	50	—	75
Op. 19. Sonate	8	50	4	—
Op. 23 Nr. 10a. Prelude Ges dur arrangiert von A. Brandoukoff)	1	—	—	50
Andante cantabile, aus dem Klavierkonzert in Fis moll, bearb. von F. Schertel	1	60	—	75

Kammermusik.

	M.	Pf.	R.	K.
Op. 4 Nr. 4. O, schönes Mädchen. Lied. Für Violine, Cello, Harmonium und Piano, arrangiert von A. Dischkewitsch	2	60	1	20
Op. 9. Trio élégiaque für Pianoforte, Violine und Cello	11	—	5	—
Op. 21 Nr. 5. Flieder (Les Lilas). Lied. Für Piano, Violine u. Cello, arrangiert von A. Schaefer	1	65	—	75

Mehrstimmige Gesangwerke.

	M.	Pf.	R.	K.
Op. 20. Der Frühling. Kantate für Bariton-Solo, Chor u. Orchester.				
Orchester-Partitur . . . n.	8	—	4	—
Orchester-Stimmen . . . n.	13	—	6	—
Klavier-Auszug . . . n.	4	50	2	—
Chorstimmen . . . n.	1	70	—	75
Op. 24. Der geizige Ritter. Oper.				
Orchester-Partitur . . . n.	40	—	20	—
Orchester-Stimmen (nach Übereinkunft).				
Klavier-Auszug mit russisch-deutschem Text . . . n.	9	—	4	—
Op. 25. Francesca da Rimini. Oper.				
Orchester-Partitur . . . n.	40	—	20	—
Orchester-Stimmen (nach Übereinkunft).				
Klavier-Auszug mit russisch-deutschem Text . . . n.	11	—	5	—
daraus einzeln:				
Arioso des Lanceotto „O steig herab"	—	60	—	30
Textbuch (russ.)	—	50	—	25
Алеко (Aleko). Oper in einem Aufzuge.				
Klavier-Auszug (russ.)	6	—	3	—
daraus einzeln:				
Nr. 3. Erzählung des Greises (Baß)	1	—	—	50
„ 10. Cavatine des Aleko (Bariton)	1	20	—	60
„ 12. Romanze des jungen Zigeuners (Tenor)	—	80	—	40
Textbuch (russ.)	—	40	—	20
Pantaleon der heilende (russ.). Für gemischt. Chor (a cappella).				
Partitur	1	50	—	75
Stimmen	1	20	—	60

Für Orchester.

	M.	Pf.	R.	K.
Op. 1. Konzert in Fis moll. Partitur und Stimmen in Abschrift.				
Op. 12. Capriccio bohémien.				
Orchester-Partitur . . . n.	9	—	4	—
Op. 18. Zweites Konzert in C moll.				
Orchester-Partitur . . . n.	15	—	7	—
Orchester-Stimmen . . . n.	17	50	8	—
Op. 27. Symphonie E moll.				
Orchester-Partitur . . . n.	35	—	16	—
Orchester-Stimmen . . . n.	52	—	24	—
Op. 29. Die Toteninsel. Symphonische Dichtung zum Gemälde von A. Böcklin.				
Orchester-Partitur . . . n.	11	—	5	—
Orchester-Stimmen . . . n.	18	—	8	—
Op. 30. Drittes Konzert in D moll.				
Orchester-Partitur . . . n.	22	—	10	—
Orchester-Stimmen . . . n.	28	—	13	—
Op. 35. Die Glocken.				
Orchester-Partitur . . . n.	—	—	—	—
Orchester-Stimmen . . . n.	—	—	—	—

Eigentum des Verlegers.

MOSKAU  A. GUTHEIL

Hoflieferant und Kommissionär der Kaiserlichen Theater.

Breitkopf & Härtel — Leipzig — Berlin — Brüssel — London — New York.

St=Petersburg, bei A. Johansen, Perspective de Nevsky, Nr. 60. Kieff, bei L. Idzikowsky. Warschau, bei Gebethner & Wolff.

Plate 10: List of compositions in Edition A. Gutheil

Plate 11: Vespers, op. 37: MS of piano arrangement of no. 5

ВСЕНОЩНОЕ БДЕНИЕ op. 37
[All-Night Vigil (Vespers)]

For 4-part unaccompanied mixed chorus.

1.	Приидите, поклонимся	O come, let us worship (Venite adoremus)
2.	Благослови, душе моя	Praise the Lord, O my soul (Benedic anima mea)
3.	Блажен муж	Blessed is the man (Beatus vir)
4.	Свете тихий	Gladsome Radiance
5.	Ныне отпущаеши	Nunc dimittis
6.	Богородице Дево, радуйся	Ave Maria
7.	Шестопсалмие	Glory be to God [Six psalms]
8.	Хвалите имя Господне	Praise the name of the Lord (Laudate Dominum)
9.	Благославен еси Господи	Blessed be the Lord
10.	Воскресение Христово видевше . . .	The Veneration of the Cross [Christ's resurrection witnessed]
11.	Величит душа моя Господа	Magnificat
12.	Славословие Великое	Gloria in Excelsis
13.	Тропарь 'Днесь спасение'	The day of salvation
14.	Тропарь 'Воскрес из гроба'	Christ is risen
15.	Взбранной воеводе	To the Mother of God

Date: January–February 1915, Moscow (acc. Asafyev).

Dedication: Памяти Степана Васильевича Смоленского [*To the memory of Stepan Vasilyevich Smolensky*] (in facsimile of SR's inscription, at end of first edition).

Voices: mixed chorus S.A.T.B. divided; solo alto in (2), solo tenor in (5). OvR 263 speaks of 'boys and mens voices'.

MS: GMM; EB 101 (MS 68), score with piano arrangement below, undated; ff 42 (holograph), 3 (duplicated).

Riesemann (OvR 252) published the fifth movement in facsimile of a MS piano arrangement, stating (op. cit. 250) that this was 'taken from the archives of the Russian Music Publishers (Éditions Russes) in Paris, as the work is no longer on the market'. (The last clause, even if the work was then – 1934 – nominally out of print, seems meaningless: surely material was available for hire?) The full extent and present whereabouts of this MS being unknown, we reproduce the page in question here (plate 11). Equally, the form of this MS is unspecified: did it consist only of the piano reduction for rehearsal purposes as now printed in the score? The heading etc. in English adds to the mystery (perhaps this was specially written for Riesemann's illustration?). This piano arrangement, though agreeing with that in the original Russian edition, differs a little from that published in the English version.

Facsimile of no. 5: OvR 252 (see above and *plate 11*).

Publication: 1915, vocal score with piano reduction underneath, Russian Music Publishers, Moscow, 'Copyright for the British Empire J. & W. Chester, London & Brighton', PMИ 275–289, pp. 91, thick brown paper covers. Russian titlepage and text only. Engraved by V. Grosse, Moscow; this edition was apparently never re-engraved by Röder of Leipzig after the first War.

1920, vocal score with piano reduction (marked 'for practice only'), The H. W. Gray Company, Inc., New York, as 'Songs of the Church: Fifteen Anthems for Mixed Chorus ... Authorized by the Composer; Edited with the English Text by Winfred Douglas'. Separate numbers spiral wire bound up as one. English text only.

1947, no. 6 only ('We do worship and praise Thee'), Bayley & Ferguson, London & Glasgow, 'edited and adapted to English words by A. M. Henderson', Choral Album no. 1558.

1978, vocal score, Boosey & Hawkes, London. A photolithographic copy of the original Russian edition, 'with the phonetic text (transliteration) and working translation prepared by Bill Tamblyn for the publishers ...'.

Current edition: Boosey & Hawkes (as above); Belwin Mills.

Performance: 10 March 1915, Moscow, Great Nobility Hall, S. I. Zimin, S. P. Yudin, Synodical Choir, cond. Nikolay M. Danilin.
9 December 1971, London, St. John's, Smith Square, Bruckner-Mahler Choir, cond. Wyn Morris.

Notes: Movements 1, 3, 6, 10 & 11 are entirely original; 2 & 15 incorporate chants of the Greek rite; 4 & 5 of the Kiev rite and 7, 8, 9, 12, 13 & 14 Znamenny chants. See SR to Yasser, 30 April 1935 (B/L 311–2).

Ever since my childhood I had been attracted by the magnificent melodies of the Oktoekhos. *I always felt that a special style was needed for their choral treatment, and this I hoped to have found in the* [Vespers], (OvR 176; ibid 243–4 also).

For details of an orchestral parergon to the second part of no. 9 see Norris 109 and notes to op. 45, in the last movement of which extensive use of that section of the present work occurs. The two *Urmotive* of the Dies irae, the descending second and descending third, coalesce and appear simultaneously as they outline the waving accompanying harmonies of the Nunc dimittis, no. 5.

In 1882, Tchaikovsky had completed his Vesper Service, op. 52, consisting of a harmonization of 17 liturgical songs for mixed chorus.

ШЕСТЬ СТИХОТВОРЕНИЙ op. 38
Six poésies pour chant et piano

1. Ночью в саду у меня.
(In my garden at night.) Lento, G minor. (e – b′ ♭)
Date: 12 September 1916, Ivanovka.
Text: Avetik Isaakian (1875–1957), *Ivushka* [The little willow], in a Russian translation by Aleksandr Blok (1880–1921).

2. К ней.
(To her.) Andante, F major. (f – b′ ♭)
Date: 12 September 1916, Ivanovka.
Text: Andrey Bely (pseudonym of Boris Bugayev, 1880–1934).

3. Маргаритки.
(Daisies.) Lento, F major. (f – a′ ♭)
Date: MS undated.
Text: Igor Severyanin (pseudonym of Igor Lotaryov, 1887–1941).

4. Крысолов.
(The rat-catcher; first published English translation: The pied piper.) Non allegro, scherzando, C major. (e – a′)
Date: 12 September 1916, Ivanovka.
Text: Valery Bryusov (1873–1924).

5. Сон.
(The dream; first published English trans: Dreams.)
Lento, D flat major. (f – b′ ♭)
Date: 2 November 1916, Moscow.
Text: Fyodor Sologub (pseudonym of Fyodor Teternikov, 1863–1927).

6. Ау!
(A—oo; first published English trans: The quest).
Andante, D flat major. (c – b′ ♭)
Date: 14 September 1916, Moscow.
Text: Konstantin Balmont (1867–1943).

Dedication: N. P. Koshits (the soprano Nina Koshetz). (Name misspelt 'Konshin' by VB and, following him, OvR).

MSS: (a) Pencil drafts, including those for two other songs only posthumously published: L. of C., ML 31., H 43a. no. 88 case, pp. 32, unsigned and not dated, folded vertically (formerly, coll. Nina Koshetz). This MS was originally a 32-page book of 12 braced stave paper, B & H No. 4E; the cover is missing but a portion of the original blue paper still adheres to the glue on the last page. The contents are as follows:

1. Ау! (= no. 6) (p. 1)
2. Крысолов (= no. 4) (p. 4 system 2)
3. К ней (= no. 2) (p. 9 system 2)

4. Молитва (see below) (p. 13)
5. Маргаритки (= no. 3) (p. 17)
6. Ночью в саду у мена (= no. 1) (p. 20 system 2)
7. Все хочет петь (see below) (p. 22 system 2)
8. Сон (= no. 5) (p. 28)

For further details of nos. 4 and 7 in this list see separate entry below (II/58). Some slight differences from the final, e.g. the ending of no. 6 (1) are to be noted.

(b) GMM; EB 122 (MS 132), ff 19. Containing the six published songs only.

Publication: 1916, Édition Russe de Musique, Moscou-Petrograd, РМИ 327–332 (separate numbers), pp. 3, 5, 5, 7, 7, 7. Russian words only. (Engraved by V. Grosse, Moscow.) Reprinted 1923 by Muzsektor, Moscow, 2059–64, ibid.

1922, Russischer Musikverlag, Berlin. 'Edited by F. H. Schneider'; also including 'paroles françaises de M. D. Calvocoressi, English translation by Edward Agate and K. Schindler, Deutscher Text von B. Feiwel', RMV 327–332, but no dedication included. (Re-engraved by C. G. Röder GmbH, Leipzig.) High keys only.

Coll. Ed. 78–83.

Current edition: Boosey & Hawkes, Songs, vol. 2, pp. 116–141; Muzyka, Romansy, vol. 2, pp. 135–157.

Performance: 24 October 1916, Moscow, Nina Koshetz and SR.

Arrangements: no. 3 Daisies.

(a) Transcribed by the composer for piano solo.
MS: L. of C., part of ML 30. 55a. R3, pp. 5 (= 3–5 of an 8-page sewn section) in pencil, with engraver's annotations. Titlepage: *'Daisies'/S. Rachmaninoff.*
Publication: [acc. to B/L 416, Edition Tair 1924; not traced and unrecorded at the Bibliothèque Nationale. As Tair was not set up until 1925, and their pl. no. 1 only appears on the score of the Fourth Concerto in 1928, some doubt must surround this entry; maybe the date was misprinted?]. 'Revised and as played by the composer, TAIR, Copyright 1940 by Charles Foley, New York, R13–3, no. 2004, pp. 5.

Coll. Ed. III (i)/81–3, 1950.
Performance: 20 May 1922, London, Queen's Hall (Lyle 181).
Recording: (1940), II.

(b) Transcribed by Fritz Kreisler for violin and piano. 'Marguerite (Albumleaf)'.
Publication: 1926, Carl Fischer Inc., B 2033, CC 24024–8, pp. 7, 3. Ditto, B. Schott's Söhne, Mainz, 31985, pp. 4, 3 (different engraving) [Transkriptionen, no. 21]. 'Mit Bewilligung der Orig. Verleger: Russische [Musik] Verlag, Berlin.' A repeat in the upper octave extends this transcription.

(c) Transcribed by Jascha Heifetz for violin and piano, 1945.
Publication: 1947, Carl Fischer Inc., B 2819, 30358–4, pp. 5, [1].

Notes: In her reminiscences, the minor Symbolist poet (and, later, Soviet author) Marietta Shaginian (1888–) says: 'From that time [1912; i.e. after she had suggested some texts for SR's songs op. 34] I repeatedly copied down for him and suggested to him poetry by Russian poets. He was not very favourable towards the Symbolists, but I always tried to make him appreciate something in them. He set V. Bryusov's *Krysolov*, F. Sologub's *Son*, A. Isaakian's *Ivushka* in A. Blok's translation – texts that I had copied down and suggested.' (M. Shaginian, 'Vospominaniya o S. V. Rakhmaninove', in VR/A, vol. 2 p. 125).

See also B/L 416; Norris 53, 193.

For German and French titles, see Appendix (i).

Neuf Etudes-Tableaux pour Piano

op. 39

1. Allegro agitato — C minor
2. Lento assai — A minor
3. Allegro molto — F sharp minor
4. Allegro assai — B minor
5. Apassionato [sic] — E flat minor
6. Allegro — A minor
7. Lento lugubre [not in MS] — C minor
8. Allegro moderato — D minor
9. Allegro moderato, Tempo di Marcia — D major

Dates: as given on MSS: 1, *5 October 1916, Moscow*; 3, *14 October 1916, Moscow*; 4, *24 September 1916, Moscow*; 5, *17 February 1917, Moscow*; 6, *8 September 1911, Ivanovka, revised 27 September 1916, Moscow*; 9, *2 February 1917.* Nos. 2, 7 & 8 undated on MSS, but doubtless contemporaneous. (Coll. Ed. gives '1917' *tout simple* for each number).

Dedication: none.

MS: (a) GMM; EB 66 (MS 104), ff 35, dated. Whether the MS of no. 6 is that originally of op. 33 no. 4 (see above) with subsequent overworkings, or an entirely new copy is not clear; the former is probable, in view of the double dating.

(b) Pencil drafts of portions of nos. 2 and 3 occur in a sketchbook (B & H 4E) now in the L. of C. (see Introduction, p. 17 above, and op. 44 below) forming part of ML 30. 55a. R3.

Publication: 1917, Édition Russe de Musique, Moscou-Petrograd, РМИ 333–341 (separate numbers, with gray wrappers), pp. 9, 7, 9, 7, 11, 9, 9, 9, 9. 'Copyright 1917 for the British Empire and the United States of America by J. & W. Chester, London, W. and Brighton.' (Engraved by V. Grosse, Moscow.)

1920, Édition Russe de Musique (Russischer Musikverlag GmbH), RMV 333–341, as above but in silurian and later in brown wrappers, re-engraved. 'Copyright 1920 by S. Rachmaninoff, New-York.' (Stich u. Druck von C. G. Röder GmbH, Leipzig.)

Coll. Ed. II/124–187, 1948.

Current edition: Boosey & Hawkes 16871–9; (IMC, Leeds).

Performance: 29 November 1916, Petrograd, SR. (Including the E flat minor piece, no. 5 – see review in *Russkaya muzykalnaya gazeta* (B/L 201) – despite date on MS as given above. Eight études were given a little later in Moscow (B/L 201–2), again including no. 5 (and presumably excluding no. 9). First complete performance, 21 February 1917, Petrograd, SR.

Recording: no. 6 only (1925), II.
Ampico roll, ditto. (? date).

Arrangements: nos. 2 (La mer et les mouettes), 7 (Marche funèbre), 6 (Le chaperon rouge et le loup), 9 (Marche) orchestrated by Ottorino Respighi as nos. 1, 3, 4 & 5 of *Cinq Etudes-Tableaux de S.R. Orchestration de Ottorino Respighi*, 1930.

Orchestra: 3 (Picc). 2. CA. 2. BsCl. 2. Contra – 4. 3. 3. 1 – Timp. Piatti, Tamt. (nos. 1, 3 & 4), Tambno. (no. 3), Campanelli (nos. 3 & 4), Campane (no. 3), Triangolo, Tamburo Basco, Cassa (no. 5) – Arpa (no. 5) – Strings.

MS: Boosey & Hawkes archives, London; pp. 100, dated *Roma – 30 Settembre 1930.*

Publication: 1931, Edition Russe de Musique, RMV 527, pp. 102 (complete); 1973, Muzyka, Moscow, 7611, pp. 111 (with preface by I. Iordan and G. Kirkor).

Performance: December 1931, cond. S. Koussevitzky.

Notes: see also op. 33 above.

Notes: no. 6 is the 'recasted' version of op. 33 no. 4, withdrawn from that opus before publication, q. v. On the extent of the rewriting, the Moscow editors are silent: the final version, however, as published, has all the technically advanced features, pianistic, harmonic and rhythmic, which differentiate op. 39 from any earlier solo piano pieces by SR. In its published form, op. 39 no. 6 was one of the items most frequently played by the composer.

According to OvR 237, though the details there given are somewhat garbled, no. 1 ('F minor' [sic]) was inspired by Böcklin's painting *The Waves*; no. 6 by the fairy tale of Red Riding Hood and the Wolf. For SR's own comments (on nos. 2, 6, 7 & 9) see SR to Respighi, 2 January 1930 (B/L 262–3).

The L.H. of no. 2 outlines the opening notes of *Dies irae*; and in this, in its key, and in its melodic arches closely resembles a major earlier score based on that chant: The Isle of the Dead (op. 29).

See also Yu. Engel, *Russkiye vedomosti*, 5 December 1916 (B/L 202).

4 ^{me} CONCERTO pour Piano et Orchestre op. 40

1. Allegro vivace (Alla breve) G minor
2. Largo – attacca subito C major
3. Allegro vivace G minor – major

Date: Commenced before SR's departure from Russia (B/L 231; Igumnov's recollections; also *Muzyka*, 12 April 1914, p. 318). The coda of the Largo introduces a passage from the Etude-Tableau in C minor op. 33 no. 3 (dated 18 August 1911 but subsequently withdrawn and only posthumously published, q. v.). The original MS full score is dated *January–August 25* [1926] *New York–Dresden.*

The work was substantially revised in June–July 1927 (i.e. after the first performance but before first publication). It was revised again in the summer of 1941, equally substantially; and it will facilitate the ordering of the considerable amount of material concerned if the three resulting versions are described separately. Perhaps we shall not be begrudged the space needed for an adequate commentary on a work whose composition spanned over half the author's working life.

Dedication: (on published editions) *à Monsieur Nicholas Medtner.* (Medtner returned the compliment by dedicating his Concerto no. 2 in C minor, op. 50, to SR in 1927.)

Orchestra: 2. 2. CA. 2. 2 – 4. 2. 3. 1 – Timp. – Strings. In (3) only: Trgl. Tbno. T.Mil. Piatti & Cassa; Piccolo.

First Version (completed 1926 – unpublished):

MS: (a) *Full score*, L. of C., part of ML 30. 55a. R3, in ink but bar lines ruled in pencil. Titlepage reads *Concert pour Piano (Nº 4) / op. 40. / S. Rachmaninoff.* Paginated throughout.

1. pp. 1–66. At head of p. 1 *S. Rachmaninoff / (op. 40)* in pencil.
2. pp. 67–83.
3. pp. 84–171. At end *January–August 25 / New York–Dresden.*

The arrangement of the orchestral accompaniment for a second piano is written at the foot throughout this orchestral score, but the bars are not joined on. Some bowings were apparently added later.

There are only a few alterations in this score, no paste-overs and no engraver's markings. At the back is loosely inserted a 4-page section giving another (?earlier, as unpaginated) version (deleted in pencil) of the passage roughly corresponding with pp. 10–13 of the full score published in 1928.

(b) A copyist's copy of this MS must have been made, together with the original performing material, intended for use also as the *Stichvorlage*: this has not been traced, but will be referred to again under the Second Version below.

(c) A copyist's copy of the arrangement for two pianos was also made, pp. 110 (v. SR to Medtner, 9 September 1926, B/L 246). The subsequent history and present location of this copy is also given under the Second Version below.

(d) *Sketches.* In L. of C., ML 30. 55a. R3, among the miscellaneous pencil sketches, a considerable amount of material referring to this work is to be found, as follows:

(i) A 32-page book of MS paper, B & H 4E, contains fairly complete 4-stave pencil drafts of the first version of the first movement, the opening section appearing towards the end of the book. This book almost certainly came with the composer from Russia. Many details of the piano writing differ from the other sources.

(ii) Another similar book (whose pre-1917 provenance is proved by its inclusion of a pencil draft of the setting from St. John, q. v. p. 172) contains similar pencil drafts of the latter part of the first movement; also of the third movement, extending from after the section in D flat major until the coda.

(iii) A double sheet gives a draft of the D flat major section of the last movement.

(iv) A separate gathering of paper bears a pencil draft of the second movement.

(v) On the reverse of a pencilled page from the Cadenza to Liszt's Second Hungarian Rhapsody (q. v. p. 196) is a rough draft of the passage occurring around cue **55** in the published scores (third movement).

(vi) A book of Breitkopf MS paper (similar to those noted above) received by the L. of C. as part of the Siloti legacy is marked on the cover in an unidentified hand: Сергей Васильевич Рахманинов / 1920–21гг./ Америка. This contains pencil sketches for the transition section in the first movement; a fragment of the high-lying violin melody in the D flat section of the finale; and notes for the following section of the finale (*Tempo I* before **57** until **62**, 1928 score).

Facsimile: of p. 152 from the original MS full score (a) above, 3rd movement, in Emanuel Winternitz, *Musical Autographs* (1955, rev. Dover Publications Inc., New York 1965) Vol. 2, plate 177. (This passage does not appear in any other version, published or unpublished.)

Publication: none in this version, except for the above-noted facsimile page.

Performance: 18 March 1927, Philadelphia, SR and the Philadelphia Orchestra, cond. Leopold Stokowski.

Notes: After the badly-received first group of American performances of the work in early 1927, a number of revisions, to which we now refer, were carried out thus establishing the Second Version. These little-known changes introduced into the work before its first publication are too extensive to be listed in their entirety but too important to be ignored. We compromise by

Plate 12: Fourth Concerto: p. 96 of MS of two-piano arrangement

reference to the salient points in which the First and Second Versions differed, using the score printed and published in 1928 (v. inf.) for comparison (cue numbers refer to this score).

1. The introductory orchestral tutti originally involved more elaborate harmonies, with chromatic parts for clarinets and bassoons; also at cue **1** the woodwind tonguing had no breathing rests and the strings' *pizz.* and *arco* were reversed from those in the printed score. Refinements in details of layout, orchestration and piano writing were made up to the passage **17–20**, which was more radically reworked; detailed rewritings continuing from **23** to **27**. The piano part from **27**–4 to **29**–2 had already been rewritten in the original MS: the printed 1928 edition follows first one, then another, of the alternatives. At **29**–2 the 5 bars as printed in 1928 replace 21 of the original MS (passing through *A tempo più vivo* to *Allegro vivace*); six bars of entirely different detail (piano with crotchet sextuplet chords) were replaced by **30**–3 &4. Again, minor rescoring thinned the orchestral parts; the cor anglais solo at **32** was originally played by a solo violin; and the final *Allegro vivace* included a piano part in semiquavers!

2. In the *Largo*, fewer changes occur. The 3/4 bar between **34** and **35** was compressed from a 4/4 one; the scoring at **35** respaced. At **36** a 2-bar reprise of the principal theme (with piano *Auftakt* in the second bar) points the derivation of the diminished version that follows. Again, a very few minor orchestral changes occur in the rest of the movement.

3. 16 bars, distilling the E flat – D motto of the Finale from the motif of the Largo, were eliminated and replaced by the present 3 opening bars. Changes next occur at the *Tempo meno mosso* in D flat, whose theme stood thus in the original MS:

Much of the subsequent setting was adjusted accordingly: at **51** the piano R.H. arabesques were originally played by flute and clarinet whilst the violin cantabile stood at first in the piano part. The solo passage and cue **52** remained unchanged; the orchestral parts for 5 bars at **53** are new. Minor rewritings follow, with a 5-bar deletion before the *pp* cymbal roll; at **56** an A-clarinet line crossed the pianist's *ascending* triads. From **61** to **65** considerable rewriting to the piano part took place; at **66** heavier scoring and an entirely different syncopated chordal piano part have been reworked. **67–69** remain unaltered, but the soloist now remains silent at **69**; **70–72** was much fuller in the MS, the melody being taken first by trumpets and trombones, then by the 4 horns, with piano 'off-beat' chromatic chords. Seven bars have been eliminated before **72**, which was scored as at the opening, and from **72** + 6 to the end was entirely rewritten (the measured tremolo was originally taken by the piano).

At that point, originally 9 bars (with the cor anglais again playing the rising scale motif) led to *A tempo meno mosso* (p. 144 of the MS full score) in B major. Here a reprise of the essence of the central D flat section occurred, continuing for some pages in this new key; an *Agitato e sempre accelerando* led to *Vivace* (G major) on p. 156 of the MS, with a low D pedal (somewhat similar to that commencing on p. 127 of the 1928 printed score, but without the section now printed there as **75–78**). From **78** to the end the two versions differ as so often in detail rather than in major features: the *Presto* indication now at **80** was originally reached three pages earlier, but the passage now at **82–83** is new for the printed edition. A crotchet stood originally in place of the rest in the last bar (♫ ♩).

Second Version (1927 – published 1928):

After 1½ months of assiduous work I have finished the corrections to my concerto ... The first 12 pages are rewritten, and also the whole of the coda (SR, Dresden, to Yuly Konyus, 28 July 1927 – RP/A 529, p. 515).

It seems certain that the copyist's copy of the full score, (b) above, was updated for use as the *Stichvorlage* by SR pasting over the necessary portions to establish his changes. As already noted, the present whereabouts of this copy is unknown (maybe it remained with the original Paris engraver or printer?), but our deductions as to its existence and revision are supported by the following:

The copyist's copy of the arrangement for two pianos, (c) above, still survives in the archives of Boosey & Hawkes Music Publishers Ltd., London. The revisions made before the first publication are written in in ink by SR's own hand and/or pasted over. In the course of this surgery, not only the pagination but also occasionally the cue numbers have got out of kilter; this MS now contains 102 pp. and it was used as the *Stichvorlage* for the publication in 1928, v. inf.

Facsimile: of p. 96 from this two-piano arrangement, in SR's hand, *see plate 12* (This passage does not occur in the final version, but appears at p. 70 of the 1928 edition.)

Publication: 1928, full and study scores, Édition TAIR, Paris, pl. no. 1, pp. 144, gray wrappers. 'Copyright 1928 by S. Rachmaninoff New York.' Parts, ditto, pl. no. 2.

1928, Réduction pour 2 Pianos à 4 mains par l'auteur, ditto, pl. no. 3, pp. 75, ditto.

Performance: for the earliest performances in the UK, 2 December 1928 (BBC Manchester, cond. Sir Henry Wood); 8 May and 27 September 1929 (London, RAM); 27 September 1929 (Harrogate, cond. Basil Cameron) the PRS returns have no record of the soloists. SR, writing to Watson Lyle from New York on 26 March 1929, referred to a concert when 'Mr. Pushnoff' [Leff Pouishnoff] played the work.

18 November 1929, London, SR and LSO, cond. Albert Coates.

Notes: The performances of this version, in London in 1929 and on the Continent in 1930, were hardly more successful than the earlier ones given in America. Still unsatisfied with the work, which he had thought of 'correcting' in 1938 (v. SR to Somov, 31 July 1938, B/L 344) SR finally revised it again in 1941.

Third Version (1941 – published 1944):

MS: (e) The 'copy' for this version was originally a printed score of the 1928 publication 'cannibalized' by SR with MS alterations and additions in his own hand. This score is now in L. of C. forming part of ML 30. 55a. R3.

(f) The existence, despite our ignorance of their current location, of the composer's first proof sheets of the new edition can be deduced from the following three facts: In L. of C., among some miscellaneous papers, are a number of pieces of MS paper, written in SR's hand and still with Sellotape stickers attached, giving some re-orchestrated passages. These pieces of paper do not fit score (e), hence the existence of (f) is assumed. Secondly, there are also a few smaller patchovers in a copyist's hand, also in L. of C., making other slight amendments; and thirdly, a number of places (for which no such patches appear to survive) differ between score (e) and the revised (1944) published edition. By reference to this latter publication, the principal differences from (e) – all in the Finale – may be quickly disposed of as follows:

- at **53**, 5 bars of the piano part now differ from the version written in (e).
- the 4 bars before **58** were a semitone higher and the strings differed, in (e).
- the double-lining of the piano part at **68–9** was not in (e).
- the three brass chords on p. 118 were originally four crotchets long in (e) (copyist's small patch-overs refer).
- from **74–76** and **77–8** the orchestration was altered by the further patch-overs prepared by SR. (These may have postdated the 1941 recording, as some unprinted woodwind parts at **75**–4 have survived therein.)

(That these alterations have all been patched into the plates of the current edition is evident from close examination.)

Publication: 1944, full score (study score following later), Charles Foley, New York, no pl. no., pp. 136, silurian covers, 'As revised by the composer in 1942' [sic].

1946, Two Pianos – Four Hands (this arrangement was completed by Robert Russell Bennett), 2302, pp. 79, ditto. A number of (chiefly minor) inaccuracies occur in this last, posthumous, publication; careful collation of the solo part with that in the 1944 full score thus being necessary to establish the authentic text in every detail.

Both the above editions, of 1944 and 1946, utilize the plates of the Tair editions of 1928 where possible and appropriate. The remaining (altered) pages and passages were lithographed, in rather cruder style, and assembled together as well as may be.

1956, full score, Muzgiz, Moscow, 25195, pp. 162. Edited by G. Kirkor (it is no surprise to see that this edition draws attention to many of the discrepancies between the above 1944 and 1946 editions).

Current editions: Belwin Mills; Eulenberg 1225 (a reprint of Foley's 1944 score, with incorrect date in the copyright line!).

Performance: 17 October 1941, Philadelphia, SR and the Philadelphia Orchestra, cond. Eugene Ormandy.
The first London concert performance (29 November 1947, RT and the Modern Symphony Orchestra, cond. Arthur Dennington) was preceded by a broadcast performance by Sidney Harrison.

Recording: SR and the Philadelphia Orchestra, cond. Eugene Ormandy (1941), V.

Notes: Apart from further compressions, as shown in the table below, and many minor pianistic and orchestral improvements, this final revision included rewriting of the piano part in the closing section of the *Largo* and recomposition (for the second time) of the middle episode and entire coda of the Finale. We are indebted to the patient study by Edward N. Waters (then Chief, Music Division, Reference Department, L. of C. – letter to RT 30 March 1966 refers) for the following schedule which documents the extent of these changes:

	Stage 1 (Autograph 1926)	*Stage 2* (First published edition 1928)	*Stage 3* (Final version published 1944)
1st. movt.	367	346	313
2nd. movt.	82	80	77
3rd. movt.	567	476	434
TOTAL	1016 bars	902 bars	824 bars

As the Second and Third Versions have both been published, we shall not discourse further here on their differences to the degree we have already done on the initial version. Suffice it to say that the tightening of the structure and rethinking of some of the texture has ensured a more concise and homogeneous result. One other consequence of all these rewritings has been the progressive elimination from the finale's coda of any reprise of material from the D flat middle section. As we have seen above, the First Version involved a substantial recapitulation of this episode, in B major; the Second Version reduced this to a (considerably transmogrified) partial repeat of the material. The final version, as with that of the First Concerto, thus reduces the original sonata-like form to a simpler episodical one. Also, the gradual acceleration expressed in the coda in the earlier versions, though maybe implied, is not indicated in the final, definitive reading.

Through all these changes, it is to be noted that the *Dies irae* motif – as prevalent in SR's later music as DSCH in that of his younger fellow-countryman – is outlined by the solo part in the passage at *Tranquillo*, cue **30** + 5.

See: RT: R's revisions and an unknown version of his Fourth Concerto (*Musical Opinion*, Feb. 1973, pp. 235–7).
GN: R's Second Thoughts (*Musical Times*, April 1973, pp. 364–8).

Although the need for a critical edition of SR's compositions is in some ways lessened by his own meticulous proof-reading and editing, it is to be hoped that an improved reissue of the hurriedly-prepared posthumous two-piano score of the present work, eliminating errors and expunging discrepancies, might form the first step in any such undertaking. The publication currently circulating, an exact reprint of that of 1946, contains around 150 errors of one sort and another, on a conservative estimate.

TROIS CHANSONS RUSSES op. 41
pour Orchestre et Choeur

1. Moderato (alla breve) – Allegro assai	E minor
2. Largo	D minor
3. Allegro mod^{to} (Alla marcia, al rigore di tempo)	B minor

Date: *16 November 1926* (no. 2).

Dedication: *à Monsieur Léopold Stokowsky.*

Orchestra: Picc. 2. 2. CA. 2. BsCl. 2. Contra – 4. 2. Tromba Alto in F. 3. 1 – Timp. Trgl. Verghe. Tamb. Militair. Piatti & Cassa. Campanelli – Harps, Piano – Strings.

Chorus: (according to published editions) 1. 15–20 Bassi; 2. 15–20 Alti; 3. 20–25 Alti & 20–25 Bassi. The last 6 bars of the Alto part are marked Solo in the full score but not in the piano score; this word was added in pencil, in another hand, in the MS.

MS: *Full score*, L. of C., part of ML 30. 55a. R3. In pencil, no titlepage, first page of music headed: *'Russian Songs' / I / S. Rachmaninoff / op. 41*, pp. 53. No. 1, pp. 1–16; no. 2, pp. 17–29; p. 30 blank; no. 3, pp. 31–53. Dated (as above) at end of no. 2 only. Words, in English only (!) in another hand (?).

This MS is a clean score, with no engraver's marks. Six bars, four before and two after cue no. **8** are pasted over; also, in the chorus parts, from **27–29** the notes are deleted though the words still appear. This MS specifies only 8–10 Alti and 8–10 Bassi for the chorus.

In the absence of a piano reduction at the foot of the full score, the existence of such a MS (presently unlocated), possibly indeed another MS including the reduction and the Russian words, may be assumed as a *Stichvorlage.*

A sketch sheet (1 page, in pencil) for no. 2 is also to be found in L. of C. among the miscellaneous sketches.

Publication: 1928, full and study scores, Édition TAIR, Paris, pl. no. 4, pp. 59, gray wrappers. 'Copyright 1928 by S. Rachmaninoff New York.' Parts, pl. no. 5.

1928, Réduction pour Piano et Chant par l'Auteur, ditto, pl. no. 6, pp. 28, ditto. Chorus parts, pl. no. 7, pp. 7, 7.

SR to Somov (B/L 254), 17 June 1928, refers to the copyright registration of this work in Washington.

1959, full score, Muzgiz, Moscow, 27300, pp. 73. Edited by G. Kirkor. Footnotes draw attention to a few discrepancies in the early editions.

Current edition: Belwin Mills.

Performance: 18 March 1927, Philadelphia cond. L. Stokowski.

Texts: 1. Через речку.
2. Ах, ты, Ванька.
3. Белилицы, румяницы вы мои.

English translation by Kurt Schindler; French by M. D. Calvocoressi; German by Heinrich Möller.

'The text and melodies of these songs, which were quite unknown outside their place of origin (the most isolated corners of Russia) had been communicated to R. in New York by ... Mme. Nadejda Plevitskaya ... and by Feodor Chaliapin from the inexhaustible store of his memory.' (OvR 199).

Notes: For an earlier version (solo voice with piano accompaniment) of no. 3, see II/86 inf.

A letter to RT dated 12 May 1970 from Edward N. Waters, answering an enquiry about the extent of any differences between MSS and published editions of this and the other later scores, is quoted here for its valuable and authoritative view:

'... I have looked at the holograph scores of [opp. 41, 42, 43, 44, 45] and compared them to the published versions. The manuscripts are almost *Reinschriften*, but this does not mean that he never re-touched them. They all have occasional measures crossed out and re-written, and sometimes erasures, but these corrections, second thoughts, eliminations, etc., were apparently done before publication took place, so it's fairly safe to say that the published versions are the same as the extant manuscripts. There are a few places in these publications that differ slightly from the manuscripts, and these places may result from changes that Rachmaninoff made in reading proofs (which we don't have).'

'... you realize how extensively he revised [the Fourth Concerto, op. 40]. So we'll refer to that no more ... he did not [rewrite the other works] as he did ... op. 40 – but he did make some changes which went into the printed versions. On the other hand, one can say that the publications, as far as we can tell from comparison with the manuscripts, represent his final thoughts for or on these pieces. Does this satisfy you?' (ibid.)

VARIATIONS <on a theme of Corelli> op. 42

for piano solo

Theme	Andante	D minor
Var. 1	Poco più mosso	”
2	L'istesso tempo	”
3	Tempo di Minuetto	”
4	Andante	”
5	Allegro (ma non tanto)	”
6	L'istesso tempo	”
7	Vivace	”
8	Adagio misterioso	”
9	Un poco più mosso	”
10	Allegro scherzando	”
* 11	Allegro vivace	”
* 12	L'istesso tempo	”
13	Agitato	”
–	Intermezzo	–
14	Andante (come prima)	D flat major
15	L'istesso tempo	”
16	Allegro vivace	D minor
17	Meno mosso	”
18	Allegro con brio	”
* 19	Più mosso. Agitato	”
20	Più mosso	”
–	Coda. Andante	”

* [see under Notes below]

Date: completed *19 June 1931, Le Pavillon* [Clairfontaine].

Dedication: *To Fritz Kreisler.*

MS: L. of C., part of ML 30. 55a. R3.

In ink; draft of wording for cover (as the printed first edition) and titlepage (... sur un thème [de Corelli] [rewritten over words erased] / 'La Folia' [crossed out]) in another hand. ff 24 (numbered thus by SR), i.e. pp. 48 (of which 2 and 46 are blank). Dated at end: *'Le Pavillon' 19 June 1931.*

This clean and very well-spaced MS appears, from the evidence of engraver's marks, to have been used as the *Stichvorlage.* (It also shows obvious signs of having been folded up at some stage.)

The following altered bars are to be noted in this MS:

Var. 3, bars 4 & 12 were rewritten.
7, the last bar was originally different.
10, bars 12–14 rewritten; also many knife erasures.
11, the last bar was originally different.
12, shows alterations in bars 5, 10 and 17–20.
16, shows alterations in bars 2, 4 and the last bar.

Coda: the 2/4 bar is the second half of what was originally a 4/4 bar; from the change to 3/4 until the last two bars the music is rewritten.

Also in the L. of C. is a spirex-bound sketch book containing extensive drafts to this work (including some rejected material) in pencil (French paper, 12 stave small folio, pp. 60).

Publication: 1931, Edition TAIR, Carl Fischer Inc., New York, P 1924, pp. 27.

1932, Édition TAIR (S. A. des Grandes Éditions Musicales, Paris), pl. no. 9, pp. 27. Blue wrappers with large facsimile signature at head. 'Copyright 1931 by Carl Fischer Inc.' (cf. W. Lyle, pp. 202–3). Reprinted by Charles Foley, R–2041.

Coll. Ed. II/188–214, 1948.

Current Edition: Belwin Mills.

Performance: 12 October 1931, Montreal, Canada, SR.
29 April 1933, London (Queen's Hall), SR.

Notes: The theme, as used in A. Corelli's Violin Sonata XII, is in fact *La Folía.* The dedicatee's version, which may have initially inspired this composition, is no. 18 of his 'Klassische Manuskripte'; for other composers' settings, cf. Scholes, *The Oxford Companion to Music*, articles 'La Folía' and 'Melody'.

For the title of this composition, see also Yasser (*Novoye russkoye slovo*, New York, 10 November 1931; *Pamyati Rakhmaninova*, New York 1946; B/L 278). The first edition was entitled 'Variations' *tout simple* 'op. 42', beneath a facsimile signature of SR on cover and titlepage; only above the commencement of the music did the reference to Corelli appear.

Variations 11, 12 and 19 (marked * above) are each footnoted: *Cette variation peut être omise.* For SR's droll comment on this aspect of the work, see his letter to Medtner, 21 December 1931 (B/L 280–1; Norris 70–1). In the American edition, at the foot of p. 14, the last word reads 'smize' [sic!] – possibly a proof that this edition predates the French one. In this context also, cf. Lyle, 203, implying that on 29 April 1933 SR said to him 'It is not yet published here [= London]'. On that day, however, RT purchased his own copy of the latter publication at Queen's Hall, during the recital! See also Swan (B/L 277).

On the morning of the London première of this work, RT received a note in that incredibly fine hand (and jetblack ink), a reproduction of which is fittingly entered here; (the signature printed in facsimile on the cover and titlepage of the Tair edition may be compared):

Thank you for your letter.
Sergei Rachmaninoff.
1933.

RAPSODIE <en forme de Variations> op. 43
sur un thème de Paganini pour Piano et Orchestre

[the bracketted words, said to be originally on the MS titlepage, were struck out by the composer (B/L 307). Earlier projected titles were 'Symphonic Variations' (SR to S. Satina, 19 August 1934) and 'Fantasia' (SR to Wilshaw, 8 September 1934), B/L 304–5].

Introduction	Allegro vivace	A minor
Var. 1	Precedente	"
Tema	L'istesso tempo	"
Var. 2	L'istesso tempo	"
3	L'istesso tempo	"
4	Più vivo	"
5	Tempo precedente	"
6	L'istesso tempo	"
7	Meno mosso, a tempo moderato	"
8	Tempo I	"
9	L'istesso tempo	"
10	(♩ = ♩)	"
11	Moderato	–
12	Tempo di Minuetto	D minor
13	Allegro	"
14	L'istesso tempo	F major
15	Più vivo. Scherzando (Orch. tacet)	"
16	Allegretto	B flat minor
17	(♩ = ♩.)	"
18	Andante cantabile	D flat major
19	A tempo vivace	A minor
20	Un poco più vivo	"
21	Un poco più vivo	"
22	Un poco più vivo (alla breve)	"
23	L'istesso tempo	"
24	A tempo un poco meno mosso – Più vivo	"

Date: 3 July – *18 August 1934, Senar* [Hertenstein b/Luzern].

Dedication: none.

Orchestra: Picc. 2. 2. CA. 2. 2 – 4. 2. 3. 1 – Timp. Tamburo (e poi Triangolo). Piatti & Cassa. Campanelli – Harps – Strings.

MS: *Full score*, L. of C., part of ML 30. 55a. R3, pp. 1–176 in ink. There are a few alterations to the piano part, establishing the printed version, in variations 4 & 5, and the string parts are altered by paste-overs in variation 13. At the end *18 August 1934 / 'Senar' / Slava Bogu!*

This generally very clean score has no titlepage at present, and there is no heading to the music; also, no engraver's marks appear (from which the existence of a copyist's *Stichvorlage* may be deduced). It is bound in dark blue leather cloth. Unlike the MSS of the Third and Fourth Concertos (q. v.), this MS does not include the orchestral reduction for the second piano at the foot. The whereabouts of the MS of this arrangement is presently unknown.

Two spirex-bound sketchbooks (French paper, pp. 72 but many pages cut out of the earlier one) also in the above collection, contain extensive pencil drafts for the work (including some rejected material e.g. a more extended cadenza than that now between vars. 22 & 23). Although the variations are numbered, no clear indication of their sequence is defined, and the original order appears to have differed in some respects. (The earlier of these two notebooks also contains a draft of the Mendelssohn Scherzo transcription, q. v.). A few sketches on loose sheets are also to be noted. See also *Notes* below.

Facsimile: of a page from Variation 20, L. of C. Quarterly Journal, Vol. 9 no. 1, November 1951, opposite p. 40.

Publication: 1934, full and study scores, Edition TAIR, Carl Fischer Inc., ed. no. R1, pp. 119. 'Copyright 1934 by Charles Foley, New York.' Full score bound in dark blue leather cloth, padded, gilt stamped.

1935, Réduction pour 2 pianos à 4 mains par l'auteur, ditto, 02457, ed. no. R8, pp. 89, silurian wrappers. (These editions were later taken over by Charles Foley.)

1957, full score, Muzgiz, Moscow, 25840, pp. 154. A re-engraved reprint of the text of the original edition.

Current editions: Belwin Mills; Eulenberg 1224 (a reprint of Foley's score).

Performance: 7 November 1934, Baltimore, SR and the Philadelphia Orchestra, cond. L. Stokowski.
7 March 1935, Manchester, SR and the Hallé Orchestra, cond. N. Malko.
21 March 1935, London (Queen's Hall), SR and the London Philharmonic Orchestra, cond. Sir Thomas Beecham.

Recording: SR and the Philadelphia Orchestra, cond. L. Stokowski (1934), V.

Arrangement: 'Paganini: Fantastic Ballet in Three Scenes by S. Rachmaninoff and M. Fokine.' Choreography by Michel Fokine.

Performance: 30 June 1939, London, Covent Garden; Dimitri Rostoff, Irina Baranova, Tatiana Riabouchinska. LPO cond. Antal Dorati; piano solo, Eric Harrison. See SR to Fokine, 29 August 1937 (B/L 333; Seroff 188–9).

For this arrangement the score was extended, with the composer's co-operation, on lines suggested by choreographer and conductor, as follows: After playing the complete work as published, the first 9 bars of Var. 11 were repeated to introduce the return of Var. 18 now transposed up into D major. The last five bars of this variation were echoed on the strings as a close. See SR to Fokine, 3 April 1939 (B/L 348); also B/L 346–350.

An arrangement of the famous Eighteenth variation – one more of SR's 'hits' – for piano and violin was made by Fritz Kreisler (transposed into D major) and published in 1953 by Charles Foley, ed. no. 1170, pp. 5 (1).

Notes: The Theme used is that of the A minor caprice for unaccompanied violin by Niccolo Paganini (1782–1840), op. 1 no. 24, in which it also forms the text for (11) variations. Liszt transcribed the work (as the sixth of his Paganini studies) twice; first in 1838, then in a revised version in 1851. (Busoni produced his own version of Liszt's transcription in 1913 and it was also included, a little altered, in his complete *Klavierübung* as published posthumously in 1925.) Brahms' *Studien für Pianoforte* ([28] *Variationen über ein Thema von Paganini*) op. 35 (1866) use only the theme, as did SR in his *Rapsodie.* Schumann's Studies after Paganini, opp. 3 & 10, do *not* include this theme at all. These details have been added because programme annotators still frequently refer to this work of Paganini's as being 'arranged also by Liszt, Brahms and Schumann'.

In Var. 7, the first phrase (seven notes) of *Dies irae* is introduced, and a continuation follows in similar style (unlike Berlioz' use in his *Symphonie Fantastique*, and Liszt's in his *Totentanz*, which both utilized much more of the actual chant). This plain-chant theme is again used as a counter-melody in Var. 10 and is also introduced at the climaxes of Vars. 22 & 24.

Seven bars (**28** to **29**) of the solo part in Var. 10 and eleven bars (**37** to **38** + 2) in Var. 14 are marked 'To be played ad libitum'.

Variation 1 (the 'inverse power' of the Theme, which it precedes) is probably an afterthought: in the original sketchbook the introduction runs straight into the Theme and all variations are numbered one less than in the final; Var. 1 appears in the other sketchbook. The MS also reveals that all variation numbers have been increased by one. Although the pagination runs on, the first bar of the Theme originally had notes in the parts (and a chord in the piano solo) which completed the cadence at the end of the introduction. These notes were cancelled and the piano part altered, to read as published.

THIRD SYMPHONY (A minor) op. 44

1. Lento – Allegro moderato — A minor
2. Adagio ma non troppo – — C sharp minor
   Allegro vivace – Tempo come prima — F minor
3. Allegro — A major

Date: 1. *18 June – 22 August 1935, corrected 18 May – 1 June 1936.*
2. *26 August – 18 September 1935, Senar.*
3. *6–30 June 1936, Senar. Finished. I thank God!*
Final corrections July 1938 (v. SR to Somov, 19 July, 31 July 1938, B/L 343–4).

Dedication: none.

Orchestra: Picc. 2. 2. CA. 2. BsCl. 2. Contra – 4. 2. Tromba c-alta in F. 3. 1 – Timp. Trgl. Tbno. Tamburo (mil.) Piatti. Cassa. Tamtam. Xyl. – Celesta. 2 Harps – Strings. *The work requires two harps. If no second harp is available a small upright piano may be substituted. If Tromba c-alta is not available an ordinary Tromba may be used.* [last sentence in revised score only].

MS: (a) *Full score*, L. of C., part of ML 30. 55a. R3, in ink.
1. pp. 64 (not continuously paginated); dated at end (as above).
2. pp. 55 ditto, plus 1 blank page; ditto.
3. pp. 74 ditto, plus 2 blank pages; dated and inscribed at end (as above).

This score has no titlepage at present and no signature or title at head of music; no engraver's marks appear. It is bound in dark green cloth (by Hans Uttinger, Luzern), lettered in gold 'S.R.' at bottom right of front board. Many bowing, etc. indications have been added in pencil in another hand. There are many alterations made with a knife; also a number of pages and bars were pasted over. Some of these pasteovers have now been, or have become, detached; revealing the earlier writings as follows:

1. p. 1: the 'motto' was originally played in octaves by the four horns and the three trumpets (!)
   6 bars were pasted over at cue **5**–1.
   5 bars were pasted over before **9**.
   The 4 bars originally 6 before the double-bar were deleted.
   The bar at **18**, also bars 4–6 after **18**, were pasted over.
   The bar 4 before **20** was pasted over.
2. A bar was added at **38** +4 on a foredge strip.
   5 bars were pasted over 4 preceding **62**.
   String parts were pasted over for 4 bars at **64**.
3. 5 bars were pasted over 4 at **115**; also the next 2 bars.

The result of these alterations is to establish the text, as originally published in 1937, see below.

(b) A copyist's (conductor's) copy of this score, bound in the same style as the above, is also in L. of C.

(c) The *Stichvorlage* for the revised edition published in 1939 was made by patching the necessary alterations into a printed copy of the 1937 score.

(d) *Sketches.* Among the miscellaneous pencil sketches in L. of C., also part of ML 30. 55a. R3, the following, chiefly on 4–6 staves, relating to op. 44 may be identified:

a gathering of a pencil draft of the first movement;
another ditto containing all the second movement and the finish of the third;
a third ditto containing sketches of the third movement;
a fourth ditto, on larger paper, consisting of a draft for the third movement;
in another gathering of pencil drafts, some presently unidentified material precedes part of the first movement of op. 44;
a Breitkopf B & H 4E book of MS paper, dating from the days in Russia (as is proved by its containing sketches for the Etudes-Tableaux op. 39 nos. 2 and 3, q. v.) also reveals a draft for the opening of the second movement of op. 44, the accompanying chords being marked *Arpe e Piano*, but here appearing in a different key from that of the final version; also an early sketch later used in the third movement.

Publication: 1937, full score, Edition TAIR, no pl. no., pp. 208. 'Copyright 1937 by Charles Foley, New York' *stamped* at foot of p. 1. (Also see *Notes* below.)

[Revised score, 1939], TAIR, Edition Charles Foley, New York, pp. 206. Copyright statement now *printed.* (For details of these revisions see *Notes* below.) Neither edition has title details on fly.

Both these editions were full bound in dark blue mottled leather cloth, gilt stamped, with full title details on cover.

1954, full (and, in 1960, miniature) score, Muzgiz, Moscow, 23624, pp. 5–167 (11–173), edited by G. Kirkor, (following the 1939 score); eleven pages of variants between the 1937 and 1939 scores in an appendix. (Though valuable, this information is neither complete nor wholly accurate – see notes below.) The miniature score also has a lengthy introduction by V. Bryantseva.

1973, study score, Belwin Mills SB 899, pp. 206. (This edition, though it is said to be based on the 1937 score, in fact follows the revised one of 1939.) The author of the unsigned Foreword also claims reference to SR's 'flexible and well-nuanced conducting of the work... In accord... additional tempo and dynamic markings have been inserted in the score in brackets... corrections... made to obvious wrong notes and other discrepancies. Other performance directions found in the composer's manuscript but not printed in the first edition have been added in parentheses'. 'Copyright renewed 1965. Additional material copyright 1972 by Belwin-Mills Publishing Corp.'

1975, Muzyka, Moscow, 8800, pp. 194.

Current edition: Belwin Mills.

Performance: 6 November 1936, Philadelphia, cond. L. Stokowski.
18 November 1937, London (Queen's Hall), LPO cond. Sir Thomas Beecham.
(A performance in Vienna projected for 10 April 1938, to be conducted by SR, but abandoned.)
10 December 1939, New York, Philadelphia Orchestra cond. SR.

Recording: Philadelphia Orchestra cond. SR, (1939), IV.
(An earlier proposal, to record the work in London in September 1937 with the LPO, did not materialize.)

Notes: see: Robin Hull, Rachmaninov's Third Symphony (*Monthly Musical Record*, Nov. 1937, pp. 201–3). Henry J. Wood, *My Life of Music* (London, 1938), 451–2.

The revisions made in the 1939 score may be summarized as follows:

(i). At *Poco meno mosso*, cue **13** + 7, the string parts have been rewritten (the Muzgiz edition appendix omits the cello and bass parts here); at **13** + 8/9 the trumpet notes were originally given to oboes and clarinets. At the *Allegro molto* a four-bar reference to the introductory motto has been deleted.

(ii). From **17–18** the layout has been changed: originally harp, flutes, oboes and clarinets were off the beat, whereas the violins had the melody on the beat; the harp's L.H. then followed the violas and cellos. (This is not shown in the Muzgiz appendix.)

(iii). At **19**, 3 bars analogous to those at **18** have been deleted.

(iv). From **38** + 4 until a bar before **41** the texture has been simplified.

(v). At **101** 2 bars have been deleted.

(vi). One bar after **105** 2 bars were deleted (The Muzgiz appendix marks the deletion a bar too late, and the second of the deleted bars is incorrect as there quoted).

(vii). The 2 bars before **110** replace 4 similar bars.

(viii). After **116**, the third bar and the first beat of the fourth have been added.

For completeness, one should add that, in his own recording of the work, SR omitted 2 bars from **26** + 1½ in the first movement!

References to the first four notes of the *Dies irae* occur in the third movement, at **94** onwards and again from 4 bars before **108** onwards.

The first edition of 1937 by TAIR appears to have been originally 'Im Selbstverlag des Komponisten' (shades of Schoenberg and Scriabin).

SYMPHONIC DANCES op. 45
for orchestra

1. Non allegro – Lento – Tempo I — C minor – C sharp minor
2. Andante con moto (Tempo di valse) — G minor
3. Lento assai – Allegro vivace — D minor

Date: 1. *22 September – 8 October 1940.*
2. *27 September 1940.*
3. *29 October 1940, New York. I thank Thee, Lord.*

Dedication: *Dedicated to Eugene Ormandy and the Philadelphia Orchestra* [on full score only].

Orchestra: Picc. 2. 2. CA. 2. BsCl. Saxophone contralto in E flat (in 1 only). 2. Contra – 4. 3. 3. 1 – Timp. Trgl. Tbno. Tamburo. Piatti. Cassa. Tamtam. Xyl. Glsp. 3 Campane (in 3 only) – Piano (tacet in 3). 2 Harps – Strings.

MS: (a)*Full score*, L. of C., part of ML 30. 55a. R3.

1. pp. 1–62, dated at end (as above), plus title: *Symphonic Dances / S.R. / I.*
2. pp. 63–107, dated at end (as above).
3. pp. 108–177, ditto, and inscribed (as above), plus title: *'Symphonic Dances' / op. 45 / Sergei Rachmaninoff.* At **90** + 1, the word *ALLILUYA* added by SR.

The MS is in black ink, with some amendments in red ink and some in pencil; also some knife erasures. No. 1 is on a smaller paper than nos. 2–3. The whole spirex bound together; this process has partly obliterated the inscription at the end, and Sophia Satina has added a note 'The final date is not easily legible and is in Russian *29 October 1940, New York. I thank Thee, Lord.*' There are no engraver's markings in this score.

The following altered passages are to be noted:

1. From **6**–2 to **6** + 7 deleted and newly inserted.
   At **14**, originally 'Violino solo' and 'Cello solo'; altered to 'Violini soli' and 'Celli soli'. At **17** 'Tutti violini'.
   At **17**, four bars deleted and rewritten.
   From **25**–2, five bars in celli and basses pasted over.
   At **28**, two bars in oboes, clarinets and bassoons ditto.
2. Clarinets pasted over in bars 5–6 and 13–14.
   At **30**–1 for four bars, muted trombones have evidently replaced stopped horns.
   Eight bars have been deleted in pencil before the present **37** (see appendix to Muzgiz edition); in the next 2 bars flute and strings were altered, then 4 more bars were deleted.
   A vi–de of the 12 bars is marked by a pencil deletion from **39** + 6.
   A bar before the 6/8 after **44** + 2 deleted (see appendix to Muzgiz edition).

Viola, horn and trumpet parts altered in pencil in another hand, and sellotaped over, at **52–3**.

3. Five bars from **90**–4 rewritten in ink (red) and sewn over; likewise the string parts to **91**.

A footnote on p. 23 reads: *In case good saxophone is not available the small notes* [in red] *indicate which instrument substitutes for the saxophone.* On p. 24, at **11**, a footnote reads: *In case good saxophone is not available the English Horn starts his melody 4 bars later.*

(b) The MS in L. of C. to same call number, listed and boxed as the 'Arrangement for two pianos' is not in fact such: it is a pencil 4-stave particell of the work.

1. pp. 22 un-numbered (pp. 1–2, sketches).
2. pp. 20 do. (last p. blank).
3. pp. 32 do. (p. 1 reads *III*, pp. 2 & 32 blank, p. 31 sketches).
At end, *10 August 1940, Long Island.*

(c) Pencilled notes of the chords at cue **1** are found in an early MS notebook in the Siloti collection (v. p. 17 supra, also entry under op. 40); also pencilled notes of the opening melody at **2** were found among the loose papers 'on the shelf near his piano in New York'.

Publication: 1941, full score, TAIR, Edition Charles Foley, New York, ed. no. R4, pp. 148. 'Copyright 1941 by Charles Foley, New York.' Full bound in dark blue leather cloth, gilt stamped.

1942, Two pianos – Four hands [Arranged by the Composer], ditto, ed. no. R 2314, pp. 103, lithographed; silurian covers.

Coll. Ed. ditto, ditto, IV (ii) / 109–214 (1951).

1953, full score, Muzgiz, Moscow 23381, pp. 159. Edited by I. Iordan and G. Kirkor. Two pages of variants in an appendix (bars in no. 2 deleted in MS and not appearing in first publication). This edition also cues the saxophone in in the first movement (following the MS).

1973, study score, Belwin Mills EL 2298, pp. 148 (a photo reduction of the first edition of 1941 'copyright renewed 1969 / copyright assigned 1970 to Belwin-Mills Publishing Corp.').

Current edition: Belwin Mills.

Performance: 3 January 1941, Philadelphia, cond. Eugene Ormandy.

Notes: This work was originally to be entitled *Fantastic Dances* (see SR to Ormandy, 21 August 1940, see B/L 359) and SR had planned that the movements should be called *Noon, Twilight* and *Midnight* (B/L 360) (*Morning, Noon* and *Evening* according to Seroff, 202).

According to the choreographer K. Ya. Goleyzovsky, part of the music incorporated in the present work emanates from that written in 1914–15 for the ballet *The Scythians*, planned to a libretto by the same (v. p. 183 inf.).

Understandably, if unconsciously, this last score represents in many ways what SR would have called a 'totalling of the sum'. A number of reminiscences, too clearly defined to be mere fingerprints, support this view; of which we only draw attention to a few, viz:

(i) at the link to the saxophone's entry, there is a reminiscence of the accompaniment pattern from the beginning of the Third Symphony.
(ii) at **21**, a clear reference to the end of the Etude-Tableau op. 33 no. 7 and to the first choral entry in *The Bells*, op. 35.
(iii) at the end of the first movement, from the change to C major, both content and texture recall the parallel passage in the Second Suite op. 17; whilst the melody resembles a softened version of that of the First Symphony.
(iv) in the third movement also, the first clause of the *Dies irae* chant is introduced; implicit in more than one motif in the principal section, it is stated prominently at **93** + 3, **94** + 5 and, for the last time, at **95**.
(v) from **96** + 2 to the end, this last movement is almost an orchestral version of the second half of no. 9 from the Vespers, op. 37; as is confirmed at **99** + 1 by SR's indication *ALLILUYA* in the MS, at a point corresponding to the entry of that word in the choral work.
(vi) the very last bars, with the unmuted gong left resounding through the closing D minor harmonies, again recall the ending of the composer's first major orchestral score: the First Symphony.

II. Works without opus numbers

[Study in F sharp] II/10
for piano solo

The questions surrounding SR's very earliest composition cannot at present be decided beyond all doubt. OvR 55–6 refers to a *Study in F sharp* 'nearly two pages' long, written one evening at Zverev's at a date not stated but which may be deduced to be late 1886. M. L. Presman, his fellow student at Zverev's, recalls in his reminiscences SR's beginnings as a composer during their 'working holiday' in the Crimea, probably during the summer of that same year – a piece dedicated by its youthful author to Presman himself (B/L 13–14; Norris 6). This piece is said by Victor Seroff (op. cit. 21 f.n. 1) to survive in MS in GMM: he then proceeds to footnote the early Four Pieces – of which the first is a *Romance*, certainly in the key of F sharp minor. It is perhaps noteworthy that this key, said to be that of his first *Study*, is indeed the key of the equally early first *Nocturne*, as also of this first piece (*Romance*) in the set originally intended to form opus 1. It is likewise the key of the 'real' op. 1 – the First Concerto – after which it is only occasionally used by SR in his piano works: the Polichinelle from op. 3, the first prelude from op. 23 and the Etude-Tableau op. 39 no. 3, for example.

['Songs without words' for piano solo] II/11

Only one of a possible ten survives, viz.

Lento D minor

Date: 1887?

Dedication: none.

MS: copy written from memory by the composer in 1931, for publication (v. inf.), Basil Verkholantzeff, Zürich (B/L 402).

Publication (in Facsimile): in OvR 253, 1934. *Not in Coll. Ed.*

Performance: May 1888, Moscow Conservatoire, SR (v. inf.).

Notes: see also OvR 61, 250. OvR has caused some slight confusion by mentioning (op. cit. 55) 'ten of these little songs' which consisted of 'altering simple melodies harmonized in two parts into four- or five-part harmonies' during the last year with Arensky's harmony class. He goes on to say that, at Arensky's instigation, SR played these 'two-part songs without words' to the examiners, who included Tchaikovsky. At OvR's request, SR wrote down the one listed above in the autumn of 1931 for inclusion in the much-criticised, but still valuable, *Rachmaninoff's Recollections.*

[Four pieces for piano solo, originally numbered Opus 1 nos. 1–4] II/12

1. *Romance*	Andante	F sharp minor
2. *Prélude*	Allegro	E flat minor
3. *Mélodie*	Andante	E major
4. *Gavotte*	Allegro	D major

Date: 1887 (according to the date, in an unidentified hand [?Goldenweiser's – B/L 17] on the MSS); 'a later date is likely' (B/L 17).

Dedication: none.

MS: GMM; EB 46 (MSS 75–78), ff 10. Numbered by the composer *Op. 1 no. 1* etc.

Publication: 1948, Muzgiz, Moscow, ed. Pavel Lamm, in Coll. Ed. I/259–275, 1948, M 18453 Г.

Performance:

Notes:

Three Nocturnes for piano solo II/13

1. Andante cantabile	F sharp minor
2. Andante maestoso – Allegro assai	F major
3. Andante	C minor

Date: 1. *14–21 November 1887.*
2. *22–25 November 1887.*
3. *3 December 1887 – 12 January 1888.*

Dedication: none.

MS: GMM; EB 45 (MS 731), ff 12, dated.

Publication: 1949, Muzgiz, Moscow, edited and with preface by I. Belza (we have been unable to consult this).

1973, E. B. Marks (Belwin Mills), pp. 16.

Coll. Ed. III (i)/3–17, 1950.

Performance:

Notes: The ending of the third piece is lost, as the pages containing it have been removed from the notebook in question. A conclusion (by repeating the opening bars) was suggested by the original editor.

[Piece (Canon) for piano solo] II/14

[Moderato] D minor

Date: 1884 (!) according to Coll. Ed. (v. inf.).
1890–1 according to EB.

Dedication: none.

MS: GMM; EB 67 (MS 105), ff 2.

Publication: 1949, Muzgiz, Moscow, in *Two Pieces*, edited and with preface by G. Kirkor (we have been unable to consult this).

1951, Leeds Music Corporation, Radio City, New York, in 'Two Fantasy-Pieces, published for the first time (from recently-discovered manuscripts), edited [and with a Foreword] by Alfred Mirovich', no. 2. P–416, L872–5, pp. 3–5. Here headed 'Allegro con brio'.

Coll. Ed. III (i)/18–20, 1950.

Performance:

Notes: The publications of this piece, in juxtaposing it with the Morceau de Fantaisie dated 11 January 1899, have tended to obscure its doubtless much earlier origin. Pavel Lamm, in the notes on p. 178 of the Coll. Ed. vol. cited above, states: 'The MS in pencil is in draft form and very rough; its transcription may therefore slightly vary.' He gives variant readings in footnotes on p. 19 of the volume concerned. Taking him at his word (or using some other authority, unspecified), Mirovich's edition adopts a number of different readings, not all based on Lamm's footnotes; omitting a bar (9 from the end) and generally making a serious endeavour to 'tidy up' this sketch for its new context.

Lamm further states: 'The theme of this piece was in all probability given to SR by his professor A. S. Arensky. Arensky used this theme for a fughetta of his own.' It is curious therefore that Lamm dates the piece, both at the head and at the end, 1884 – an impossibly early year since SR only entered Arensky's harmony class in autumn 1886 and fugue class three years later.

B/L 409 lists the piece clearly under 1899, stating however '(untitled, undated, possibly an earlier work)'. It seems likely that their entry on p. 403 for 'Sketches for a fugal development by Arensky', said to be in GMM, refers to this same piece. EB 67 had catalogued 'Two sketches...', stating that one of them was included in G. Kirkor's 1949 publication, and B/L may have confused these *Two sketches* with Kirkor's *Two pieces.*

The 'beginning and end of the [fugue] examination problem in 1890 [sic; ?1891] when SR finished the fugue class of the Moscow Conservatoire' were written out by SR for inclusion in OvR, where they appear in clear and characteristic facsimile, on pp. 254–5.

Prélude II/15
for piano solo

Commodo F major

Date: *20 July 1891, Ivanovka.*

Dedication: none.

MS: GMM; EB 47 (MS 79), ff 2, dated.

Publication: 1948, Muzgiz, Moscow, ed. Pavel Lamm, in Coll. Ed. I/276–9, 1948, M 18453 Г.

Performance:

Notes: SR to Slonov, 24 July 1891: *I also wrote a prelude for piano; after the prelude I have become somewhat calmer and stronger in my weakened spirit.*

Six months later, this piece was arranged by SR for cello and piano and was first published in that form as op. 2 no. 1, q. v.

[Four Improvisations for piano solo] II/16
by A. Arensky, A. Glazunov, S. Rachmaninoff and S. Taneyev

1. [Moderato] E minor
2. Allegretto C major
3. [Allegro scherzando] B flat minor
4. Largo F minor

Date: Autumn 1896, St. Petersburg.

Dedication: none.

MS: Autograph, pencil drafts, Central Bakhrushin Theatre Museum, Moscow.

Publication: 1925, Muzsektor, Moscow; in *S. I. Taneyev*, ed. Kuznetzov; pp. 7 (appendix).

Coll. Ed. III (i)/174–7, 1950.

Notes: B/L 409 is a misleading entry, speaking as it does of an 'Improvisation' by SR, one of 'Four Improvisations' by the four above-named composers and describing the work as 'Themes and variations'. In fact, each of the four pieces was commenced by a separate author, but then the other three all contributed in turn to the continuations of each other's pieces. (One pictures a not-too-serious party game as the occasion.) The publication in Coll. Ed. III (i) quite clearly attributes each participant's share, as does the original publication.
See also *S. I. Taneyev* ut supra, pp. 160–1.

[Two pieces for piano solo] II/17

[1.] *Morceau de fantaisie*	Allegro	G minor
[2.] [Fughetta]	Moderato	F major, 6/8

Date: 1. *11 January 1899.*
2. *4 February 1899.*

Dedication: none.

MS: GMM; EB 51, 52 (MS 90, 91), ff 1, 1, dated. The title of the first piece, *Morceau de fantaisie* is followed in the MS by the word *'Delmo'*. The MS of the second piece has no title.

Publication: 1. 1949, Muzgiz, Moscow, in 'Two Pieces', edited by G. Kirkor.

1951, Leeds Music Corporation, Radio City, New York, in 'Two Fantasy-Pieces, published for the first time, (from recently-discovered manuscripts), edited [and with a Foreword] by Alfred Mirovich', no. 1. P–416, L872–5, pp. 1–2.

Coll. Ed. III (i)/21–22, 1950.

2. *Unpublished.* (B/L 409 gives Muzgiz 1950 for the publication of both items, but this was the date of the re-issue – of item 1 only – in the Coll. Ed., vol. III, which had specifically referred to the previous 1949 issue of that piece, ed. Kirkor, on p. 178 f.n. 1).

Performance:

Notes: Convenience in cataloguing is our reason for entering these two works together; some further justification is also perhaps to be found in that the composition of each dates from the same, otherwise rather fallow, period. This 'Fughetta' is apparently the sole surviving piano solo by SR to remain unpublished.

Polka de W. R. II/18
for piano solo

Allegretto A flat major

Date: 11 March 1911.

Dedication: *A Monsieur Leopold Godowsky.*

MS: presently unlocated.

Publication: 1911, Édition Russe de Musique, in 'Nouvelle Collection de Musique', Premier Cahier, item 4, pp. 10–17, RMV 97. Later offprinted to the same plate no., pp. 9; the whole 'Cahier' later becoming Vol. 2 of the 'Album Russe'.
Coll. Ed. III (i)/23–31, 1950 (with some minimal differences in the penultimate line).
Current edition: Boosey & Hawkes 16327.

Performance:
6 May 1922, London, Queen's Hall, SR.

Recording: 1919, I.
1921, I.
1928, II.
Also Ampico roll (1919).

Arrangement: orchestrated by Harold Perry; *publ.* 1955, Boosey & Hawkes 17674; 2 (Picc). 1. 2. 1 – 2. 2. 3. 0 – SD. BD. Glock. – Harp – Strings – Piano conductor. This version, transposed up into B flat major, is considerably cut; principally by the omission of the middle section from *meno mosso* to the reprise.

Notes: The original polka, though it may well have been a favourite of the composer's father Vasily [Wasili] Arkadyevich Rachmaninoff, was not in fact composed by him: its origin is to be found in *Lachtäubchen* – Scherzpolka (La rieuse – Polka badine) by Franz Behr (1837–98), op. 303. There the tempo direction is Allegretto grazioso and the key, F major (*see plates 14–15*). The first published identification of this source appears to have been in VR/A, Vol. II, pp. 450–4, where the original work is reproduced complete; see also Norris (1978 edn.); maybe another connoisseur of the genre may yet identify the Polka Italienne also arranged by SR, v. inf.

See also entry under Behr, III/2 inf.

The other items appearing in the original album publication were as follows:

Feuillet d'Album (A. Goedicke)
Crépuscule [op. 24 no. 1] (G. Catoire)
Fragment lyrique, op. 23ª [no. 1] (N. Medtner)
Feuillet d'Album op. 58 (A. Scriàbine)
Prélude et Fugue op. 29 (S. Taneëv)

[Three pieces for piano solo] II/19

[1.] [Prelude (posthumous)]	Andante ma non troppo	D minor
[2.] [Oriental Sketch]	Non allegro	B flat major
[3.] [Fragments]	Andante semplice	A flat major

Date: 1. *14 November 1917, Moscow.*
2. *14 November 1917, Moscow.*
3. *15 November 1917, Moscow.*

Dedication: none.

MS: all three pieces, L. of C., part of ML 30. 55a. R3.

1. 'Unidentified [sic; rather 'untitled'] piano work', pp. 4 in ink, dated.
2. Untitled; pp. 1–5 of an 8-page gathering, in ink, dated.
3. Untitled; pp. 6–7 ditto, in ink, dated.

All the above are on the same German paper (B & H no. 4) and are obviously original fair copies.

The *Stichvorlage* of 2, headed in another hand 'Oriental Sketch' / S. Rachmaninoff, consists of pp. 7 in ink (autograph) in the same collection. Some slight pianistic amendments were made by the composer in this MS which then served for the engraver's use (his numbers appear thereon). Whereas the original MS also had some fingering, and (like op. 39) used the 3/4 signature, only to disregard it where necessary, these features were now omitted.

The present whereabouts of the *Stichvorlage* of 3 ('Fragments') is unknown; with the consequences referred to in the Notes below.

Facsimile of the first page of item 1 in B/L 209, also in 'A Commemorative Collection' (v. inf.), p. vi.

Publication: 1. *Prelude (posthumous).* 1973, Belwin-Mills Publishing Corp., Melville, N.Y., in 'A Commemorative Collection', EL 2408, pp. 1–3. Also published separately, PA 2146, pp. 5 (with facsimile of first page, as above).

2. *Oriental Sketch.* 1938, Sole selling agents: Carl Fischer, New York, P2171, R9–4, pp. 5. 'Copyright 1938 by Charles Foley, New York.'

3. *Fragments.* 1919, Theodore Presser Co., Philadelphia, in *The Etude*, October 1919; later issued as a separate sheet no. 16663, pp. [1]. Also see *Notes* below.

Coll. Ed. item 2: II/215–8, 1948, (giving date as '1938').
items 1 & 3: *not in Coll. Ed.*

Current edition: Belwin-Mills Music Ltd. All three items in 'A Commemorative Collection', pp. 1–3, 56–9, 4–5.

Performance: item 1, 27 November 1978, London, Wigmore Hall, Leslie Howard.
item 2, 12 November 1931, New York, Juilliard School, SR.

ditto, 2 March 1935, London, Queen's Hall, SR.
item 3, ?

Recording: item 2 only, 1940, II.

Arrangement: *Oriental Sketch*, transcribed (3 Nov. 1945) for violin and piano by Jascha Heifetz, *publ.* 1947 Carl Fischer Inc. B 2820, 30359–7, pp. 7, 3. Copyright 1938, 1947 by Charles Foley, New York.

Notes: The unsigned preface to 'A Commemorative Collection' states that in items 1 and 3 'editorial additions and suggestions have been placed between brackets'. As regards the reprint of *'Fragments'* therein, the (anonymous) editor also states that the 1919 publication in *The Etude* [and presumably the offprint likewise] included 'many inaccuracies which have now been corrected after careful examination of the manuscript'. With due respect to the care thus obviously taken, however, not only here but throughout this 'Centennial Edition', one may be permitted to question whether the *Stichvorlage* for this little work still exists. If it does, examination may reveal whether or not SR made the changes noted at this stage, as he did for the *Oriental Sketch* (or on the proof sheets). Is this not in any case more likely, than that he permitted a faulty publication to circulate?

Convenience of cataloguing – and closely-related dates of composition – are, it is hoped, sufficient justification for the grouping together of these three items.

For a reminiscence of SR's compelling playing of the *Oriental Sketch*, see Swan op. cit., quoted in B/L 279.

POMAHC II/20
[Romance]
for piano duet

[Moderato] G major

Date: ?1894.

Dedication: none.

MS: GMM; EB 71 (MS 107), ff 1.

Publication: 1950, Muzgiz, Moscow, ed. Pavel Lamm, in Coll. Ed. III (ii)/82–85, 1950, M 2014a Г. (in score).

Performance:

Notes:

Polka italienne notée par S.R. II/21
[Italian Polka]
for piano duet (two versions)

[no tempo indication] E flat minor – major

Date: ?1906 (or later).

Dedication: Sergey I. Siloti [brother of Aleksandr].

MS: (a) ?lost.
(b) L. of C., part of ML 30. 55a. R3, pp. 5 (in score), in ink. Headed in pencil *Polka/arranged by S.R.*

Publication: (a) ?1906, J. Jurgenson, St. Petersburg (OvR 265).

Coll. Ed. III (ii)/70–73, 1950 (in score).

(b) 1938, Carl Fischer, New York, R11–8, pp. 9 (opposite pages). 'Copyright 1938 by Charles Foley, New York.' This version, which harmonically is considerably elaborated from the above, also includes the trumpet fanfares, v. inf.

Coll. Ed. III (ii)/74–81, 1950 (in score); the Coll. Ed. apparently reverses the sources of the two versions in its appendix, p. 110.

Current edition: Rob. Forberg / P. Jurgenson; Belwin Mills. Although the Forberg publication is marked *Originalausgabe*, it has in fact the same text as the Foley edition (minus the fanfares), set out on opposite pages, pp. 9.

Performance:

Recording: (private), Sergei and Natalya Rachmaninoff. 1938, II.

Arrangements: Transcribed for piano solo by A. Siloti, transposed to D minor – major.
Publ. 1925, A. Gutheil, pp. 3 (based on (a)).
Current edition: Boosey & Hawkes 19380.

Arranged for the Band of the Imperial Marine Guards, with fanfares added by SR (B/L 166, 412; SR to Edwin Franko Goldman, 27 December 1937) (see above).

Transcribed for violin and piano by Fritz Kreisler, transposed to D minor – major.
Publ. 1949, Charles Foley 1034, pp. 7, 3 (based on (b)).
We leave unrecorded a number of other arrangements, some for unlikely ensembles.

Notes: According to the received anecdote (as recounted by Anna Trubnikova [SR, *Ogonyok*, Moscow, 1946, no. 4]; B/L 125) the tune was played outside SR's lodgings in Florence by itinerant musicians. As the owner of the original copyright does not appear to have come forward – unlike the somewhat parallel case of the second barrel-organ tune in Stravinsky's *Petrushka* (cf. E. W. White, *Stravinsky, the composer and his works*, p. 200) – we have not conducted a sufficient enquiry into the extensive repertoire concerned to identify this specimen.

[Two pieces for piano six hands] II/22

1. *Valse*	Tempo di Valse (Allegro)	A major
2. *Romance*	Andante sostenuto	A major

Date: 1. *15 August 1890, Ivanovka.*
2. *20 September 1891, Moscow.*

Dedication: (for Natalya, Lyudmila and Vera Skalon).

MS: The editor of the first edition, v. inf., maintains an impenetrable silence as to the whereabouts of the MSS, and a fortiori of his sources. (Though listed in B/L as if in GMM, no entry is to be found in EB.)

Publication: 1948, State Music Publishers, Moscow, pp. 27 (in score), no pl. no.; edited and with preface by Nestor Zagorny. Reprinted in:

Coll. Ed. III (ii) / 86–109, 1950.

Performance:

Notes: The theme of the Valse is by Natalya Skalon (B/L 25); *I dedicate this Valse to the composer of the theme I have used* (inscription by SR on terzo part). *Arensky liked your Valse very much* (SR to N. Skalon, 10 January 1891; B/L 31). The preface to the first edition quotes a letter from SR to Natalya Skalon, 2 November 1891, sending her the Romance and indicating that there was to have been a 'Polonez' to complete the suite. This was never written.

The introductory five bars of the Romance, which do not recur later in the piece, are all but identical (except for key) with the accompaniment figure at the solo piano's entry in the second movement of the Second Concerto, op. 18, q. v.

РУССКАЯ РАПСОДИЯ

Rhapsodie russe pour deux pianos

Moderato – Vivace – Meno mosso	E minor
Andante – Con moto	G major

Date: *12 – 14 January 1891.*

Dedication: none.

MS: GMM; EB 72 (MS 108), ff 21, dated.

Publication: 1951, Muzgiz, Moscow, ed. Pavel Lamm, in:

Coll. Ed. IV (i) / 3–52, 1951 (in score), M 20886 Г. A rejected variant reading is footnoted on pp. 5–14 and 19–33.

1955, Leeds Music Corporation (no pl. no.), ed. Michael Fredericks, pp. 35 (in score). This edition does not include the variant readings.

Performance: A planned performance by SR and his fellow-student L. Maksimov, at a student concert at the Moscow Conservatoire on 24 February 1891, did not take place (see SR to the Skalon sisters, 5 February 1891, B/L 32); the work was played there however on 17 October 1891 by SR and Josef Lhévinne, as recalled by Goldenweiser (*SR*, ed. Tsitovich, Moscow 1947; B/L 41).

Notes: For the probable origin of the work, see Wilshaw to SR, 5 June 1934 (B/L 31–2).

This is apparently the first of the composer's instrumental works to utilize a Russian theme as its basis.

[First Quartet] for 2 violins, viola and cello (unfinished) II/30

[1.] (missing)		
[2.] *Romance*	Andante espressivo	G minor
[3.] *Scherzo*	Allegro	D major
[4.] (missing)		

Date: 1889 (according to date, in an unidentified hand, on the MS); but perhaps 1890 (see *Notes* below).

Dedication: according to B/L 403 'inscribed by the composer to 'Sasha' ' [? Siloti]; but the editor's preface to the published edition does not refer to this.

MS: GMM; EB 43 (MS 62), ff 12.

Publication: 1947, Muzgiz, Moscow, M 18644 Г, edited and with preface by B. V. Dobrokhotov and G. Kirkor, score and parts, pp. 3–9, 10–17.

Performance: October 1945, Moscow, Beethoven Quartet.

Arrangement: for string orchestra by the composer, 1890 (*Andante* and *Scherzo*). The MS of a pencil sketch for the double bass part is also included in EB 43 (MS 62).

Performance: 24 February 1891, Student concert, Moscow Conservatoire, cond. V. Safonov (cf. Seroff, op. cit., 223).

See SR to Natalya Skalon, 10 December 1890 (B/L 30 and f. n.).

The 'String Quintet' 'mentioned in the Belyayev list' (B/L 404, OvR 264), but not elsewhere recorded, is possibly to be identified in the above arrangement of the present work.

Arranged for viola (or cello) and piano by Philip Clark, 1976; publ. Oxford University Press (no pl. no.), pp. 16, 6, 6.

Notes: SR to Natalya Skalon, 8 September 1890 (B/L 27): *For Christ's sake look for my music ... My songs and the quartet.*

Romance II/31
for violin and piano

Lento – Andante cantabile A minor

Date: '... probably written in the 1880s'.

Dedication: none.

MS: no information given in the sole published edition.

Publication: 1951, Leeds Music Corporation, New York, V–130, L889–9, pp. 8, [3], edited with special annotations by Louis Persinger.

Performance:

Notes: 'Published for the first time (from recently discovered manuscripts)'. *Foreword* and *Suggestions for Performance* by the editor. 'R's *Romance* for violin and piano, recently brought to light, was probably written in the 1880s...' No source, MS or otherwise, is specifically quoted. B/L 405 states 'from MS found in Moscow'.

Lied [Romance] II/32
for violoncello and piano

Andantino F minor

Date: *6 August 1890, Ivanovka.*

Dedication: Vera D. Skalon.

MS: GMM; EB 79 (MS 852), ff 2; entitled *Lied.* Dated.

Publication: 1948, Muzgiz, Moscow, as *Romance* [not seen].

Performance:

Notes:

'Melodie on a theme by S. Rachmaninoff' for violoncello or violin with piano II/33

Moderato D major

Date: 1890, according to preface to published edition.

Dedication: 'Dedicated to and arranged by Modest Altschuler'.

MS: lost; formerly in the possession of Modest Altschuler.

Publication: 1947, The Composers Press Inc., New York, CP 252, pp. 7, 2 (2). 'Melodie on a theme by S. Rachmaninoff. Dedicated to and arranged by Modest Altschuler ...' With preface by the arranger.

Performance:

Notes: In his preface, Altschuler states that the original MS was 'written out on several loose scraps of paper...' He further states that he 'subsequently... copied off the Rachmaninoff MS on regular music paper in order to facilitate performances'. In the mid-1920s the original MS was lost, it is stated.

Trio élégiaque for piano, violin and violoncello II/34

Lento lugubre G minor

Date: *18 January – 21 January 1892, Moscow.*

Dedication: none.

MS: GMM; EB 40 (MS 58), ff 14, dated. According to OvR 265 (following VB) this MS was at one time 'in the possession of P. Lodyzhensky'.

Publication: 1947, Muzgiz, Moscow (2nd edition 1957) M 18732 Г, pp. 28, 5, 5; edited by B. V. Dobrokhotov; p. 28 has notes and variants.

Performance: 30 January 1892, Moscow, Vostryakov Hall; SR, David Kreyn, Anatoly Brandukov.

Notes: B/L 41–2.

[Second quartet] for 2 violins, viola and cello (unfinished) II/35

1. Allegro moderato — G minor
2. Andante molto sostenuto — C minor

[3. ?]
[4. ?]

Date: ?1896 (B/L); ?1910–13 (EB p. 11).

Dedication: none.

MS: GMM; EB 44 (MS 63), ff 9, in pencil.

Publication: 1947, Muzgiz, Moscow, M 18644 Г, edited and with preface by B. V. Dobrokhotov and G. Kirkor, score and parts, pp. 18–30, 31–42. Followed by a page of annotations and variants from the MS.

Performance: October 1945, Moscow, Beethoven Quartet.

Notes: Taneyev's diary for March 1896 records: 'Friday [22], in the evening, Rachmaninoff came. He is writing a quartet. We talked of quartet style...'

Scherzo II/40
for orchestra

Allegro D minor

Date: *5–21 February 1887.*

Dedication: none.

Orchestra: 2. 2. 2. 2 – 1. 1. 0. 0 – Timp. – Strings.

MS: GMM; EB 14 (MS 28), ff 11, dated. Entitled 'Scerzo' [sic].

Publication: 1947, Muzgiz, Moscow, M 18897 Г, pp. 23. Edited and with preface by Pavel Lamm.

Performance: 2 November 1945, Moscow, cond. N. Anosov.

Notes: The MS is headed *Second movement* according to Lamm's preface, but *Third movement* according to EB, op. cit. (and confirmed to GN by Mme. E. N. Alekseyeva of GMM, letter of 1 Nov. 1973).

Both B/L 402 and Seroff 222 give the key as F major, which is obviously incorrect as a glance at the score will reveal.

The 'model' for this earliest orchestral effort is undoubtedly Mendelssohn's Scherzo from the music to *A Midsummer Night's Dream.*

Concerto II/41
for piano and orchestra

1. Allegro molto C minor, 4/4
   [unfinished]

Date: *November 1889.*

Dedication: none.

Orchestra: not scored.

MS: GMM; EB 31 (MS 37), ff 11. An unfinished draft, for two pianos, of the first movement only. Dated.

Publication: none.

Performance: none.

Notes: We have been assured by Mme. Ekaterina Alekseyeva that, despite the tonality, tempo and time-signature, there is no resemblance at all between the music of this early sketch and the later Second Concerto, op. 18, in the same key.

'Manfred' II/42
Symphonic Poem [? Suite for orchestra]
(? unfinished)

Date: 1890–91.

Dedication: ?

Orchestra: *full symphony orchestra* (v. inf.).

MS: lost.

Publication: none.

Performance: none.

Notes: SR to Natalya Skalon, 2 October 1890: *Manfred made extraordinary progress. In two evenings the first movement was composed, and during the next two days it was written down...* ibid. [9/10] October 1890: *I am thinking ... how to do one bit in the second movement of Manfred.*

ibid. 6 January 1891: *I've been writing all the time ... only now have I finished orchestrating my suite.* ibid. 10 January 1891: *I have had no luck with my orchestral suite – it will not be played because it is written for a full symphony orchestra.*

(v. B/L 29–31). B/L 31 states that the orchestral suite referred to 'has not been identified and must be placed among the several lost works ... along with the *Manfred* composition'. The assumption we have made, namely that the suite and *Manfred* are one and the same work, is incidentally supported by B/L 403 and OvR 265 (following VB), where the latter finds a place but not the former.

Symphonie in d-moll II/43
for orchestra

I-re partie:
Grave – Allegro molto D minor

Date: *28 September 1891.*

Dedication: none.

Orchestra: 2. 2. 2. 2 – 4. 2. 3. 1 – Timp. – Strings.

MS: GMM; EB 15 (MS 30), ff 33, headed *1st movement.* Dated.

Publication: 1947, Muzgiz, Moscow, M 18908 Г, pp. 58, as 'Youthful Symphony'. Edited and with preface by Pavel Lamm.

Performance:

Notes: Only this first movement survives, if appears.
... Arensky demanded several compositions: a symphony ... I began working on the symphony at once ... Arensky was not pleased with the separate movements as I showed them to him... I finally finished the work ... (OvR 77–8).

КНЯЗЬ РОСТИСЛАВ II/44
[Prince Rostislav]
Symphonic poem for large orchestra
on A. K. Tolstoy's ballad

D minor

Date: *9–15 December 1891.*

Dedication: Посвящает дорогому своему профессору Ант. Ст. Аренскому-автор. [*To my dear teacher, prof. Anton Arensky*].

Orchestra: Picc. 2. 2. CA. 2. 2 – 4. 2. 2 Pistoni. 3. 1 – Timp. Piatti. Gran Cassa. Tamtam – Harp – Strings.

MS: GMM; EB 16 (MS 29), ff 13, dated.

Publication: 1947, Muzgiz, Moscow, M 18898 Г, pp. 85. Edited and with preface by Pavel Lamm; text of Tolstoy's poem appended.

Performance: 2 November 1945, Moscow, cond. N. Anosov.

Notes: A. K. Tolstoy's ballad of the same name is dated April 1856.

Two episodes à la Liszt after Byron's 'Don Juan' for orchestra II/45

1. Don Juan
2. Don Juan and Haidée; Lambro; and the death of Haidée. [unfinished]

Date: summer 1894 (commenced 20 June).

Dedication: none.

Orchestra: ?

MS: presumably destroyed by the composer, v. inf.

Publication: none.

Performance: none.

Notes: SR to M. Slonov, 24 July 1894 (B/L 64): *I ... even threw away most of it, but worst of all, I might perhaps throw away all that now exists ...*

ibid. (B/L 65, but date incorrectly referenced as 3 September): *I have not given up the idea of Byron's* Don Juan. (SR expected the work to last 40 minutes!).

B/L 408 associate with this work a choral setting of words from *Tolstoy*'s 'Don Juan', v. II/62 inf. This, despite its implication by the editor of SR's letters (cf. RP/A, ibid.) is probably an unjustifiable assumption, on the evidence presently available.

[Symphony] (sketch) II/46

Date: *5 April 1897.*

Dedication: none.

Orchestra: –

MS: GMM; EB 26 (MS 53), ff 1, dated.

Publication: none.

Performance: none.

Notes: 'Sketch with indications of orchestration. On the first page, in the composer's hand: *Sketches of my new Symphony, in which I judge nobody is likely to take any interest. S. Rachmaninoff, 5 April 1897.'* (EB op. cit.)

[Two songs] (1890) II/50
for bass voice and piano

[1.] У врат обители святой.
(At the gate of the holy abode.)
Andante, G minor. (AA – e♭)
Date: 29 April 1890.
Text: Mikhail Lermontov (1814–1841), 'The beggar' (1830).
Dedication: M. A. Slonov.

[2.] Я тебе ничего не скажу.
(I shall tell you nothing.)
Allegro, C major. (C – f)
Date: 1 May 1890.
Text: Afanasy Fet (pseudonym of Afanasy Shenshin, 1820–1892).
Dedication: none.

MS: according to B/L 403, GMM; but not listed by EB.

Publication: 1947, Muzgiz, Moscow, in *Posthumous vocal works*, ed. Pavel Lamm.
Coll. Ed. 1–2.
Current edition: Muzyka, Romansy, vol. 1, pp. 7–14.

Performance:

Notes: Four years earlier, in 1886, Tchaikovsky had used the same words as the second of the above songs in his op. 60 no. 2.

The close dates of composition are our slender justification for grouping these two songs together.

ОПЯТЬ ВСТРЕПЕНУЛОСЬ ТЫ, СЕРДЦЕ II/51
(Again you leapt, my heart)
Song for high voice and piano

[Andante sostenuto] G minor (d – a′♭)

Date: [1890] in Coll. Ed. (EB gives [1893]).

Dedication: none.

Text: Nikolay Grekov (1810–1866).

MS: GMM; EB 109 (MS 136), ff 2, undated.

Publication: 1947, Muzgiz, Moscow, in *Posthumous vocal works*, ed. Pavel Lamm.
Coll. Ed. 3.
Current edition: Muzyka, Romansy, vol. 1, pp. 15–19.

Performance:

Notes:

[Two songs] (1891) II/52
for high voice and piano

[1.] C'était en avril.
[Moderato], E flat major. (d – a'♭)
Date: 1 April 1891.
Text: Edouard Pailleron (1834–1899), 'Chanson' from *Avril* (Amours et Haines, 1889).
Dedication: none.
Notes: 'Set by the composer to a French poem.' The Muzgiz (and subsequent) editions give a Russian translation (Апрель! Вешний праздничный день) by V. Tushnovaya.

[2.] Смеркалось.
(Twilight has fallen.)
[Moderato], G major. (d – b')
Date: 22 April 1891.
Text: A. K. Tolstoy (1817–1875).
Dedication: none.

MS: again, according to B/L 403 these are to be found in GMM; but no mention of them occurs in EB.

Publication: 1947, Muzgiz, Moscow, in *Posthumous vocal works*, ed. Pavel Lamm.

Coll. Ed. 4–5.

Current edition: Muzyka, Romansy, vol. 1, pp. 20–27.

Performance:

Notes: B/L 403 add the note '[These two songs were intended for publication as part of the planned Op. 1; see "Four pieces for piano", above]'.

The words of no. [2] were also set to music by César Cui as his op. 10 no. 3.

[1.] Песня разочарованного.
(Song of the Disillusioned.)
[Andante], F minor – A flat major (bass). (C – f)
Date: [1893].
Text: Daniil Rathaus (1869–1937).
Dedication: none.

[2.] Увял цветок.
(The flower has faded.)
[Andante], A minor (m). (c – g′)
Date: [1893].
Text: Daniil Rathaus.
Dedication: none.

[3.] Ты помнишь ли вечер.
(Do you remember the evening?)
[Moderato], E major (m). (e – a′)
Date: ?
Text: A. K. Tolstoy (1817–1875): 'Crimean sketches no. 4', (no separate title). 'The composer has made some changes in the text' [f. n. to Coll. Ed.]. (SR omits verses 3 and 4 of the poem and rewrites the last line of verse 2.)
Dedication: none.

MS: nos. 1–2; GMM; EB 108, 107 (MSS 139, 140), ff 2, 2; undated.
no. 3: 'lost; published from copy' (B/L 404).

Publication: 1947, Muzgiz, Moscow, in *Posthumous vocal works*, ed. Pavel Lamm.

Coll. Ed. 6, 7, 8.

Current edition: Muzyka, Romansy, vol. 1, pp. 28–41.

Performance:

Notes: Once again, we group together three songs presumed to date from the same period.

On the last page of the MS of no. [2] there is a pencil draft of a vocal piece to the text 'I am there where there are no sufferings ...'

The words of no. [3] were also set to music by César Cui.

ИКАЛОСЬ ЛИ ТЕБЕ II/54
(Were you hiccupping?)
Song for bass voice and piano

Быстро F major (C – f)

Date: *17 May 1899.*

Dedication: at the head of the score is written, in Russian, in SR's hand: *No! My muse has not died, dear Natasha* [Natalya Satina]. *I dedicate my new song to you!*

Text: Pyotr Vyazemsky (1792–1878). (See notes below.)

MS: GMM; EB 113 (MS 142), ff 1, dated.

Publication: 1947, Muzgiz, Moscow, in *Posthumous vocal works*, ed. Pavel Lamm.

Coll. Ed. 9.

Current edition: Muzyka, Romansy, vol. 1, pp. 42–45.

Performance:

Notes: SR composed this song in 1899, revealing that, despite the depression brought on by the failure of his First Symphony, he still retained a sense of humour. He annotated the title with the comment: *Please study the poetry carefully first*, and accompanied the phrase 'Loving Natasha' (bars 16–17) with the motif that occurs in Lensky's aria 'I love you' in Tchaikovsky's opera, *Eugene Onegin.* At bars 23 & 26 the polka from the same work is quoted in the piano part.

The text SR chose is part of a poem *Epernay* which Vyazemsky wrote while he and his friend, the poet Denis Davydov (1784–1839), were enjoying themselves in the Epernay champagne cellars. SR altered some of the words (Voronezh in the song was originally Moet!) and also replaced the name Davydov with Natasha; where SR quotes from Eugene Onegin, 'Natashu – poetessu' in the song was originally 'nayezdnika poeta' [horseman – poet].

НОЧЬ
(Night)
Song for medium voice and piano

II/55

Largo A minor (c – a′)

Date: *Moscow, 1900* [B/L list under dates 1903–5].

Dedication: none.

Text: Daniil Rathaus (1869–1937).

MS: GMM; EB 114 (MS 133), ff 2, dated.

Publication: 1904, Jurgenson, for the Moscow branch of the Russian Music Society, in 'Collection of compositions by contemporary Russian composers', vol. 2, pp. 53–7.

Coll. Ed. 46.

Current edition: Muzyka, Romansy, vol. 2, pp. 3–7.

Performance:

Notes:

ПИСЬМО К. С. СТАНИСЛАВСКОМУ ОТ С. Ра. II/56
(Letter to K. S. Stanislavsky from S.R.)
for bass voice and piano

Довольно медленно E flat major (BB♭ – e)

Date: (October 1908).

Dedication: (for K. S. Stanislavsky).

Text: SR's letter of greeting to Stanislavsky on the occasion of the tenth anniversary of the Moscow Arts Theatre (RP/A, no. 328; translation in B/L 147).

MS: Museum of the Moscow Arts Theatre, Stanislavsky Archive no. 5004, pp. 4.

Facsimile: in RP/A, between pages 352–3.

Publication: [1908?] A. Gutheil, Moscow, according to RP/A, no. 328 note, OvR (not VB) and B/L; but not included in their 2-volume collection of Songs with piano accompaniment.

1956; reproduced in B/L at pp. 148–151 from a printing in *Sovetskaya muzyka*, October 1948.

Coll. Ed. 62.

Current edition: Muzyka, Romansy, Vol. 2, pp. 61–5.

Performance: 14 October 1908, Moscow Arts Theatre, F. Chaliapin.

Notes: In the song, at the point where Maeterlinck's *Blue Bird* is mentioned in the letter, a quotation from the Polka (from the incidental music to that play) by I. A. Sats (1875–1912) appears in the piano part.

Stanislavsky recalls the event at which this song was performed in some detail in his autobiographical Моя жизнь в искусстве [My Life in Art], Moscow, 1954, p. 477. According to him, the 'ecclesiastical' phrase [bb. 25–29], which gives the motto for the ritornello of the song, also comes from Sats' *Blue Bird* music.

ИЗ ЕВАНГЕЛИЯ ОТ ИОАННА

(From the Gospel of St. John)
for bass voice and piano

Довольно медленно A major (C sharp minor) (C♯ – e)

Date: *16 February 1915* (B/L, following Asafyev, gives Autumn 1914).

Dedication: none.

Text: St. John; XV, 13.

MS: A draft in pencil is to be found in a MS book (B & H 4E) now in L. of C. (see op. 40 above), part of ML 30. 55a. R3. The whereabouts of the copy sent to Jurgenson for the engraving is unknown.

Publication: 1915, Moscow, in symposium Клич, ed. Bunin and others, pp. 222–3. At end, signature and date (16 February 1915) in facsimile. Engraved by P. Jurgenson.

Coll. Ed. 77.

Current edition: Muzyka, Romansy, Vol. 2, pp. 133–4.

Performance:

Notes: 'Jurgenson published for War relief an album contributed by various writers, artists and composers, including R' (B/L 193). This most interesting volume (there is a copy in BL 12350. l. 32) contains prose and verse by many famous writers; reproductions of pictures (including Repin's magnificent portrait of Tolstoy, and drawings by L. Pasternak); and a musical section comprising:

pp. 222–3, Rachmaninoff (as above)
224–5, Glazunov, Russian song
226–9, Ippolitov-Ivanov, Arioso
230–2, Grechaninov, 2 Slovak songs
233, Scriabin, Prelude op. 74 no. 2
234–7, S. Vasilenko, Спящая река (from Suite Antique)
238–40, Arseny Koreshchenko, Mirage for violin and piano.

[Two Sacred Songs]
for high voice and piano

1. Молитва – Prayer.
   [Slowly, with deep feeling], D. (f♯ [c] – a′♭)
   Text: Konstantin Romanov (cf. op. 15 no. 4).
2. Всё хочет петь [All things wish to sing] – Glory to God.
   [With animation], E major. (c – a′♭)
   Text: Gregor [sic] Sologub (cf. op. 38 no. 5).

Date: 1916.

Dedication: Dedicated to Nina Koshetz.

MS: Pencil drafts, L. of C. ML 31. H 43a. no. 88 case, undated (formerly coll. Nina Koshetz). Originally intended to form part of the group now published as op. 38, see description of the MS under that number, above.

Facsimile: of the first pages of both songs, in Belwin Mills publication as listed below.

Publication: 1973, Belwin-Mills Publishing Corp., Melville, N. Y., as 'Two Sacred Songs – First Printing'. Centennial Edition, F 3501, pp. 15. Edited and revised by Nina Koshetz, with facsimiles of the first page of each song, portrait of SR inscribed to Nina Koshetz and photograph of SR and Nina Koshetz, c. 1916. Russian and English words; English translations by Marina Koshetz.

Not in Coll. Ed.

Performance:

Notes: B/L 416, 200 f. n.
The facsimile clearly shows that the poet's name as given above for the second song is a misreading of SR's writing for 'Fyodor'.

DEUS MEUS <Canon> II/60

Motet for six-part unaccompanied mixed chorus

Alla breve A minor

Date: 1890 [according to EB, 1892, possibly a misprint?].

Dedication: none.

Text: *Deus meus ad te de luce vigilo*
et in nomine tuo levabo manus meas, alleluia.

Voices: Chorus, S.A.A.T.T.B.

MS: GMM; score, EB 95 (MS 70), ff 2, endorsed 'Performed in the choral class. V. Safonov'. Arrangement for piano solo, EB 96 (MS 70 also), on a separate sheet. Both OvR 265 and B/L 403 state that the MS is in the Moscow Conservatoire.

Publication: 1972, Muzyka, Moscow, 7347, in Three unaccompanied choruses (Три Хоры ...), pp. 5–7. Introduction (pp. 3–4) and edited by I. Iordan and G. Kirkor.

Reprinted 1976, Muzyka 9252, in Хоровые Произведения, pp. 29–30.

Performance: 24 February 1891, Moscow Conservatoire chorus, cond. SR.

Notes: This work was composed 'for the examination, in the special theory class (for graduation into the fugue class),' B/L 24. Subtitled *Canon*, the work, though imitative, is in fact not a canon in any strict sense of the word.

For identification purposes, we quote the first line of the soprano part, viz.

'В МОЛИТВАХ НЕУСЫПАЮЩУЮ БОГОРОДИЦУ' II/61

['O Mother of God perpetually praying']
Sacred Concerto [Motet] for four-part unaccompanied mixed chorus

1. Moderato — G minor
2. Poco meno mosso — C minor
3. Allegro — G major

Date: Summer 1893, Lebedin.

Dedication: none.

Text: ?

Voices: Chorus, S.A.T.B.

MS: GMM; score, EB 97 (MS 71), ff 4. Formerly in the possession of the Synodical School in Moscow (OvR 265, B/L 406). A copy (non-autograph) is in L. of C. (B/L 406).

Facsimile: of 'The first page [sic; ?first system] of R's. *Concert Spiritual*' in Alfred J. Swan, *Russian Music*, London 1973, plate 29 (between pp. 160–1).

Publication: ?1955, Muzgiz, Moscow [acc. to P. Piggott, loc. cit. inf.]
1972, Muzyka, Moscow, 7347, in Three unaccompanied choruses, pp. 8–24. Edited and with introduction by I. Iordan and G. Kirkor.

Performance: 12 December 1893, Moscow, Synodical Choir, 'under Orlev' (Swan, op. cit. 150).

Notes: Patrick Piggott (*R. Orchestral Music*, London 1974, p. 46) draws an interesting parallel between a phrase which occurs in this work and one prominent in the later finale of the Second Concerto.

This chorus was not included in the Muzyka 1976 issue of Хоровые Произведения.

(a) ХОР ДУХОВ **[Chorus of Spirits]** II/62
for four-part unaccompanied mixed chorus

Allegretto (32 bars) F major, 3/8

(b) [ПЕСНЯ СОЛОВЬЯ] **[Song of the Nightingale]**
for four-part mixed chorus and piano

(16 bars in F major, 4/4)

Date: ?1894 (acc. B/L 408, but v. inf.).

Dedication: none.

Text: from *Don Juan*, dramatic poem by A. K. Tolstoy (1817–1875).

Voices: Chorus, S.A.T.B.

MS: GMM; EB 98, 94 (MS 26), ff 1. Recto and verso of same sheet.

Publication: (a) 1972, Muzyka, Moscow, 7347 in Three unaccompanied choruses, pp. 25–6. Edited and with introduction by I. Iordan and G. Kirkor.

Reprinted 1976, Muzyka 9252, in Хоровые Произведения, pp. 27–8.

(b) unpublished.

Performance:

Notes: B/L 408, following the editor of RP/A, consider this work is related to the project commenced in summer 1894 but left unfinished, an orchestral work 'à la Liszt' based on *Byron*'s 'Don Juan'. This assumption appears gratuitous. See also II/45.

EB states that (a) is in D minor; although the commencement may be construed in this key, the close definitely comes in F major.

ПАНТЕЛЕЙ – ЦЕЛИТЕЛЬ

II/63

[Panteley the Healer]
for four-part unaccompanied mixed chorus

Довольно скоро E minor

Date: *4/5 1901* (B/L, probably following Asafyev, give June–July 1900).

Dedication: none.

Text: Alexey Tolstoy's poem of the same title; dated Rome, 20 February 1866.

Voices: Chorus, S.A.T.B.

MS: GMM; score, with pianoforte arrangement below, EB 99 (MS 73), ff 5, dated.

Facsimile: bars 29–39 (= p. 5 of MS) in Patrick Piggott: *R* (The Great Composers series), London 1978, p. 39. (2 systems; the lower one is also reproduced on the back cover.)

Publication: 1901, A. Gutheil, Moscow, A 8107 G, pp. 15. Score with pianoforte arrangement below; Russian text only. Engraved by V. Grosse. Also separate parts published.

1976, Muzyka, Moscow, 9252, in Хоровые Произведения, pp. 31–7.

Performance: 1901, Moscow, Synodical Choir.
29 June 1973, Chester Cathedral, Cathedral Choir, cond. Roger Fisher.

Notes:

Opera in one act

1.	*Introduction*	Andante cantabile – Agitato	D minor
2.	*Gypsy chorus*	Allegro vivace	F major
3.	*Old Gypsy's story*	Moderato espressivo	F major
4.	*Scena and chorus*	Allegro ma non tanto	A minor
5.	*Gypsy Girls' dance*	Tempo di valse	A flat minor
6.	*Men's dance*	Vivo	G minor
7.	*Chorus*	Allegretto	D minor
8.	*Duet*	Moderato	D major
9.	*Zemfira's song*	Allegro risoluto	A minor
10.	*Aleko's cavatina*	Moderato	C minor
11.	*Intermezzo*	Allegretto pastorale	F major
12.	*Young Gypsy's song*	Allegretto	B flat major
13.	*Duet and finale*	Allegro moderato	D minor

Libretto: by Vladimir Nemirovich-Danchenko (1858–1943), after Aleksandr Pushkin's poem Цыганы [The Gypsies] (1824).

Date: 1892; commenced 26 March, completed 13 April. Separate movements dated: no. 1, *April 2–3*; 2, *April 3*; 3, *April 4*; 5, *21–22 March*; 6, *23–25 March*; 7, *28 March*; 8, *28 March*; 9, *29 March.* Vocal score, May 1892 (SR to M. Slonov, 7 June 1892, refers).

Dedication: none.

Cast:	
Aleko	*Baritone*
Young Gypsy	*Tenor*
Old Gypsy	*Bass*
Zemfira	*Soprano*
Old Gypsy woman	*Contralto*
Gypsies	*(Chorus, S.A.T.B.)*

Orchestra: Picc. 2. 2. CA. 2. 2 – 4. 2. 3. 1 – Timp. Triang. Tambno. Piatti. Cassa – Harp – Strings.

MS: (a) GMM; *full score*, EB 1 (MS 1), ff 61; nos. 10–13 are missing; dated as above.

(b) Central Music Library, Leningrad; copy of the full score, presumably in the hand of M. Slonov (cf. OvR 79, 140), with SR's MS amendments. The editors of the first published full score (1953) say in their preface that

'This copy shows many signs of work on it by the composer. In R's hand there are many corrections, insertions and additions, notably in the orchestral parts. In this score, in Aleko's Cavatina, a page is crossed out after the words Я минуту разогнать умела, and on it is written in R's hand: *From here begin the insertion (7 pages), after which re-copy p. 239.* The next seven pages are written in R's hand and constitute the second version of Aleko's

Cavatina, which was not included in the first published vocal score in 1892. The next printing of the vocal score was edited by the composer and published by Gutheil with the second version of the Cavatina.'

(c) GMM: early sketch of the fourth page of the score, EB 2 (MS 54), ff 1, in pencil.

(d) GMM: vocal score of the first version, [May 1892], EB 3 (MS 3), ff 41.

(e) GMM: vocal score of extract of Aleko's Cavatina, no. 10, EB 4 (MS 5), ff 1. This is the portion of the Cavatina that R. inserted for the second version of the opera (see (b) above), and it agrees with pp. 63–65 of the second edition of the published vocal score. EB p. 6 states: 'At the end of the MS is the composer's signature and an inscription in an unidentified hand: "Written in 189... and Natalya was there at the time" '.

(f) GMM: sketch for the Finale, Gypsy chorus, extract, EB 5 (MS 6), ff 1, in pencil.

In the original MS full score (a), it appears that nos. 7 and 8 occurred in reverse order from that of the later printed editions.

Publication: 1892, vocal score by the composer, A. Gutheil, Moscow, A 6345 G, pp. ??, small folio, Russian words only. Engr. by G. Grosse. (A copy inscribed to Natalya Satina, EB V/A/2 (no. 338).)

Second impression, incorporating the rewritten version of the Cavatina, pp. 100; otherwise as above. There is a copy in BL at F. 864. g.

[post-1915] vocal score, ditto, A 6345ª G, pp. 106, A. Gutheil/Koussevitzky, Imprimerie Breitkopf et Härtel. Russian and French words (Traduction française de Louis Laloy).

1893, piano score by E. Langer, A. Gutheil, Moscow, A 6581 G, pp. 54. Russian words only. Engr. by G. Grosse (agreeing in content with the second edition of the vocal score).

Nos. 3, 10 & 12 were also published separately; so were nos. 5 & 6 in SR's own arrangement and nos. 5 & 12 in a piano arrangement by A. Dubuque (all these were published by A. Gutheil). For details of a performance by SR of nos. 5 & 6 – on 24 December 1892, i.e. before the premiere of the opera, see OvR 85–6 and B/L 51–2.

1953, full score, Gos. Muz. Iz, Moscow, M 23208 Г, pp. 7–236, ornamental cloth boards. Edited and with preface by I. Iordan and G. Kirkor, Russian text only. Reissued 1965, Muzyka, Moscow, 1429, pp. 7–236, but without preface. These editions are based on the corrected and extended MS (b) above.

Current editions: full score as above; vocal score, Muzyka 2980, pp. 119 (1966).

Performance: Played by SR to the Moscow Conservatoire examination panel on 7 May 1892. For a private performance by SR of nos. 5 & 6, 24 December 1892, see above.

Intermezzo performed 31 May 1892, Moscow Conservatoire (graduation concert), cond. V. Safonov.

Dances performed 19 February 1893, Moscow, Russian Musical Society, cond. V. Safonov.

First complete and staged performance, Moscow, Bolshoy Theatre, 27 April 1893; with Bogomir Korsov (Aleko), Lev Klementyev (Young Gypsy), Stepan Vlasov (Old Gypsy), Maria Deysha-Sionitskaya (Zemfira) ... ...
(Old Gypsy woman); choreographed by ... ...
conducted by Ippolit Altani.

18 October 1893, Kiev; cond. SR.

Gypsy Girls' dance performed 17 December 1894, St. Petersburg, Russian Symphony Concert cond. N. Rimsky-Korsakov.

27 May 1899, St. Petersburg; F. I. Chaliapin (Aleko), cond. SR.

Notes: SR composed *Aleko* as part of his finals in the composition class of the Moscow Conservatoire (his fellow-students Lev Konyus and Nikita Morozov also wrote operas on the same libretto). On 18 February 1892 he wrote to Natalya Skalon: *At the conservatoire the day of the examination for the final year theory class has already been fixed. 15 April is the important day for me. On 15 March they will give us a subject for a one-act opera. As you see, I shall have to compose it, write it out and orchestrate it in one month. No mean task ... All the best one-act operas will be performed at the end of May. If my opera is included among the best, I shall have only one task after 15 April, to attend the rehearsals of my forthcoming opera.* But, as SR reports in another letter (30 April) to Natalya Skalon: *We didn't have the exam on 15 April, and couldn't have done, because we were only given the libretto on 26 March.* This date must be incorrect, as SR had written to Natalya Skalon on 23 March: *The libretto is taken from Pushkin's poem* The Gypsies *and compiled by Vlad. Nemirovich-Danchenko. The libretto is very well done. The subject is marvellous. I don't know whether the music will be marvellous ... Two dances for* Aleko *are now ready.* He wrote to Natalya Skalon again on 30 April 1892: *I finished my opera on 13 April.*

In the *Men's dance* (no. 6), at the 'meno mosso alla Zingana', a footnote to the score states 'borrowed theme', without identifying further its source.

Among the eighteen other operas based on this same poem of Pushkin identified in the Concise Oxford Dictionary of Opera, we mention an early work by Shostakovich, later destroyed by himself.

See also RP/A, loc. cit.
Norris 15–21, 133–7.
G. Norris: 'Rakhmaninov's Student Opera', *The Musical Quarterly*, LIX (1973), pp. 441–8.
V. N. Bryantseva: *Detstvo i yunost' Sergeya Ra.* (Moscow 1970, 2/1973).

MOHHA BAHHA (**Monna Vanna**)

Unfinished opera

Libretto by M. A. Slonov based on the play by Maurice Maeterlinck (1862–1949) in the Russian translation by Mattern and Vorotnikov. See *Notes* below.

Date: 1906–8.

MS: L. of C., parts of ML 30. 55a. R3.

(a) Complete libretto and drafts (in the hand of M. Slonov) and 3 pages of preliminary drafts (in SR's hand). In the original envelope, marked in pencil on the outside: Монна Ванна.

(b) Vocal score of Act I, pp. 1–100, in ink; dated at conclusion *End of Act I/ Dresden 15 August 1907*, as follows:

pp. 1–3	[prelude]
4–14	Scene 1
15–58	Scene 2
58–100	Scene 3

(c) Two gatherings (pp. 6, 8) of pencil sketches in vocal score, presumably fragments for Act II.

Note: It should perhaps not pass without comment that the existence of the complete and obviously all-but-final vocal score of Act I reveals SR's method of composition: evidently the orchestration would follow only after completion of the work in short-score form.

Facsimile: of p. 4 of the vocal score, commencement of Scene 1, B/L 208.

Publication: none as yet.

Notes: When SR considered the continuation of his interrupted work in 1908, it appears that he was unable, even with Stanislavsky's intervention, to obtain Russian and German operatic rights to the original play: exclusive operatic rights had already been granted (through Heugel et Cie.) to Henri Février, whose opera of this title was performed (in Paris) in 1909. (K. S. Stanislavsky to M. Maeterlinck, 1908; Maeterlinck to Stanislavsky 9 December 1908); Norris 39–40; B/L 141. (OvR 140 suggests that Stanislavsky visited Maeterlinck in person.) Seroff 104 quotes Sophia Satina's letter of 25 March 1946 to Anna Trubnikova, which implies that the MS was at that time still in Switzerland, at Senar; his footnote further specifically states that Slonov's MS libretto of Act I is in GMM (but note: it is not shown in EB's listing).

A photo-copy of SR's MS has been made available to the publishers Belwin Mills; the USA copyright had earlier been registered at L. of C. by Charles Foley on 24 April 1951.

SR's letters refer, to Slonov: 3, 21 November 1906, 4 January, 27 July 1907; to Morozov: 8 May, 16 July 1907. (B/L 131–141; Seroff 104).

Miscellaneous and unfinished operatic and dramatic projects

(a) **Esmeralda** (October 1888); fragments of an opera to be based on Victor Hugo's novel 'Notre Dame de Paris'.
Introduction to Act I;
Entr'acte;
portions of Act III (one dated 17 October 1888)
(in piano score)
MS: GMM (according to B/L 402, but not listed in EB). See also B/L 19.
Unpublished.

(b) **Undine**; scenario by Modest Tchaikovsky after Zhukovsky; originally prepared for P. I. Tchaikovsky, but rejected by him and at his suggestion offered to SR ('it had actually been offered to Lyadov as well ...' B/L 56). SR's letters to Modest Tchaikovsky, 13 May and 14 October 1893 refer (B/L 56, 62; GN 137–8). No music appears to have been written.

(c) **Richard II**; (cf. B/L 82) a plan involving a libretto, said to be based on Shakespeare's play, again by Modest Tchaikovsky, was dropped in favour of the latter's work which became *Francesca da Rimini*, op. 25 supra.

(d) **Salammbô**; scenario by SR based on Flaubert's book. It was originally intended that M. P. Svobodin should write the libretto; on his delaying, N. S. Morozov wrote a scene but the project was shortly turned over to M. A. Slonov; v. SR to Morozov, 19 March, 10 April, 27 April, 4 May 1906; to Slonov, 8 May, 16 May, 24 May. (B/L 117–125). No music for this project appears to have been committed to paper.

It is perhaps worth noting that Mussorgsky too had considered this subject: his music fills over 200 pages of the Collected Edition of his works, much being transferred later to others of his compositions.

(e) Other subjects for operatic treatment considered at one time or another by SR included Turgenev's *Spring Floods, The Lull* and *A Song of Triumphant Love.* Possible use of Chekhov's *Uncle Vanya* is to be traced through the use of a passage from Act 4 thereof in the song op. 26 no. 3 (q. v.), dated 14 August 1906. Other Chekhov subjects, offered by the author but regretfully declined by SR were *The Black Monk*, and his adaptation of Lermontov's *A Hero of our Time* (v. OvR 151).

Further subjects, not confirmed by SR, concerned *The Minstrel* 'with a scenario by Chaliapin based on a poem by Maykov, and a one-act opera, also suggested by Chaliapin, *The Mysterious Island*' (B/L 142; also Seroff 77, 104).

The question of a scene from *King Lear* was raised in 1913 by the Committee for the 350-year celebration of Shakespeare (v. SR to Marietta Shaginian, 30 August 1913), but no further mention of the work exists.

(f) In a letter dated 1 November 1914 to Siloti, SR reveals his interest in writing a ballet for Fokine and referring to other similar projects (v. B/L 190). SR is also said by the choreographers A. Gorsky and K. Goleyzovsky to have 'completed the major part of a ballet, *The Scythians*' (Norris 51), the music of which was stated to be incorporated in the *Symphonic Dances*, op. 45. Twenty years later, SR and Fokine were indeed associated in the ballet *Paganini*, based on the *Rhapsody on a theme of Paganini*, op. 43, q.v.

[Two Monologues from Pushkin's drama 'Boris Godunov'] II/80

(a) *Boris's monologue* for bass voice and piano
(Three variants: 40, 34, 30 bars) D minor

(b) *Pimen's monologue* for tenor voice and piano
(Two variants: 46, 21 bars) D minor

Date: 1891? (v. *Notes* below).

Dedication: none.

Text: Aleksandr Pushkin's drama *Boris Godunov* was written in 1824–5 and published in 1830.

(a) 'Ты, отче патриарх ...'

(b) (From the Scene: Night, a cell in the Monastery; 17, 6 lines)
'Еще одно последнее сказанье ...'

MS: GMM; EB 105 (MSS 23–24), ff 2, 1, 2; 1, 1.

Publication: 1947, Muzgiz, Moscow; first variants only of both (a) and (b) in *Posthumous vocal works*, ed. Pavel Lamm.

(other variants unpublished)

Performance:

Notes: *For my accelerated graduation, Arensky demanded several compositions – ... some vocal recitatives ...* (OvR 77–8). This and the next entry may well be identified with the works in question (cf. B/L 40 f.n.).

I ... handed in the desired recitatives as well (ibid).

НОЧЬ, ПРОВЕДЕННАЯ БЕЗ СНА … II/81

for bass voice and piano

D minor

Date: 1891?

Dedication: none.

Text: Arbenin's monologue from *Masquerade*: drama by Mikhail Lermontov (1814–1841).

MS: GMM; EB 106 (MS 141), ff 1.

Publication: 1947, Muzgiz, Moscow; in *Posthumous vocal works*, ed. Pavel Lamm.

Performance:

Notes: cf. preceding entry.

[Vocal quartet] II/82

(unfinished fragment)

with piano accompaniment 13 bars, D major

Date: ?

Dedication: none.

Text: 7 lines from the first Canto of the poem *Poltava* by Aleksandr Pushkin (1799–1837). EB lists the work as 'Quartet: Mazeppa, Kochubey, Lyubov and Maria'.

MS: GMM; EB 103 (MS 25), ff 1, in pencil, in an unidentified hand.

Publication: none.

Performance: none.

Notes:

ГРЯНЕМ УХНЕМ II/83
(Russian boatmen's song)
arranged for voice and piano

Date: [before 1892].

Dedication: to Adolf Yaroshevsky.

MS: Moscow, coll. Ivan Shishov.

Publication: 1944, Muzgiz, Moscow [not seen].

Performance:

Notes: B/L 404.

[Two Russian songs] II/84
arranged for unaccompanied mixed chorus

1. At the Gate . . .
2. Чоботы [Shoes] (Ukrainian song) Allegro, D minor

Date: (no. 2) *12 November 1899.*

Dedication: none.

Voices: Chorus, S.A.T.B.

MS: (1) lost.
(2) GMM; score EB 123 (MS 72), ff 3, dated.

Publication: (no. 2) 1949, Muzgiz, Moscow.
Edited by G. Kirkor.

1976, Muzyka, Moscow, 9252, in Хоровые Произведения, pp. 39–42. (This edition gives the date for the first publication as 1950.)

Performance:

Notes:

[Arrangements of Russian songs] II/85
for voice and piano

1. Лучинушка [The little splinter]
2. Apple Tree, O Apple Tree
3. Along the Street (sketch)

Date: 1. 3 July 1920, Goshen, New York.
2. 1920.
3. (?1920).

Dedication: 1. (arranged for John McCormack).
2. (for a collection by Alfred J. Swan, v. inf.).
3. –

MS: 1. (? originally coll. John McCormack.)
Copy, L. of C.
2. The late Alfred Swan, Philadelphia. Signed and dated. 'One long strip of manuscript paper'; no title, and no words underlaid.
3. L. of C.

Facsimile of 2, in *Musical Quarterly*, Vol. 30, January 1944, opposite p. 11.

Publication: 1, 3: unpublished.
2: in *Songs from Many Lands*: 30 Folk Songs ... arranged by Celebrated Composers. Editor's note by Alfred J. Swan, Enoch & Sons, London, 1923, E & S 5835, p. 38 (2 verses under voice line; verses 3–5 at foot of page).

Performance:

Notes: cf. B/L 222, 417.

БЕЛИЛИЦЫ – РУМЕНИЦЫ ВЫ МОИ II/86
['Powder and Paint']

Russian song from the Kursk district, arranged for voice and piano, [1st version].
[no tempo indication] B flat minor

Date: 1925.

Dedication: (for Nadezhda Plevitskaya).

MS: GMM; EB 124 (MS 732), ff 4, in pencil; photocopy L. of C. With some indications of orchestration.

Publication: none in this form; but see notes inf. regarding the piano accompaniment.

Performance:

Recording: Nadezhda Plevitskaya and SR (1926), II.

Notes: The second, and definitive, version of this song later appeared as the third of the *Trois Chansons Russes pour Orchestre et Choeur*, op. 41 q.v.

The piano accompaniment to the present version appears very similar, though not quite identical, to that published in the 'Réduction pour piano et chant par l'Auteur' of op. 41 no. 3 (which incidentally was in B minor). Here, however, the solo voice part continues with more of the 'innumerable verses' (OvR 199) during those passages later scored as orchestral interludes (cues 27–29; 30–1 and 32–34 in the published score). The existence of certain minute differences between the full score and the piano score of op. 41 no. 3 is probably thus to be explained.
The recording of the song by Vladimir Ashkenazy and Elisabeth Söderström (Decca SXL 6832) uses a transcription made by Ashkenazy from the Rachmaninoff/Plevitskaya recording.

Plate 13: Rachmaninoff in the 1930s

III. Arrangements of other composers' works

BACH: III/1
Suite from the Partita in E major for Violin

Transcription for piano.

Preludio < Non allegro >	E major
Gavotte	,,
Gigue	,,

Date: *9 September 1933*; Gavotte and Gigue later revised.

Dedication: none.

MS: L. of C., parts of ML 30. 55a. R3.

(a) Preludio ... pp. 12 in ink, with pp. 4 wrapper. Some engravers' queries and marks. This also bears Carl Fischer's numbers, indicating it was their *Stichvorlage.* Not signed or dated.

(b) Almost complete pencil sketches of this movement are also in the same collection.

(c) Gavotte et Gigue / J. Bach / arranged by S. Rachmaninoff, pp. 3–9 headed *Gavotte en Rondeau*, p. 10 blank, pp. 11–13 *Gigue*, p. 14 blank; pp. 15–16 (inverted) contain pencil sketches of this arrangement of the Gigue. In ink, sewn into one 16-page section, dated at end *9 September 1933 / 'Senar'.* This MS differs considerably in detail from the version not published until 1941.

(d) *Gavotte and Gigue / from Bach's Partita (No. 3, E major) / S. Rachmaninoff* on p. 1 of a 4-page wrapper; sewn inside is a 16-page section consisting of the Gavotte (pp. 9), Gigue (pp. 4) and 3 blank pages. All in pencil, and showing engraver's marks, this MS is evidently the *Stichvorlage* for the delayed 1941 publication.

(e) A pencil draft for this final version of the Gavotte was found among the loose papers listed as 'on the shelf near his Piano in New York'. This is now also in L. of C.

Publication: 1933, Edition TAIR, Carl Fischer Inc., New York, P 1966, CC 26487–9, pp. 11 (Preludio from the E major Sonata for Violin); Édition TAIR, Paris, pl. no. 11, pp. 11 (Prélude de la Sonate pour Violon en Mi maj. de J. S. Bach) (simultaneous publication); 'Copyright 1933 by Carl Fischer Inc., New York'. The French edition copies the Fischer engraving, apparently.

1941, Charles Foley, New York (Suite from the Partita ... Preludio, Gavotte and Gigue). Preludio pl. no. CC 26487–9 'Copyright 1933 by Charles Foley', Gavotte and Gigue ed. no. R–2060 'Copyright 1941 by Charles Foley', pp. 18.

Coll. Ed. III (I) / 84–99, 1950.

Reprinted in 'A Commemorative Collection, Centennial Edition', Belwin-Mills Publishing Corp., 1973, ed. no. EL 2408, pp. 6–21, copying the Tair (Fischer) and Foley editions.

Current edition: Belwin Mills.

Performance: (Prelude only) 20 February 1933, Portland, Oregon, USA.
29 April 1933, London, Queen's Hall.
(Suite) 9 November 1933, Harrisburg, Penn. USA.

Recording: (1942), II.

Original: J. S. Bach (1685–1750), Six Sonatas and Partitas for unaccompanied violin, Sonata 6 (Partita 3) in E (BWV 1006), movements 1, 3 & 7. Bach himself transcribed the whole work (BWV 1006a) for (?pedal) harpsichord, transposing it down an octave (SR's transcription retains the violin pitch). Saint-Saëns also transcribed the Gavotte for piano solo as no. 10 (in Vol. 2) of his Bach transcriptions. The music of the Prelude reappears in Bach's 29th Cantata as the basis of the overture, and this was also arranged by Saint-Saëns as the opening number of his collection; this version is in D major.

Notes: It appears from the details of MSS given above that SR was evidently not satisfied with the transcriptions of the Gavotte and Gigue in their original form; hence the first publication consisted of the Prelude alone, its two companions only following, in their final version, eight years later.

BEHR: III/2
Lachtäubchen – Scherzpolka

A transcription of this polka by Franz Behr (1837–98), op. 303, forms the basis of a piano solo published as *Polka de W. R.* q. v. (II/18 supra). Although therefore not an original work – no more so, in fact, than the two Kreisler transcriptions – we have judged it better to make our entry for this item under the title, however misleading a one, by which it is still published. The present cross-reference allocates a place to it amongst the other arrangements, where it more rightfully belongs; and we reproduce two pages of the original piece for interest (see *plates 14–15*).

Plate 14: Franz Behr: Lachtäubchen – Scherzpolka: first page

Plate 15: Franz Behr: Lachtäubchen – Scherzpolka: last page

BIZET: III/3

Minuet from *L'Arlésienne* Suite no. 1

Transcription for piano (two versions)

Tempo di minuetto C minor

Date: (a) *13 September 1900* [EB gives year as 1900, but Coll. Ed. gives 1903]. (b) ?1922.

Dedication: none.

MS: (a) GMM; EB 69 (MS 92), ff 3, dated.

(b) L. of C., ML 96, R135. This MS is the *Stichvorlage*, pp. 8, in ink, of the American publication. Signed (in pencil) at head, but not dated. Originally headed *Menuetto / Bizet – Rachmaninoff.*

Publication: (a) 1950, Muzgiz, Moscow, ed. Pavel Lamm, in *Coll. Ed.* III (1) / 100–106.

(b) 1923, Carl Fischer, Inc., New York, P 1321, CC 22711–6, pp. 7. In *Coll. Ed.* III (1) / 107–112 (quoting as source Tair, which however was not operative until ca. 1925). Reprinted in 'A Commemorative Collection ...' Belwin Mills 1973, pp. 110–115, but re-engraved.

Current edition: J. B. Cramer & Co. Ltd., (a reprint of the original Fischer edition).

Performance: (b) 19 January 1922, Tulsa, Okla., USA.

Recording: (1922), I; also Ampico roll.

Original: Georges Bizet (1838–1875): op. 23, incidental music to Alphonse Daudet's play *L'Arlésienne.* The minuet, marked *Allegro giocoso* in the original, is an Intermezzo (no. 17) between the third and fourth acts. It forms the second movement of the Suite [no. 1] Bizet arranged from the incidental music. It was also arranged for piano solo by the composer.

Notes: SR to Librarian of Congress, 28 March 1923: *I take pleasure in sending you today the only manuscript I have in my possession. I regret that it is not a larger or more important one, but when I left Russia, I could not take any of my larger manuscripts with me.*

GLAZUNOV:
Symphony no. 6, op. 58

Transcription for piano duet.

Date: 1896.

Dedication: à son ami Mr. Felix Blumenfeld (on original work).

MS: ?Belyayev archives formerly.

Publication: 1897 (but 1898 on original multicoloured titlepage), M. P. Belyayev, Leipzig, 1594. Réduction pour piano à quatre mains par S. Rachmaninoff.

Current edition: none.

Performance:

Original: Aleksandr Glazunov's (1865–1936) Sixième Symphonie en Do mineur pour grand orchestre.

1. Adagio – Allegro passionato	C minor
2. *Tema con Variazioni*	
Tema Andante.	G major
Var. 1 Più mosso, Allegro moderato.	"
Var. 2 Allegretto.	"
Var. 3 *Scherzino.* Allegro	E major
Var. 4 *Fugato.* Andante mistico.	E minor
Var. 5 *Notturno.*	B major
Var. 6 Allegro moderato.	
Var. 7 *Finale.* Moderato maestoso.	G major
3. *Intermezzo.* Allegretto	E flat major
4. *Finale.* Andante maestoso	C major

Notes: SR to Morosov, 29 June 1908 ... *I sat at it for two months ... 200 rubles. That is precisely the fee I received for the Glazunov symphony ...* (B/L 146).

KREISLER:
Liebesleid **and** *Liebesfreud'*

Concert transcriptions for piano.

Liebesleid:	Tempo di valse	A minor – major
Liebesfreud':	Allegro	C major

Date: ? 1921, 1925.

Dedication: none.

MS: *Liebesleid:* L. of C., part of ML 30. 55a. R3: pp. 12, in ink, with engraver's annotations, undated. Title in another hand.

Liebesfreud': untraced at present.

Publication: *Liebesleid:* 1923, Carl Fischer Inc., New York, P 1322, 22712–10, pp. 11. B. Schott Söhne, Mainz und Leipzig, 1758 (31293), pp. 9 (a different engraving).

Liebesfreud': 1926, Carl Fischer Inc., New York, P 1498, 23730–15, pp. 16. B. Schott Söhne ..., 1757 (31912), pp. 15 (a different engraving). (This latter edition quotes 1922 as Fischer's copyright date; the notes to the Coll. Ed. and the Belwin-Mills reprint correctly give 1926.)

The Fischer editions later taken over by Charles Foley. The Schott editions bear portraits (pencil sketches) of SR and Kreisler on the wrappers.

Coll. Ed. III (1) / 113–122, 123–136, 1950 (referring to 'Foley' editions of 1926 [actually Fischer] and 1943). Both reprinted in 'A Commemorative Collection ...', Belwin Mills 1973, pp. 70–79, 80–94 from the Fischer, not the Schott, editions.

Current editions: Belwin Mills.

Performance: *Liebesleid:* 20 November 1921, Chicago, Ill., USA.
6 May 1922, London, Queen's Hall.
Liebesfreud': 29 October 1925, Stamford, Conn., USA.
November 1929 UK tour (Glasgow, 13th; London, Royal Albert Hall, 24th.).

Recording: *Liebesleid:* (1921), I; also Ampico roll.
Liebesfreud': (1925), II, (1942), III.

Original: Fritz Kreisler (1875–1962), Klassische Manuskripte nos. 10–11, Alt-Wiener Tanzweisen, nos. 1–2, for violin and piano. Kreisler – himself an accomplished pianist – made his own regular piano versions of both these pieces (Schott).

Notes: OvR 265 states 'Unpublished in Europe' against his entries for these two pieces: a statement disproved by the Schott editions listed above.

LISZT: III/6

Cadenza to the 2nd Hungarian Rhapsody

Piano solo.

Date: ?1919.

Dedication: none.

MS: 'This cadenza was apparently never written down by the composer and survives only in a few treasured Edison records' (Joseph Reither, *Tempo* 22, 1951–2, p. 36). '... the work existed in a manuscript in the possession of the Rachmaninoff family' (v. inf. Introductory Note to publication).

In L. of C., among the miscellaneous sketches included in ML 30. 55a. R3, is a sheet bearing a pencil draft of part of this cadenza (cf. pp. 5–6 of published version) on one side and part of the Fourth Concerto on the other.

Publication: 1955, Mercury Music Corporation, New York, pp. 8. Edited (and with Introductory Note) by Jan Holcman. 'Copyright 1955 by Charles Foley, New York.' (English agents: Francis, Day & Hunter). [Holcman reconstituted the work from the Edison recording.]

Not in Coll. Ed.

Performance: 10 January 1919, Boston, Mass., USA.
20 May 1922, London, Queen's Hall.

Recording: (1919), I.

Original: Franz Liszt's (1811–1886) Rhapsodie Hongroise no. 2 dates from 1847 and was published in 1851. An opportunity for a 'Cadenza ad libitum' is indicated before the final flourish.

Notes: – It is possible that in all these years you have not written a single note?
– *Oh yes, I have written a cadenza to Liszt's Second Rhapsody.*
(OvR 198).

The sketch-sheet listed above corresponds closely to the printed version as follows: p. 5, bars 2–16; p. 6, bars 1–8; p. 5, bars 17–20; p. 6, bars 9–18. Though differing frequently in enharmonic 'spelling', the accuracy of Holcman's reconstitution is thus demonstrated to be of a high order.

MENDELSSOHN: III/7
Scherzo from *A Midsummer Night's Dream*

Transcription for piano.

Allegro vivace G minor

Date: 6 March 1933 acc. to B/L 419; but also v. inf. *Notes.*

Dedication: none.

MS: L. of C., part of ML 30. 55a. R3: pp. 20, in ink. No title, date or signature at present, but this MS is evidently the *Stichvorlage* for the Fischer edition. A pencil draft is also to be found in the spirex-bound sketchbook otherwise devoted to the Rapsodie, op. 43.

Publication: 1933, Edition TAIR, Carl Fischer Inc., New York, P 1965, CC 26476–15, pp. 17; Édition TAIR, Paris, pl. no. 10, pp. 17 (Scherzo tiré du *Songe d'une nuit d'été)* (simultaneous publication); 'Copyright 1933 by Carl Fischer Inc., New York'. (The French edition apparently copies the Fischer engraving.) Reprinted by Chas. Foley R–2028.

Coll. Ed. III (1) / 137–152 (quoting a Fischer edition of 1938). Reprinted in 'A Commemorative Collection ...', Belwin Mills 1973, pp. 41–55, copying the Tair (Fischer) publication.

Current edition: Belwin Mills.

Performance: 23 January 1933, San Antonio, Texas, USA.
29 April 1933, London, Queen's Hall.

Recording: (1935), II.

Original: Felix Mendelssohn-Bartholdy (1809–1847); op. 61, incidental music to Shakespeare's play *A Midsummer Night's Dream.* The Scherzo (no. 1) is to be performed after the first act. A concert transcription of this piece for piano solo was also made by Camille Saint-Saëns (Durand).

Notes: Watson Lyle (op. cit. 202) states: 'this was written in America as long ago as 1921', but gives no further authority for this assertion.

MUSSORGSKY: III/8
Hopak

Transcription for piano.

Vivace G major

Date: *1 January 1924.*

Dedication: none.

MS: L. of C., part of ML 30. 55a. R3: pp. 5 (= 3–7 of an 8-page section), in ink, with engraver's annotations. (p. 1) titlepage: *Hopak / Moussorgsky – Rachmaninoff.* At end *N. Y. / January 1 1924.*

Publication: 1924, Carl Fischer Inc., New York, P 1375, CC 23051–4, pp. 5.

Coll. Ed. III (1) / 153–6 (giving Fischer's date, erroneously, as 1921). Reprinted in 'A Commemorative Collection ...', Belwin Mills 1973, pp. 66–9, copying the Fischer edition.

Current edition: Belwin Mills.

Performance: 13 November 1923 (sic), Scranton, Penn., USA.
October 1924 English tour (Bournemouth, 2nd; London, Queen's Hall, 6th).

Recording: (1925), II; also Ampico roll (1923).

Arrangement: for violin and piano (by SR).

MS: L. of C., ref. as above, pp. 4, in pencil. Untitled, but dated *11 May 1925 / New York* at end. This MS is amongst the miscellaneous sketches.

Publ: 1926, Carl Fischer Inc., New York, B 2014, 27082–8, pp. 7, 3 (also Edition Tair acc. to B/L 419; but unrecorded by the Bibliothèque Nationale).

Original: to be found in Modest Mussorgsky's unfinished opera *Sorochintsy Fair:* Mussorgsky (1839–1881) himself made a separate arrangement for piano solo of the Hopak; his tempo direction is *Allegretto scherzando.* It forms the conclusion of the opera in both N. Tcherepnin's and V. Shebalin's versions.

Notes: 'Though a disciple of Tchaikovsky, he [SR] woke my appreciation of Mussorgsky and Rimsky-Korsakov' (Chaliapin, *Pages from my Life*, cf. B/L 82).

RIMSKY-KORSAKOFF: III/9
The Bumble Bee

Transcription for piano.

Presto A minor

Date: ?1929.

Dedication: none.

MS: untraced at present.

Publication: 1931, Carl Fischer Inc., New York, P 1923, pp. 7. 'Copyright 1931 by Carl Fischer, New York.' Large facsimile signature on wrapper and titlepage.

Coll. Ed. III (1) / 157–161 (incorrectly quoting the original publisher as Foley). Reprinted in 'A Commemorative Collection ...', Belwin Mills, 1973, pp. 60–5, copying the Fischer edition.

Current edition: Belwin Mills.

Performance:
13 March 1937, London, Queen's Hall.

Recording: (1929), II; also Ampico roll.

Original: Nikolay Rimsky-Korsakov (1844–1908): opera in 4 acts with a prologue (7 scenes) *The Tale of Tsar Saltan* (1899–1900), based on Pushkin. The scherzo entitled *The Bumble Bee* forms the closing episode of Act 3 scene 1, and as such does not occur in the suite from the opera, op. 57 (which consists only of the preludes to Acts 1 & 2 and to the closing scene). The composer's own arrangement is to be found in the piano score of the opera (Bessel); there is also another 'concert transcription' for piano by J. Strimer.

Notes: *Just to read a score by Rimsky-Korsakov puts me in a better mood ...* (SR to S. Bertensson, B/L 303).

SCHUBERT:
The Brooklet

Transcription for piano.

Allegretto G major

Date: 1925.

Dedication: none.

MS: untraced at present.

Publication: 1926, Carl Fischer Inc., New York, P 1511, 23731–7, pp. 9.

1929, Édition TAIR, Paris, pl. no. 8, pp. 7 ('Le Ruisseau'). 'Copyright 1926 by Carl Fischer Inc., New York.' (This edition was re-engraved in Paris by Grandjean.)

Coll. Ed. III (1) / 162–7 (giving Fischer's date erroneously as 1936). Reprinted in 'A Commemorative Collection ...', Belwin Mills 1973, pp. 104–9, but re-engraved.

Current edition: Belwin Mills.

Performance: 29 October 1925, Stamford, Conn., USA.
November 1929 UK tour (Glasgow, 13th).

Recording: (1925), II.

Original: Franz Schubert (1797–1828): op. 25, song cycle *Die schöne Müllerin* (Wilhelm Müller), 1823; no. 2, *Wohin?* Schubert's tempo direction is *Moderato.* This song was also transcribed by Liszt in 1846, as no. 5 of his set of [6] *Müllerlieder.*

Notes: The musical content of the 1926 and 1929 editions listed above agrees; in the re-engraving the original 7 pages of music were compressed into six, by increasing the number of systems on certain pages.

SMITH:
The Star-Spangled Banner

Transcription for piano.

Date: 1918.

Dedication: none.

MS: ?

Publication: none.

Performance: 15 December 1918, Symphony Hall, Boston.

Recording: Ampico roll (1919).

Original: John Stafford Smith (1750–1836), whose melody 'Anakreon in Heaven' was used for the national anthem of the United States.

Notes:

TCHAIKOVSKY:

'Manfred' Symphony

Transcription for piano duet.

1. Lento lugubre – Moderato con moto – Andante	B minor
2. Vivace con spirito	B minor
3. Andante con moto	G major
4. Allegro con fuoco	B minor – major

Date: 1886.

Dedication: the original work was dedicated to M. Balakirev.

MS: lost.

Publication: none.

Performance: this arrangement was played to Tchaikovsky, at Zverev's house, by Rachmaninoff and his fellow student Matvey Presman, possibly on 8 December 1886.

Original: P. I. Tchaikovsky (1840–1893): op. 58, *Manfred*, Symphonie en 4 Tableaux d'après le poème dramatique de Byron (1885). Published by P. Jurgenson in 1886; the published arrangement for piano duet is by Tchaikovsky himself.

Notes: 'Without any guidance whatever young Rachmaninoff had made himself acquainted with the problems and secrets of score reading and had immediately applied his newly-acquired knowledge in this very practical fashion' (OvR 57). The symphony was first performed (in Moscow) on 11 March 1886.

TCHAIKOVSKY: III/13
Ballet: 'The Sleeping Beauty'

Transcription for piano duet.

Date: summer 1890; corrected and revised, summer 1891.

Dedication: the original work was dedicated to I. A. Vsevolozhsky.

MS: lost.

Publication: 1892, P. Jurgenson, Moscow. Partition complète; Intro. et nn. 1–30 séparèment, pour le Piano à 4 mains par S. Rachmaninoff; 17016–44/44ª/45.

Suite tirée de la partition du ballet, ditto; 17025 (according to Jurgenson's catalogue).

Current edition (of Suite): Rob. Forberg / P. Jurgenson, 17025a, pp. 53 (opposite pages).

Performance:

Original: P. I. Tchaikovsky: op. 66, *La belle au bois dormant*: ballet en trois actes, précédé d'un prologue (1888–9).

The suite from the ballet, as now known (op. 66ª), was chosen by Siloti at Tchaikovsky's suggestion but was only published posthumously by Jurgenson in 1899 (v. preface by David Lloyd-Jones to Eulenberg score no. 1329); it consists of five movements, viz:

Introduction. La Fée des lilas. [from Act I, 9, Finale]
Adagio. Pas d'action. [from Act I, 8]
Pas de caractère (le chat botté et la chatte blanche). [Act III, 23]
Panorama. [Act II, 17]
Valse. [Act I, 6]

B/L 419 states that the transcription of the suite was also published in 1892, but at that date the latter probably did not exist in its present entity.

Notes: A. Siloti had made the piano solo arrangement of the complete ballet score in 1889 at Tchaikovsky's request. 'Because of a minor injury to his hand, Siloti was unable to write much and suggested that R. should be allowed to do [the four-hand version] under his supervision for a fee of 100 roubles' (GN 10). For Tchaikovsky's reaction when he first saw the proofs of this arrangement, see his letter to Siloti of 14 June 1891 (B/L 35–6). See also SR to Natalya Skalon, 11 July 1891: *Tchaikovsky criticizes me terribly for the transcription, quite reasonably and justly.* Assistance from Siloti at this stage evidently appeased the composer sufficiently for publication to ensue.

It appears from the plate numbers that nos. 6, 13b and 22 (part) had already appeared in Siloti's 4-hand arrangement, nos. 16156/7/8.

Lullaby

Transcription for piano.

Andantino A flat minor

Date: *12 August 1941.*

Dedication: none.

MS: L. of C., part of ML 30. 55a. R3: pp. 10 (= pp. 3–12 of a sewn 16-page section), in pencil, with engraver's annotations. (p. 1) titlepage: *Lullaby / by / P. Tschaikowsky / arranged by / S. Rachmaninoff.* At end *12 August 1941.*

Publication: 1941, Charles Foley, New York. R–2059, pp. 7. 'Copyright 1941 by Charles Foley, New York'.

Coll. Ed. III (1) / 168–173. Reprinted in 'A Commemorative Collection ...', Belwin Mills 1973, pp. 36–40, copying the Foley edition.

Current edition: Belwin Mills.

Performance: 14 October 1941, Syracuse, N.Y., USA.

Recording: (1942), II.

Original: P. I. Tchaikovsky: op. 16, Six Songs (1872); no. 1, Lullaby (words by Maykov); publ. Bessel, 1873. An arrangement of this song as a piano solo was published by Tchaikovsky himself; another arrangement, made by P. Pabst, appears as no. 7 of 'Sept pièces pour piano', the other six being the *Six morceaux*, op. 21 (Bessel).

Notes: It is perhaps appropriate that SR's last musical work, this arrangement of the well-known song by his so much admired Tchaikovsky, closes our listing of his musical legacy.

Appendices

(i) German and French versions of song titles

op. 4

1. O nein, ich fleh', geh nicht von mir	Ne t'en vas pas
2. Der Morgen	Le matin
3. Wenn Nacht mich hüllt u. Schweigen	Dans le silence et l'ombre
4. O schönes Mädchen	Chanson géorgienne
5. O du wogendes Feld	O mon champ bien-aimé
6. Wie lang ist's her	Ma bien-aimée, ton regard triste

op. 8

2. Die Wasserlilie	La Nymphéa
2. Du bist wie die taufrische Blume	Enfant, belle fleur
3. Reflexion (Grübelei)	Rêverie
4. Wohl zu eignem Leid hab' ich Lieb' geweiht	La femme du soldat
5. Traum	Un rêve
6. Gebet	Prière

op. 14

1. Ich harre dein	O viens à moi
2. Das Inselchen	L'ilôt
3. Längst beut mir Liebe	L'amour ne m'a causé que peines
4. Ich war bei dir	J'étais près d'elle
5. Diese herrlichen Nächte	O les nuits estivales
6. Dich lieben alle so	De tous tu es aimée
7. Glaub's nicht mein Lieb!	Je mens, amie
8. O, traure nicht!	Ne me regrette pas
9. So schön wie Tag	Elle est le rayonnant soleil
10. Die Liebe flammt	Dans mon coeur l'amour pénètre
11. Frühlingsfluten	Parmi les champs couverts de neige
12. 's ist Zeit	O viens

op. 21

1. Schicksal	Le destin
2. Am frischen Grabe	Sur la tombe
3. Dämmerung	Crépuscule
4. Die Antwort	Réponses
5. Flieder	Les lilas
6. Bruchstück aus A. de Musset	Un fragment d'Alfred de Musset
7. Hier ist es schön	Tout est si beau
8. Auf den Tod eines Zeisigs	Sur la mort d'un oiseau
9. Melodie	Mélodie
10. Vor dem Gottesbilde	Devant l'image sainte

11. Bin kein Prophet	Ne suis guerrier ni magicien
12. Wie mir's weh tut	Oh, je souffre

op. 26

1. Viel Töne wahrt	Des chants murmurent
2. Gott nahm mir alles	Dieu m'a ravi mes biens
3. Wir werden ruhen	Un doux repos
4. Zwei Abschiede	Deux adieux
5. Verlassen wir, mein Lieb	Ma bien-aimée fuyons
6. Der Herr erstand	Le Christ renaît
7. An die Kinder	Aux enfants
8. Um Schonung flehe ich	De grâce, épargne moi
9. Wieder bleib' ich allein	De nouveau je suis seul
10. Vor meinem Fenster	Dans mon jardin je vois
11. Die Fontaine	La fontaine
12. Trübe Nacht ist's	L'ombre est triste
13. Als wir uns trafen	Je la vis s'arrêter
14. Der Ring	L'anneau
15. Wie alles geht	Tout passe

op. 34

1. Die Muse	La muse
2. Die Seele selbst birgt jederzeit	Chacun de nous cache
3. Der Sturm	La tempête
4. Tag und Nacht vergleichend	Une brise passe
5. Arion	Arion
6. Auferweckung des Lazarus	La résurrection de Lazare
7. Zu grausam ist's	Oh! non jamais
8. Musik	Musique
9. Du kanntest ihn	Tu l'as connu
10. Des Tags gedenk ich	Ce jour d'extase
11. Der Leibzins-Entrichter	Le redevancier
12. O welche Wonne	Bonheur suprême
13. Dissonanz	Dissonance
14. Vocalise	Vocalise

op. 38

1. Nächtlich im Garten	L'ombre au jardin
2. Zu ihr	À Elle
3. Margariten	Les marguerites
4. Der Rattenfänger	Le joueur de chalumeau
5. Der Traum	Le rêve
6. A... U...!	Vers les cimes

(ii) Notes on the Dedicatees

Aleksandrova, Nadezhda Aleksandrovna (? – ?); a well-known gypsy singer. (op. 14/8).

Arensky, Anton Stepanovich (1861–1906); composer, pianist, teacher and conductor. Professor at the Moscow Conservatoire, where SR entered his harmony class in 1886. (op. 3).

Brandukov, Anatoly Andreyevich (1856–1930); cellist, teacher and conductor. Professor at the Moscow Conservatoire from 1921. (opp. 2, 19).

Chaliapin, see *Shalyapin.*

Conus, Julius, see *Konyus.*

Dahl, Dr. Nikolay Vladimirovich (1860–1940); specialist in treatment by hypnosis and an accomplished amateur musician. (op. 18).

Deysha-Sionitskaya, Mariya Adrianovna (1859–1932); soprano, who performed at the Bolshoy Theatre, Moscow, where she created the role of Zemfira in *Aleko* (1893). (op. 8/6).

Godowsky, Leopold (1870–1938); Polish pianist, teacher and composer.

Goldenweiser, Aleksandr Borisovich (1875–1961); pianist, fellow-student of SR at the Moscow Conservatoire of which he was later director, 1939–42. (op. 17).

Golenishcheva-Kutuzova, Olga Andreyevna (d. 1924); wife of the poet Arseny Golenishchev-Kutuzov. (op. 4/6).

Gutheil, Mariya Ivanovna (? – ?); wife of Karl Aleksandrovich Gutheil, SR's principal publisher until 1914. (op. 14/5).

Hofmann, Josef Casimir (1876–1957); Polish pianist, pupil of Anton Rubinstein. (op. 30).

Ivanova (married name, *Shatalina*), *Mariya Aleksandrovna* (d. 1925); daughter of the Satin family's cook; later housekeeper to SR. (op. 21/10).

Kerzin, Arkady Mikhaylovich (1857–1914) and *Mariya Semyonovna* (1865–1926); leading patrons of the arts, especially music. They formed the Circle of Lovers of Russian Music, at one of the concerts of which (in 1907) SR's songs op. 26 were first performed.

Klokachova (née *Pribytkova*), *Anna Georgiyevna* (? – ?); cousin of SR, daughter of his aunt and uncle Anna Arkadyevna and Georgy Filippovich Pribytkov. Subsequent married name Zhukovskaya. (op. 14/7).

Komissarzhevskaya, Vera Fyodorovna (1864–1910); Russian actress. She was a close family friend of SR's cousin A. Ziloti. (op. 34/7).

Konyus, Yuly Eduardovich (1869–1942); violinist and composer. His son Boris married SR's younger daughter Tatyana. (op. 6).

Koshetz, Nina Pavlovna (1894–1965); Russian soprano. She sang with Zimin's Private Opera Company in Moscow and also sang in concerts with SR accompanying her. (op. 38).

Kreisler, Fritz (1875–1962); Austrian violinist of world fame. Recorded sonatas by Beethoven, Schubert and Grieg with SR. (op. 42).

Kreytser (married name *Zhukovskaya*), *Elena Yulyevna* (1875–1961); singer and teacher. Had piano lessons from SR in her childhood. (op. 21/4).

Lanting, Natalya Nikolayevna (? – ?); cousin of SR's wife Natalya. Her mother, Olga Aleksandrovna Lanting, was sister to SR's father-in-law, Aleksandr Aleksandrovich Satin. (op. 21/9).

Lavrovskaya, Elizaveta Andreyevna (1845–1919); Russian contralto. She sang at the Mariinsky Theatre, St. Petersburg, and taught at the Moscow Conservatoire from 1888 to 1919. (op. 14/9–10).

Leschetizky, Theodor (1830–1915); the most famous teacher of the pianoforte of his day, whose fame lived on in that of his many pupils, from Paderewski to Brailowsky. (op. 22).

Litvin, Feliya (Litvinova, Fekla Vasilyevna) (1861–1936); Russian dramatic soprano. She sang at the Mariinsky Theatre from 1891. (op. 34/13).

Liven (Lieven), (Princess) *Aleksandra Andreyevna* (d. 1914); president of the Ladies' Charitable Prison Committee, and one of the organizers of charitable concerts in which SR and others participated (op. 21/6).

Lodyzhenskaya (née *Aleksandrova*), *Anna Aleksandrovna* (? – ?); sister of the gypsy singer Nadezhda Aleksandrova. (opp. 4/1, 13).

Lodyzhensky, Pyotr Viktorovich (? – ?); a friend of SR's in Moscow. Husband of the above-named. (op. 12).

Lysikova, E. N. (? – ?); wife of a Kharkov merchant. SR and his friend Mikhail Slonov stayed on the Lysikovs' estate at Lebedin in the summer of 1893. (op. 4/5).

Medtner, Nikolay Karlovich (1879–1951); Russian composer and pianist and friend of SR. (op. 40).

Mengelberg, Josef Willem (1871–1951); conductor of the Concertgebouw Orchestra in Amsterdam 1895–1945. (op. 35).

Morozov, Nikita Semyonovich (1864–1925); fellow-student of SR in Arensky's composition class in 1892. (op. 20).

Nezhdanova, Antonina Vasilyevna (1873–1950); Russian coloratura soprano. (op. 34/14).

Olfereva, Mariya Vasilyevna (? – ?); common law wife of SR's father. (op. 8/4).

Ormandy, Eugene (1899–); conductor of the Philadelphia Orchestra from 1936. (op. 45).

Ornatskaya, Anna Dmitriyevna (? – ?); SR's first professional piano teacher. (op. 14/11).

Pabst, Pavel (1854–1897); professor of piano at the Moscow Conservatoire. (op. 10).

Presman, Matvey Leontyevich (1870–1941); pianist and teacher. Fellow-student of SR's at Zverev's. (op. 36).

Pribytkova, Zoya Arkadyevna (1892–1962); daughter of SR's cousin Arkady Georgiyevich Pribytkov (whose mother, Anna Arkadyevna, was the sister of SR's father). (op. 14/3).

Sakhnovsky, Yury Sergeyevich (1868–1930); composer, conductor and music critic. He was a close friend of SR's from their student days in Moscow. (opp. 4/2, 14/4).

Satin, Vladimir Aleksandrovich (1881–1945); SR's cousin and brother-in-law. (op. 21/12).

Satina, Natalya Aleksandrovna (1877–1951); SR's cousin, and his wife from 1902. (opp. 4/4, 21/7).

Satina, Sofiya Aleksandrovna (1879–1975); SR's cousin and sister-in law. (op. 14/2).

Shaginian, Marietta Sergeyevna (1888–); poet and, later, writer of prose fiction. Her verse anthology *Orientalia* (1913) was dedicated to SR. (op. 34/1).

Shalyapin, Fyodor Ivanovich (1873–1938); famous Russian bass. (opp. 21/1, 34 (part)).

Siloti, see *Ziloti.*

Skalon (married name *Rostovtsova*), *Lyudmila Dmitriyevna* (1874–1962); one of three sisters who were cousins of SR by marriage. (op. 14/1).

Skalon (married name *Valgard*), *Natalya Dmitriyevna* (1869–1943); the eldest of the three Skalon sisters. (op. 8/5).

Skalon (married name *Tolbusin*), *Vera Dmitriyevna* (1875–1909); the youngest sister of the above. (op. 4/3).

Slonov, Mikhail Akimovich (1869–1930); singer and teacher. He was a reader at Jurgenson's publishing house, and was one of SR's closest friends. (op. 8/2).

Smolensky, Stepan Vasilyevich (1848–1909); professor of church music at the Moscow Conservatoire. SR studied briefly under this great authority on the subject. (op. 37).

Sobinov, Leonid Vitalyevich (1872–1934); Russian tenor. (op. 34 part).

Stokowski, Leopold (1882–1977), conductor; from 1914 to 1936 of SR's 'favourite' Philadelphia Orchestra. (op. 41).

von Struve, Nicolas (d. 1920); close friend of SR from the Dresden years, later associated with the Russischer Musikverlag in Berlin. (op. 29).

Taneyev, Sergey Ivanovich (1856–1915); composer, teacher and pianist. Director of the Moscow Conservatoire from 1885 to 1889. (op. 27).

Tchaikovsky, Pyotr Ilyich (1840–1893); most famous Russian composer. (opp. 5, 9, 34/8).

Trubnikova, Olga Andreyevna (1877–1942); cousin of SR. Her mother, Mariya Arkadyevna, was the sister of SR's father. (op. 21/8).

Vrubel (née *Zabela*), *Nadezhda Ivanova* (1867–1913); Russian soprano, who sung at the Moscow Private Opera Company and at the Mariinsky Theatre. (op. 21/3).

Yakovlev, Leonid Georgiyevich (1858–1919); Russian baritone. He sang at the Mariinsky Theatre, St. Petersburg. (op. 8/3).

Yaroshevsky, Adolf Adolfovich (1863–1910); Russian pianist, professor at the Moscow Conservatoire from 1898. (op. 8/1).

Zatayevich, Aleksandr Viktorovich (1869–1936); composer and collector of folk-songs. (op. 16).

Ziloti, Aleksandr Ilyich (1863–1945); SR's cousin, pianist, pupil of Liszt and Zverev. His mother, Yuliya Arkadyevna, was sister of SR's father. (opp. 1, 23).

(iii) A Conspectus of Rachmaninoff's compositions, set out in categories, and in their approximate chronological positions

	Piano solo	*Chamber music*	*Orchestral*	*Vocal solo*	*Choral*	*Dramatic*
1886	Study in F sharp	'Manfred' (Tchaikovsky) trans.				
7	4 pieces 3 Nocturnes		Scherzo			
8		? Romance, Vl. pf.				'Esmeralda', sketches
9		2 quartet movts. Romance, Vc. pf.	Pf. Concerto (unfin.)			
1890	Piece in D minor	2 pieces (6 hands) 'Sleeping Beauty' trans.	'Manfred' suite First Concerto, op. 1	songs, incl.	Deus meus	
1	Prelude in F	Russian Rhapsody (2 pts.)	'Prince Rostislav'	op. 4		
2	Morceaux de Fantaisie, op. 3	2 Cello pcs., op. 2; Trio in G minor	Capriccio bohémien, op. 12			'Aleko', opera
3	Morceaux de Salon, op. 10	Fantaisie, op. 5 2 Violin pcs., op. 6	Fantaisie, op. 7	6 songs, op. 8	Sacred concerto	
4		Trio élégiaque, op. 9 6 Morceaux, op. 11 (duet)	(Capriccio finished)			
5			First Symphony, op. 13		6 choruses, op. 15	
6	Moments musicaux, op. 16	2 quartet movts. Trans. of Glazunov, Sym. 6		12 songs, op. 14		
7			Symphony (sketch)			
8						
9	Morceaux de Fantaisie, Fughetta			Song-jest	2 Russian songs	
1900	Bizet Minuet trans.			Song ('Night')		Duet for 'Francesca'
1	Prelude in G m. op. 23/5	Second suite, op. 17 Cello sonata, op. 19	Second Concerto op. 18	Song ('Fate') op. 21/1 11 Songs, op. 21 nos. 2–12	'Panteley the healer' 'Spring', cantata, op. 20	
2	Chopin variations, op. 22					

	Piano solo	*Chamber music*	*Orchestral*	*Vocal solo*	*Choral*	*Dramatic*
1903	Preludes op. 23					'Der geizige Ritter', opera, op. 24
4						'Francesca da Rimini', opera, op. 25
5						
6		Polka italienne	Second Symphony op. 27	15 Songs, op. 26		
7	Sonata, op. 28	Trio, op. 9, revised				
8			'Die Toten-insel', op. 29	Letter to Stanislavsky		'Monna Vanna', opera (unfin.)
9			Third Concerto, op. 30			
1910	13 Preludes, op. 32			Song, op. 34/7	Liturgy, op. 31	
1	9 Etudes-Tableaux, op. 33 Polka de W. R.					
2	'Lilacs' trans.			12 Songs, op. 34 (exc. 7 & 14)		
3	Second Sonata, op. 36				'The Bells', op. 35	
4				'From St. John'		
5				Vocalise, op. 34/14	Vespers, op. 37	
6				6 (8) songs, op. 38		
7	9 Etudes-Tableaux, op. 39		Revision of First Concerto			
8	3 pieces					
9	Cadenza to Liszt 2nd Rhapsody					
1920				Russian songs		
1	'Liebesleid' trans.					
2	Bizet Minuet trans.					
3	'Daisies' trans.					

	Piano solo	*Chamber music*	*Orchestral*	*Vocal solo*	*Choral*	*Dramatic*
1924	'Hopak' trans. 'Liebes-freud' ' trans.			'Powder and paint'		
5	'The Brooklet' trans.					
6			Fourth Concerto, op. 40		3 Chansons russes, op. 41	
7			ditto, revisions			
8						
9						
1930	Revision of Second Sonata Corelli variations, op. 42					
1	'Bumble Bee' trans.					
2						
3	Bach and Mendelssohn trans.					
4			Rapsodie sur un thème de Paganini, op. 43			
5						
6			Third Symphony, op. 44		partial revision of 'The Bells'	
7						
8			Revisions of Third Sym.			
9						'Paganini', ballet
1940	Revisions of early piano pieces		Symphonic Dances, op. 45			
1	Tchaikovsky 'Lullaby' trans.		Final revision of Fourth Concerto			
2						
3						

Index of names and titles

Note: for German and French titles of the songs, see Appendix (i); for names of dedicatees see Appendix (ii).